the art
of friday
night
dinner

*For Mum, Dad, Flo and Ollie,
my favourite people to share
a Friday night with*

the art of friday night dinner

Eleanor Steafel

BLOOMSBURY PUBLISHING

LONDON · OXFORD · NEW YORK · NEW DELHI · SYDNEY

Thank God for sausage pasta (see pages 146–7)

Contents

Introduction

I sometimes wonder if even the shoddiest weeks are worth it for the heady relief that comes with making it to Friday night. With that first sip of something cold, that first frantic handful of crisps, the week begins to retreat. By the time the kitchen is filled with the scent of a good dinner coming together, all is forgiven. It's the start of a two-day exhale, where everything that has been hazy and difficult slowly comes into focus. It's the sensory full stop at the end of the week that says: 'You did it, you made it to Friday night – have an olive, and a gin and tonic.' Nothing beats the feeling of a weekend stretching out in front of you, all shiny with the promise of good food and good people or quiet pots of coffee and no people. It's like the first night of holiday when your shoulders finally drop, and the only question you have to ponder is: 'Do you want a glass of rosé next, a plate of cheese, or both?'

I learned early on the magic of a Friday night in. As a child it was when I was allowed to stay up and have dinner with my parents after my younger brother and sister were asleep. While they were cajoled into bed, I would hide in the downstairs loo so as not to raise suspicion that something fun might be about to happen. When the coast was clear, out came the crisps and on went *Top of the Pops*. If there's a heaven, I think it might be a saggy red sofa in a 1990s living room, with endless salt-and-vinegar Kettle Chips and the dulcet tones of the *Ground Force* theme tune. I've been chasing that high ever since, and spent more nights out longing to be in than I am proud of.

There is a kind of secret glamour to an evening on the sofa, totally alone, with no one to please but yourself.

The sort of night when a fried cheese sandwich is a perfectly acceptable dinner, perhaps accompanied by a very dry, briny martini, because it's your Friday night and you make the rules. I like pouring red wine into a big glass and eating spaghetti in my dressing gown in front of old *West Wing* episodes. I like making breakfast for dinner – seven-minute Burford Browns smushed on to toast that has been spread thickly with cream cheese and Marmite and topped with pickled shallots; golden American home fries with peppers, onions and sausage. I like cradling a bowl of something delicious on the sofa while sobbing along to videos of people being reunited with long-lost family members and old Oscars acceptance speeches. It might sound tragic but, honestly, there is nothing so cathartic as watching Tom Hanks's 1994 acceptance speech for *Philadelphia* at the end of a ropy week. Really blows the cobwebs away.

I often find I shop in a way I never would Monday to Thursday. The end of the week seems to bring along with it an end to structure and sensible decision-making. Instead, Friday night ushers in a resounding 'sod it'. After a week spent foraging for leftovers and finding new ways to justify how adding a feeble handful of spinach to everything makes for a balanced meal, I'll get an urge to go to the posh deli on the way home and splurge a month's salary on overpriced bits. A piece of English sheep's

cheese, a sourdough baguette, and a paper bag containing three heritage tomatoes for £16? Don't mind if I do. A perfect bavette from the butcher to devour with baked potatoes, soured cream and chives? Just call me Katie. (And if that reference is lost on you, then for the love of God, please put this down and go and watch *The Way We Were* immediately.)

I love the intoxicating freedom of a Friday night. That 'anything-is-possible' feeling when you leave work, perhaps with only a vague plan, but with some intangible fizz in the air and a little voice telling you it's going to be a good night. On nights when I don't know where the wind is going to take me, I always have one eye on what I'm going to make when I get home in the wee hours, having skipped dinner. A fried mozzarella, salami and honey sandwich; a tuna melt to silence all other tuna melts; a mound of egg fried rice. Tired eyes, sore feet, stupid grin and the prospect of a full stomach. There's nothing like it.

Occasionally, Friday nights are for shutting the world away and revelling in a moment of fallow time before the weekend.

Sometimes it's a night for sitting opposite your oldest friend; a chance to pour your souls out to each other over a mound of pad Thai and then sink an entire bar of Tony's (the purple one, with the pretzels, obviously) while watching *Sleepless in Seattle* for the millionth time. Sometimes it's a night to set the table properly and tuck into something special once small people are in bed; a chance to look each other in the eye for the first time all week, to make plans and reminisce, to air some of the things that have been troubling you and to retell all those stories you've told so many times before. And sometimes, all you want to do is to assemble a gang of your favourite people around a groaning table for one of those nights that roll on and brilliantly on.

The words 'Come over, I'll cook!' might well be my epitaph.

What usually happens is someone suggests getting together, various bars are floated and pubs debated at great length on WhatsApp, while I sit on my hands trying not to say those four little words. Eventually, I can't help myself. I don't think I'll ever tire of getting a gang of people round for dinner, whether they know each other or not. I love filling little bowls with good things to be snacked on – black olives (the soft, greasy kind, or sweet little niçoise), a mound of ice-cold radishes to swipe through butter and flaky salt, a jar of cornichons, a plate of good anchovies dressed with lemon zest and chilli, some sort of creamy, herby dip laced with garlic, little saucers of oil and thick, fruity vinegar, a board piled high with torn hunks of bread. I love lighting candles and putting on lipstick and mixing drinks – a jug of jalapeño margaritas or tumblers of syrupy vermouth with orange slices and too many olives.

Above all, I love creating villages from strangers. I love my little flat being full, and that feeling when you finally crawl into bed in the wee hours, filled with the deep contentment of having laughed your way through a long meal with excellent people.

A Friday night can be all these things and more. It can be anything you want it to be. But first, you need to settle on something good to eat.

Fried crumbs make everything better

Whenever my friends add what they would call 'bits' to a meal, they refer to it (proudly, but with a gentle eye roll) as 'doing an Els'. They're not wrong. There aren't many meals that I won't find a way to add a pickle, or a toasted crumb, relish or salsa to. I am, to put it mildly, addicted to all things crunchy and acidic, and in so many meals, that welcome hit of sourness often comes from the 'extras' that you might add yourself at the table or just before serving. It's always the thing that draws me to a dish on a menu, whatever the cuisine – I'm in it for the lime-spiked pol sambol alongside the dal, the little dish of pickled daikon you might get with a donburi, the highlighter pink turnips crammed into a falafel wrap, the drizzle of tart pomegranate molasses on a fattoush. It's the acid that seems to round out the other flavours and hook me in, beckoning me back for another bite.

The brilliant Samin Nosrat, whose seminal book *Salt Fat Acid Heat* is the ultimate guide to understanding flavour, says acid 'heightens our pleasure'. If ever you eat something and find it falls flat or lacks a certain something, acid is usually what your taste buds are searching for. It's like Diana Henry says: 'Nearly always, when there seems to be something missing, the answer is lemon.' You simply can't argue with that logic. Acid brightens things and creates contrast – it makes everything sparkle.

Nosrat also points out that the list of acidic ingredients extends 'far beyond' vinegar and citrus. 'Anything fermented is also acidic. That includes cheese, pickles, and beer. [...] Think of beef stew cooked in red wine or meatballs simmered in tomato sauce.'

Adding a hit of acid to a dish, then, isn't just about all things pickle. It's the sharp, salty feta crumbled over a platter of fatty, slow-roasted lamb; the slosh of white wine in a risotto. It's the lemon half, charred on the barbecue and squeezed over a whole fish at the table, or the finely chopped white onion to be added to your taco just before it goes in your mouth. It's almost infuriating how you can spend hours lovingly marinating a piece of meat or standing over a bubbling pot, but when it comes to eating the thing, it's often the scattering of something sharp and fresh that actually makes the meal. All that work, and the thing everyone is talking about is the few slices of red onion you tossed in some lime juice.

The good thing is, it's easy enough to either whip up a sprinkly bit while everything else cooks, or have a few of these things on hand in the fridge, jarred and ready for when you might need to pep up a meal. I love blitzing tired herbs with oil for green sauces. They never seem to come out the same way twice – sometimes I'll add chilli or garlic, a bit of citrus or vinegar, whatever I have knocking about – but pop them in a jar under oil and they'll keep for a few days in the fridge, ready to pep up your dinners.

If I'm honest, save for the obligatory ends of cheese, most of the time you'd be hard pressed to actually find much fresh produce in my fridge. Instead, it mainly serves as a kind of flavour cabinet, filled with treasures guaranteed to bring heat, acid and umami savouriness to my cooking. The top shelf is stacked precariously with pickles, chilli sauces and more varieties of mustard than one girl could possibly need, but the truth is I am a condiment addict, and I make no apologies. Those jars and bottles of sweet tartness and heat are the secret weapons in my culinary arsenal that smooth over mistakes and elevate even the most basic meals to something moreish and satisfying. Most plates end up with a shake, squadge or spoonful of some sort of condiment, or a little mound of something soused.

If a dish calls for pickled onions, I'll always make extra and pack the rest in a jar, adding them to everything from toasties to bowls of weeknight soup, curries, tacos, slow-cooked beans and stews. I always have some sort of pickled cucumber to hand, often just eating them whole from the fridge about five minutes after I've entered the house, but occasionally dicing them up to use in a dressing, relish or dip. There is usually something creamy in the fridge too – it's possible to save or enhance so many things, I find, with a dollop of tangy freshness from a pot of soured cream, crème fraîche or thick yoghurt.

I'm not generally a great one for a kitchen 'hack' – I'm not organised enough to have ice-cube trays filled with stock and wine, and I'll never be the kind of person who gets their breakfast ready and out on the side the night before (I'm in the 'leg it out of the door with wet hair in the direction of the nearest Americano' camp when it comes to a morning routine).

But if I could pass on one culinary trick, it's to do yourself a huge favour and keep a bag of breadcrumbs in the freezer.

I only realised you could do this a few years ago. I was preparing some crispy fried breadcrumbs for a supper club and massively overestimated how many I was going to need. I found myself with bags of the stuff and shoved them in the freezer, thinking they'd probably fuse together and I'd end up having to chuck them out. But no, I found that as long as you don't squeeze the bag too much when you stuff it in your freezer drawer, they stay conveniently separate. I've never looked back. The beauty of freezing your stale ends of bread is that you can then just grab a handful whenever the mood takes you, frying from frozen in a piping-hot pan with plenty of oil, or scattering them on a baking sheet and toasting them in the oven with garlic and salt. You can also just tear up chunks of stale bread rather than blitzing them to a crumb and freeze them for *migas* – that Spanish staple where leftover bread is torn up, rehydrated and fried in olive oil, often with chorizo, morcilla or peppers.

Do it today. Put a bag of torn or crumbed bread in your freezer, and give yourself the gift of instant salty crunch.

Forever breadcrumbs

I love ... adding crispy crumbs to probably far too many things. That salty crunch brings something to everything from pasta to pan-fried prawns, tenderstem broccoli, sautéed cabbage, risotto and even a tomato salad. It's why I like to blitz the ends of bread and freeze them, so I can have a handful of crumbs to fry off in a pan whenever I like.

Makes as many as you like
as much slightly stale
   white bread or sourdough
   as you like
plenty of olive oil
flaky salt

For the flavourings (optional)
1 garlic clove, bashed and peeled
anchovies
sesame seeds
citrus zest
flat-leaf parsley, leaves and stems
   finely chopped
chilli flakes
smoked salt

Blitz the bread in a food processor to make crumbs as coarse or as fine as you like them. Put the crumbs in a freezer bag and pop the bag in the freezer. Grab a handful whenever you need them.

When you come to cook them, set a large frying pan over a medium heat with plenty of olive oil. When the oil is piping hot, add the crumbs. Watch them, tossing them in the oil occasionally, leaving them to cook until golden brown and crispy. Transfer them to a plate lined with kitchen paper. Sprinkle with flaky salt.

If you want garlic breadcrumbs, add a bashed, peeled garlic clove to the oil as you fry the crumbs. If anchovy crumbs are what you're after, melt the anchovies in the oil first, then fry the crumbs. If you're using sesame seeds, scatter them into the pan for the final minute of frying.

Add any citrus zest, fresh herbs, chilli flakes or salt to the crumbs once they're cooked and have cooled a little.

Extremely. Addictive. Butter.

I love ... melting it on flatbreads or pizza dough, or on hot corn-on-the-cob; or cooking fat, juicy prawns in it.

250g unsalted butter, softened
5cm root ginger, peeled
2 large garlic cloves, peeled
a big handful of coriander
2 teaspoons smoked garlic granules

1 lime, zest and juice
a few dashes of hot sauce
2 teaspoons fish sauce
a good pinch of salt

Put all the ingredients in a food processor. Blitz until you get a smooth, vibrant green butter. At this point you could spoon it on to a sheet of cling film or baking paper, form it into a sausage, wrap it and freeze it, or you could use it straight away.

Tahini sauce

I love … serving this with barbecued aubergines, chicken and lamb.

Makes enough for 6–8 people
300g tahini
1 garlic clove, finely grated
a pinch of flaky salt
1 lemon, juiced
a pinch of sumac or za'atar

Using a balloon whisk, beat the tahini and garlic with the salt. Beat in the lemon juice to a thick paste, then a few drops at a time, beat in 50ml of water until smooth and creamy (you want the texture of pancake batter). To finish, sprinkle with the sumac or za'atar.

Aioli (with saffron or anchovy)

I love … having a bowl of this on the table with a roast chicken, a green salad and fried potatoes.

Makes enough for 6 people
2 egg yolks
100ml sunflower or
  rapeseed oil
125ml good olive oil
2 garlic cloves, finely
  grated
a good pinch of flaky salt
½ lemon, juiced
cracked black pepper

For the saffron aioli
a large pinch of saffron
  strands

For the anchovy aioli
6 salt-cured anchovies, finely
  chopped and mashed
  a little with a knife
a handful of flat-leaf parsley,
  leaves and stems chopped

For the basic aioli, using a balloon whisk, beat the eggs in a large bowl. Trickle in the oils very, very slowly, alternating between each, and beating continuously. Make sure each drop has emulsified before you add the next. When the aioli is thick and glossy, add the garlic, salt and season with plenty of black pepper. Then add the lemon juice and beat again. Use the same method for the saffron version, except put the lemon and saffron in a little bowl and leave to infuse for a few minutes, then stir through. For the anchovy, stir the chopped anchovies and parsley through the finished aioli.

Gremolata

I love … sprinkling this on meaty ragùs, beany soups and fishy braises (it's meant for osso buco). Make it ahead so the flavours have a chance to meld.

Makes enough for 5 people
a big handful of flat-leaf
  parsley, leaves and stems
  finely chopped
1 lemon, zest and juice
2 garlic cloves, finely grated
2 tablespoons olive oil
a pinch of flaky salt

Mix all the ingredients together and leave to sit until you're ready to serve.

Pink pickled onions

I love ... having these with leftover cold meats and for barbecues.

Makes enough for 6–8 people
200ml cider vinegar or white
  wine vinegar
2 tablespoons caster sugar
1 teaspoon salt
2 red onions, finely sliced

Optional
1 teaspoon yellow mustard
  seeds
1 teaspoon nigella seeds
1 star anise
1 cinnamon stick
a couple of small, dried
  chillies

Put the vinegar, sugar and salt in a small saucepan and bring the liquid to the boil. If you're using any aromatics, add them now. Simmer until the sugar has dissolved. Put the onions in a sterilised jar, pour the hot vinegar over them and put the lid on. Leave to cool completely at room temperature. The pickles will keep for up to 2 weeks in the fridge once opened; and longer unopened, depending on how cavalier you are.

Very quick pickled onions

I love ... making these for tacos and cheesy, chilli-topped fried eggs.

Makes enough for 4–6 people
1 red onion, finely sliced

1 teaspoon flaky salt
2 limes, juiced

Put the onion, salt and lime in a plastic container and scrunch it
all together with your fingers. Put the lid on the container and leave
the onions for 20 minutes (you can, of course, leave them for longer,
but 20 minutes is just enough to break down some of that oniony oomph),
occasionally shaking the container. Drain the liquid off and serve. If you
have leftovers, pop them in a jar under a little vinegar and they'll keep
for a few days in the fridge.

Dill pickled cucumber

I love ... eating these with fried fish and potato salads, piling them on
top of burgers and hot dogs, or finely chopping them and adding them
to a bagel with brisket, thick ham or salami and English mustard.

Makes 1 x 250ml jar
1 large 300g cucumber (or,
  better, use small pickling
  cucumbers – about 6)
1 teaspoon salt
150ml cider vinegar

50ml malt vinegar
1½ tablespoons caster sugar
½ teaspoon ground turmeric
2 teaspoons yellow mustard
  seeds
a few dill sprigs

Depending on how you want to use your pickles, you can either cut the
cucumber in half, then use a mandoline or a vegetable peeler to finely
slice it lengthways into ribbons, or you can use a knife to cut it into batons
(measure them up against the height of your jar to work out what length
they should be).

Lay the cucumber in a wide, shallow dish. Sprinkle the salt over it and
leave it for about 30 minutes.

Meanwhile, heat the vinegars with the sugar and turmeric in a small
pan, letting it come to a simmer. Cook until the sugar has dissolved
(about 3 minutes).

Wipe some of the salt off the cucumbers and pack them into a sterilised
jar, layering them with the mustard seeds and dill. Pour as much of the
hot vinegar over the cucumbers as you can get in the jar, pop the lid on
and leave it at room temperature until the pickling liquid is completely
cool. You can eat the cucumbers straight away once they're cooled, or keep
them for a couple of months in the fridge once opened (longer unopened,
depending on how cavalier you are).

Radishes in rice wine

I love … serving a little mound of these with something like glazed salmon and brown or jasmine rice. I make lots as they keep well in the fridge.

Makes enough for 8 people
2 tablespoons rice wine
3 tablespoons cider vinegar
    or white wine vinegar
2 teaspoons caster sugar
2 teaspoons black sesame
    seeds

5–6cm piece of root ginger,
    peeled and cut into
    matchsticks
a handful of radishes,
    very thinly sliced (use a
    mandoline if you have one)

Bring the wine, vinegar and sugar to a simmer in a small saucepan. Stir to dissolve the sugar, then add the sesame seeds and ginger and cook for 1 minute. Put the radishes in a sterilised jar and pour the hot vinegar (including the seends and ginger) over them. Seal and leave to cool. You can eat them straight away, or chill and eat them within about a week.

Pickle relish

I love … spooning this over Buttermilk Spatchcocked Chicken (see page 175). It's great in burgers too.

Makes enough for 4 people
2 large pickled gherkins
    (chip-shop, or the pickled
    cucumbers on page 23),
    finely chopped, plus
    1 tablespoon pickling liquid
1 small red onion, finely
    chopped

½ lemon, juiced
a good pinch of salt
a big handful of chives,
    snipped
2 handfuls of coriander,
    roughly chopped
a shake of Tabasco
1 tablespoon olive oil

Mix the pickles, onion, lemon and salt. Leave for 20 minutes, then add all the remaining ingredients. Let it sit for a bit before you serve.

Marinated feta

I love … crumbling this over tomato risotto and creamy polenta, and piling hunks of it into flatbreads with fried aubergine and onions.

Makes enough for 4 people
1 x 200g block of feta
1 lemon, zested
1 teaspoon chilli flakes

2 teaspoons fennel seeds
1 teaspoon coriander seeds,
    bashed
2 tablespoons good olive oil

Put the feta in a small dish. Sprinkle over the zest, chilli flakes and both seeds. Drizzle over the oil. Cover and refrigerate for 1 hour before serving.

Coriander dipping vinegar

I love ... spooning this over barbecued chicken, and serving it as a dip for cheese-stuffed flatbreads or Aubergine Fritters (see page 135).

Makes enough for 5 people
6 tablespoons sherry vinegar
2 teaspoons runny honey
1 teaspoon chilli flakes
a good pinch of salt

a big handful of coriander,
  leaves and stems finely
  chopped

Beat the vinegar, honey, chilli flakes and salt together with a fork. Stir through the coriander and leave to sit for a few minutes before serving.

Feta. Lemon. Herb. Crumble.

I love ... sprinkling this over slow-cooked lamb, or wilted greens and eggs on toast. It's also great mixed with olive oil, salt and black pepper and tossed through pasta for a super-quick dinner.

Makes enough for 5 people
  as a topping
1 x 200g block of feta
a big handful of flat-leaf
  parsley, leaves and stems
  finely chopped
1 lemon, zested, lemon
  reserved

Pat the feta dry with some kitchen paper, then use your hands to crumble it into a large bowl. You want fairly small pieces, so crumble it thoroughly. Add the parsley and stir to combine. Mix in the lemon zest, then cut each end off the lemon and, using a small knife, carefully remove the skin and pith. Roughly chop the flesh, taking care to discard any pips. Set the lemon flesh aside and add it to the feta mixture just before you're about to serve. (This is to avoid the lemon making the feta wet and creamy, which would make everything stick together.)

Nuoc cham

I love ... dunking spring and summer rolls in this, but I also often add a tablespoon of oil to it and use it as a dressing for a warm summer salad with some sort of griddled stone fruit and halloumi.

Makes enough for 4 people
  for dunking
30g dark muscovado sugar
2 teaspoons fish sauce
1 lime, juiced
2 teaspoons rice wine
2 teaspoons white wine
  vinegar
1 small green chilli, halved
  lengthways and finely
  sliced (with or without the
  seeds, depending on your
  preference)
1 large garlic clove, finely
  chopped
a pinch of salt

With a fork, beat the sugar, fish sauce, lime juice, rice wine, vinegar, chilli and garlic in a large bowl with the pinch of salt. Keep beating until the sugar dissolves.

Tapenade dressing

I love … spooning this over fish, particularly something meaty like tuna or hake.

Makes enough for 4 people
100g dry, salt-cured black
olives, pitted and chopped
a big handful of flat-leaf
parsley, leaves and stems
roughly chopped
6 cured anchovies (any will
do), finely chopped

2 garlic cloves, finely grated
1 lemon, juiced
1½ tablespoons red wine
vinegar
1 tablespoon olive oil
freshly cracked black pepper

In a large bowl, mix the chopped olives with the parsley, anchovies and garlic and season with black pepper. Add the lemon juice and vinegar, and lastly the olive oil.

Dressing-gown dinners

The time will come
when, with elation
you will greet yourself arriving
at your own door, in your own mirror
and each will smile at the other's welcome,

and say, sit here. Eat.
You will love again the stranger who was your self.
Give wine. Give bread. Give back your heart
to itself, to the stranger who has loved you

all your life, whom you ignored
for another, who knows you by heart.
Take down the love letters from the bookshelf,

the photographs, the desperate notes,
peel your own image from the mirror.
Sit. Feast on your life.

'Love After Love' by Derek Walcott

Toast, pastas and baked potatoes for the perfect sofa suppers

When I was a teenager, I lived in two worlds. One of them was real and filled with what I'm sure must have been a pretty classic cocktail of angst and boredom and avoiding homework and minor dramas that seemed catastrophically enormous. The other was the world inside my head, the imagined one that held the blueprint for the better, cooler, more glamorous adult version of my life. This world was far more vivid than the real thing, and it was also entirely based on romantic comedies.

To my mind, adult life was anything Richard Curtis, Nancy Meyers or Nora Ephron said it could be. Future me had a flat with a candlelit balcony and a red chaise longue like Bridget Jones and wore short skirts, big coats and red scarves (I still hear Chaka Khan every time I walk across a London bridge). She had a sweet, floppy-haired boyfriend like William Thacker, said hilarious and cutting things at weddings and wore dark lipstick like Fiona in *Four Weddings and a Funeral*. She strolled around Central Park in high-waisted jeans and had actually worked out how to get good curls. She ate in diners and held couples' dinner parties. She met men who looked like Ethan Hawke on trains to Vienna. And she wouldn't flinch before flying across the country to catch a glimpse of a man she'd heard on the radio, whose voice she'd inexplicably fallen in love with.

Tangled in my imaginings of this far-off place in the future, there was always food. There is one scene that I still love in a fantastically rubbish rom com called *Because I Said So*. Mandy Moore comes home to her shabby-chic Los Angeles apartment – all rust-coloured rugs, soft lamp light and exposed brick – after a long day and begins to make herself a bowl of pasta. Van Morrison's 'Days Like This' saunters along in the background as she drains a pan of steaming spaghetti, chops herbs and garlic, and sprinkles parmesan from a height. She moves slowly but purposefully, her shoulders visibly beginning to drop as she serves herself a generous helping in a beautiful bowl, pours a large glass of red, takes a sip and exhales.

When I was 16 years old and waiting for life to start, this seemed preposterously glamorous. The idea of coming home to your own flat, making yourself a bowl of pasta and drinking red wine with no one to bother you? To my incurably, painfully romantic teenage brain this was the apex of adult living. Now, I'm certain it's exactly the sort of meal we should all make ourselves more often.

A solo dinner can be a glorious thing. An important thing, even. In Kathleen Le Riche's 1954 book *Cooking Alone* – the essential guide to dining in solitude – there's a story about a young mother revelling in eating what she pleases while her children are out. She resolves to cook for herself when she is alone as generously as if she were her own guest. I love that. And as Bee Wilson, who wrote the foreword to the new edition, said, it's funny 'how radical a message that still seems' nearly 70 years on.

Perhaps it's something to do with having been single my entire life, but I have never understood why you wouldn't make yourself something delicious when it's just you for dinner. I seem to have so many friends (mainly, to be fair, male) who will eat a packet of plain Tesco tortellini or a sad frozen pizza when home alone rather than make themselves something really delicious. No shade on frozen pizza: a 3am slice of so-hot-it'll-take-the-roof-of-your-mouth-off frozen pepperoni is a kind of culinary nirvana. It's the attitude, not the food itself, that upsets me. You can eat what you like as far as I'm concerned, as long as it's really what you fancy. I think it's the grim functionality of it; that thing of reducing food to fuel. It's why I find energy bars so depressing: 'Get all the nutrients you need from a complete meal in one handy bar!' But why? Why would I want to get them all in one bar? Even if it is 'packed full of flax seed and cacao nibs'. Cacao nibs have a lot to answer for if you ask me.

A lot of the time, dinner needs to be cheap, quick or both. Sometimes it needs to literally do what it says on the tin and take up as little of your energy as possible. But I'm still not sure that means it shouldn't bring you joy when you eat it. And if you're the only one who is going to eat it, why not be generous with yourself? Why not give yourself the gift of a really delicious plate of food, however you define that?

There must, by now, have been infinite words written about the therapeutic powers of cooking and I wouldn't presume to have the final one (Nigella should obviously and by rights have the final word on all matters related to food and comfort). I would just like to put in a good word for pottering. Alone in my kitchen, as I am a lot of the time, I take really visceral pleasure in pottering. I love that thing of cooking with absolutely no pressure. My music (or podcast), my best pan, my clean chopping board, the good knife. A few things in the cupboard, some odds and ends in the fridge; no real plan other than the hope of a good dinner.

I remember the brilliant broadcaster Fi Glover saying once that the best radio has 'a sense of meandering purpose'. The most satisfying cooking is like that too, I find. The kind when you know what you want to eat but you've no roadmap for how to get there, nor a huge inclination to follow a recipe. Instead, you follow your nose and trust that all the meals behind you will inform the one in front of you. It's then that dinner becomes about more than the plate of food at the end; it's about the whole process of making yourself something to eat. For me, the business of cooking is what makes a great dinner so unendingly restorative. I find that thing of chopping an onion and sweating it in oil and a pinch of salt deeply soothing. But really, it's just about the quiet magic of satisfying your own hunger with something you really, really want to eat.

Now for a word on dressing gowns. I don't understand people who don't immediately get changed the second they get home. If I haven't taken my jeans off within the first 10 minutes of walking through the door then everything feels off. I just think there are indoor clothes and outdoor clothes, and if I'm going to wear denim on this side of my front door, then it's either going to be because I have people round or because they're at least a size too big, very soft and slouchy.

We all have our singular little rituals. Mine is coming home, washing my face, putting on my old dressing gown (a waffle number, now very much more greige than white and with a hole in a frankly pretty unfortunate place) and making dinner. Perhaps dressing gowns aren't for you. Maybe you're all about the big-t-shirt-and-giant-pants look; perhaps you're a matching-tracksuit person, like a novelty onesie, or have a drawer devoted to M&S granny nighties. Whatever floats your boat. My only stipulation for an evening spent revelling in your solo Friday night dinner is that you should be perfectly, exquisitely comfortable.

The recipes in this chapter are meals to be savoured entirely on your own, on a night when you need to shake off the week and slow everything down a notch. They're designed for one (though, it must be said, a very hungry one), but could all be increased to feed a crowd. Most you will be able to adapt according to what you have in or the bits you managed to pick up on the way home. They rely heavily on good store-cupboard ingredients, but might involve a small amount of shopping.

Some are pure, glorious indulgence (rarebit-smothered potatoes, a whole burrata with anchovies on toast); others are warming and satisfying (sesame and gochujang noodles, Bloody Mary rigatoni, saucy beans). Many of these dishes are the kind that you can eat straight from the pan because there's no one there to judge you, or in your favourite bowl on your lap in front of the telly. They are meals to cook gently, to eat in your dressing gown and, most importantly, to relish.

The Way We Were *baked potato with hot smoked salmon, soured cream and pickled radishes (see pages 40–1)*   37

Emergency spaghetti

There are some ingredients that, if ever I find I'm running low on them, I start to feel on edge. Garlic, olive oil, lemon, a block of parmesan, some sort of pasta – they are my store-cupboard stalwarts and the most used ingredients in my kitchen by a country mile. If I were cast away to a desert island and allowed to take only five ingredients with me, I'm almost certain it would be these five. Lemon, garlic and olive oil find their way into almost everything I cook; parmesan (either a handful, grated, or a chunk of rind) makes everything taste better, more savoury, more of itself; and I don't want to be dramatic, but I'm not sure I could actually contemplate a life without pasta.

Whenever I ponder the desert-island-ingredients question (which I do with the intensity and regularity of someone for whom being cast away to a desert island might actually be a possibility – yes I do make for a really fun first date, thanks for asking), I struggle with the idea of leaving tomatoes and potatoes behind. What if I could use them to grow my own, like Matt Damon in *The Martian*? Perhaps I could swap out the olive oil – there are bound to be a few coconuts knocking about the island. And I could salt-dry the tomatoes and preserve them, I'll have nothing else to do. Then again wouldn't I miss chocolate? Where to keep it though, it'll melt. Maybe there'll be a very cold cave to store it in...

Given the likelihood of my needing to test this list of essential ingredients is slim, I should probably get something resembling 'A Life' and stop daydreaming about a world in which I just eat very garlicky spaghetti alone on a desert island until the end of time. Then again, it sounds quite nice.

I use my top five ingredients all the time and in a million different ways, but they're perhaps at their best when they all meet in the same pan for one of those brilliant, failsafe pastas the Italians call *spaghettata di mezzanotte* – 'midnight spaghetti'. There are so many versions of this pasta, and you should feel free to make it your own too. That's the beauty of emergency spaghetti. It's different every time because it relies on ingredients you already have in your kitchen. If I don't have anchovies but find a jar of capers at the back of the fridge or a tin of briny olives, I'll swap them in. No parsley? No matter – a few fresh herbs are nice but not essential. Ideally, this pasta should require absolutely no shopping whatsoever. It's a spur-of-the-moment dinner, one that I adapt according to what I have in stock. It's the sort of meal that once I've thought of making it, I tend to find nothing else will do. It's like when someone says the word chips and then all you can think about is where and how fast you could acquire a bag of salty, vinegar-sodden, chip-shop chips. This pasta is like that for me. I can be flicking through the mental rolodex of dinners on the bus home, famished and trying to fathom 1) what I actually want to eat and 2) whether I can be bothered to make it – then I remember there's always emergency spaghetti. After that, there's no going back.

I make it after late nights in the pub, and for the first meal back after a holiday or the first dinner in a new home, and at the end of a very long week. It's emergency spaghetti, and it never, ever lets me down.

Serves 1

100g spaghetti
3 tablespoons good
  olive oil
30g coarse, stale
  breadcrumbs
2 garlic cloves, finely
  sliced
4 salt-cured anchovies
½ teaspoon chilli flakes
1 lemon, zest and juice
a small handful of
  flat-leaf parsley, leaves
  and stems roughly
  chopped
flaky salt and cracked
  black pepper
grated parmesan,
  to serve

Set a large pan of well-salted water on to boil. When the water is boiling vigorously, cook the spaghetti until al dente, then drain it, reserving a good 3 tablespoons of the cooking water.

Meanwhile, set a frying pan over a medium heat and add half the oil. Fry the breadcrumbs until golden – toss them regularly in the oil and watch they don't catch. Transfer them to a plate lined with kitchen paper and season with flaky salt.

Wipe out the pan and return it to the heat, which you should turn down low. Add the remaining oil and fry the garlic and anchovies. You want the garlic to turn golden, but not catch, and the anchovies to melt. This shouldn't take more than 2 minutes. Take the pan off the heat and add the chilli flakes. Cook for slightly less than 1 minute in the residual heat of the pan.

When the pasta is cooked, add it to the garlic pan along with the reserved cooking water, lemon zest and juice, the parsley and half the breadcrumbs. Put the pan over a low heat and use tongs to toss everything together. You want the sauce to really stick to the pasta. Keep it moving until every strand is well coated.

Tumble the pasta into a bowl and serve it topped with the remaining crumbs, a sprinkling of black pepper and some grated parmesan.

The Way We Were *baked potato with hot smoked salmon, soured cream and pickled radishes*

There is a scene in *The Way We Were* that I've always loved. Robert Redford is staying at Barbra Streisand's apartment. He hasn't realised he's in love with her yet (is he ever truly in love with her? Probably a discussion for another time ...), and on Friday night when she gets home from work, he is already on his way out. Babs has been thinking of the dinner she's going to make him all day. She has gone to the shops on the way home and picked up everything she needs. She arrives home laden with all the things surely guaranteed to woo. 'No, you can't. You can't. You can't,' she yelps. 'I got steaks and potatoes and soured cream and chives and salad and fresh baked pie. I would have made pot roast – I make a terrific pot roast – but I didn't know if you liked pot roast.' She is rambling breathlessly, a bunch of yellow daisies in the crook of one arm, a paper bag bursting with shopping in the other.

'Anyway, there wasn't time, because it should be made the day before, so I got steaks! With all my ration stamps! You can't go yet. You've got to stay for supper, that's all there is to it!' Redford just looks at her with those piercing blue eyes and says: 'What kind of pie?'

If steak is what you've a hankering for, you should absolutely go and get a steak (turn to page 84 for inspiration). For a solo dinner, I love a slightly simpler accompaniment to my jacket. These are filled with hot smoked salmon, dill, quick-pickled radishes (using the same recipe as on page 24, but omitting the rice wine, ginger and sesame seeds and using a few nigella seeds instead) and salmon roe, along with the obligatory soured cream. It's special enough to feel like a Friday night dinner, but happily low key.

This will yield too many pickled radishes, but if I were you, I'd make a decent-sized batch as they keep well for a couple of days in the fridge. If you'd rather just make a little pile of them for tonight's dinner, use the same amount of vinegar and sugar, just discard the liquid before serving. And perhaps use something closer to a pinch of nigella seeds.

(Photograph on pages 36–7.)

Serves 1

1–2 large baking potatoes, depending on greed
3 tablespoons cider vinegar (or white wine vinegar)
1 teaspoon caster sugar
1 teaspoon nigella seeds
a handful of radishes, topped, tailed and very finely sliced
2 tablespoons soured cream
2 spring onions, finely chopped
a small handful of dill (or chives), chopped
flaky salt and cracked black pepper

To serve
chilled butter
40g hot smoked salmon or trout
some salmon or trout roe (optional, but recommended)
a lemon wedge

Preheat the oven to 200°C/180°C fan/Gas 6.

Wash the potatoes and prick them with a fork. While they're still damp, sprinkle them with plenty of salt. Put them directly on the oven shelf and bake them for about 1 hour 15 minutes (or more, depending on how big your potatoes are). They are done when the skin is crisp, but the flesh feels very soft underneath.

While the potatoes are cooking, heat the vinegar with the sugar and nigella seeds in a small pan over a low–medium heat until the sugar has dissolved. Pour the liquid over the radishes and leave it to cool while you do everything else.

Mix the soured cream with the spring onions, half the dill and a little salt and black pepper.

To serve, cut open the potatoes and pile in chilled butter, the soured cream mixture and flakes of smoked fish. Finish with more dill, a pile of pickled radishes, a couple of spoonfuls of roe, if you like, and a wedge of lemon.

Very briny martini

'Can I tell you what's messed up about James Bond?' says President Bartlet à propos of not very much in *The West Wing*. 'Shaken not stirred will get you cold water with a dash of gin and dry vermouth. The reason you stir it with a special spoon is so as not to chip the ice. James is ordering a weak martini and being snooty about it.' I love a drink that comes with a bit of ceremony, where the making of it is all part of the experience. Sometimes you just want a gin and tonic any way up and quick as you can. But methodically preparing yourself a proper martini can be a strangely therapeutic thing. It also, I think, seems like the perfect cocktail for one.

As someone who can't handle more than one, I'm in awe of the writer Patricia Highsmith who, on several occasions, had seven martinis over the course of a meal. She wrote in her diary in 1945, 'I wonder if any moment surpasses that of the second martini at lunch, when the waiters are attentive, when all life, the future, the world seems good and gilded (it matters not at all whom one is with, male or female, yes or no).' It's as persuasive an advert for leaning into the good things in life as any I've ever heard. And is there anything more glamorous than a lunch martini?

Serve your martini as you like – shaken or stirred, with an olive, onion, lemon peel or nothing at all. If you like an olive, add a little of the brine as I have here (you might know it as a 'Dirty Martini'). It adds an extra salty oiliness, which I love.

Serves 1

lots of ice
60ml very cold gin
20ml dry vermouth
2 teaspoons olive brine
2 green olives
1 strip of lemon peel

Put a martini glass in the fridge to chill.

Tip the ice into a jug and pour in the gin, vermouth and olive brine. Stir it carefully with a martini spoon (or any long spoon) so you don't chip the ice.

Put the olives in your cold martini glass. Run the lemon peel around the rim, then put it in the glass with the olives. Using a strainer, pour over the ice-cold gin mixture.

Port and pomegranate

I like a cocktail that makes me feel like I could be in a Slim Aarons photograph. The ones where people with big hair and flares are gathered around a beautiful pool in Palm Springs at cocktail hour, or have stopped at an ice bar half way up a ski slope for a snifter. I like the confidence of a 1970s cocktail, when the rule seems to have been: the brighter and sweeter the better, and keep the maraschino cherries coming. Lotta crème de menthe around at that time, and drinks named after men, like a Harvey Wallbanger (vodka, orange juice, Galliano), or an Arnold Palmer (three parts unsweetened tea to one part lemonade – called a John Daly if you add vodka).

A port and pomegranate won't have quite the saccharine punch of a 70s cocktail, but it does have that gloriously retro look. I love a white port (drier and fresher than dark port) and tonic, and the dash of grenadine in this makes it a little longer and sweeter. You can serve this mixed, or lean into the retro look and pour the grenadine down the edge of the glass at the end for that sunrise look.

Serves 1

lots of ice
80ml white port
tonic water
2 teaspoons grenadine
   syrup

To serve (optional)
a few pomegranate seeds
   (or even a maraschino
   cherry)
a thin slice of orange

Fill a tall glass with ice and pour in the white port. Top with the tonic, leaving 1cm at the top of the glass free. Once the bubbles have settled, tilt the glass and pour the grenadine down the side. Top with pomegranate seeds (or cherry) and slice of orange, if you're using them.

Dressing-gown dinners

Sardines on toast with lemon and hot sauce

Few things in life are quite as reassuring as toast. Sourdough or C.W.S.B. (crap white sliced bread); spelt, soda or rye – a great piece of toast when you're ravenous knocks most things out of the park. Mostly, I'd take heavily laden toast over a sandwich. The Danes get so much right – furniture, murder shows, gender equality, cities that are set up for cycling – but their approach to sandwiches is particularly spot on. The *smørrebrød* is surely Queen of the Sarnies, mainly because you can fit double the amount of filling on one slice and then legitimately have two.

Toast for dinner gets a bad rap. It sounds lacking in inspiration – a bit unexciting. I tend to think the opposite is true. A sturdy slice of toast is a vehicle for favourite things: greens cooked with olive oil and garlic and topped with shavings of hard, sharp cheese; eggs any-which-way; onions cooked almost to a paste, with anchovies; and this, which I think makes for a pretty stylish one-person dinner.

This recipe always reminds me of the high tea that Lucy and Mr Tumnus share in *The Lion, the Witch and the Wardrobe* (the tape of which I wore out as a child): 'A nice brown egg, lightly boiled, for each of them, and then sardines on toast, and then buttered toast, and then toast with honey, and then a sugar-topped cake.' Doesn't that just sound like a meal you want to eat all the time?

Serves 1

2 tablespoons salted butter, softened
1 small garlic clove, finely grated
a few dashes of Tabasco, plus optional extra to serve
½ lemon, zest and juice, plus extra wedges to serve
2 (or more) thick slices of sourdough, not cut especially neatly (craggy bits that are extra-toasty are a good thing)
1 large, very ripe tomato, thickly sliced
1 x 80g tin of good sardines in olive oil
a few flat-leaf parsley sprigs, leaves and stems finely chopped
flaky salt

In a bowl, mash the butter with the garlic, Tabasco and lemon juice. Add a little salt if it needs it (depending on the saltiness of your butter). Set aside.

Toast your bread well. You want some proper crunch.

While the toast is still warm but not piping hot, spread it thickly with the garlic butter (or spread it while it's still hot – I just like it when the butter doesn't entirely melt). Top with slices of tomato and a couple of sardines. Finish with lemon zest, parsley and more Tabasco, if you like, and a couple of extra lemon wedges for squeezing over. Eat immediately.

Toast with whipped brown butter and little lemony shrimp

Somewhere close to the top of the list of greatest ever kitchen smells – underneath the scent of sizzling bacon on an autumnal Sunday morning but, I'd argue, possibly controversially, coming in just above freshly baked bread – has got to be the smell of butter browning. When it's approaching its peak, a few seconds away from needing to be whipped from the hob, it's as if you've stepped inside a packet of Werther's Originals. That sweet, toffee nuttiness is intoxicating. It's confusing too – I don't know whether I want to beat it with icing sugar and slather it on a cake or use it to fry a few chestnut mushrooms with garlic. Every time I make it, I wonder why I don't do so every day. It seems to make most things better, improving everything from a pan of brownies to mashed potatoes.

I like to make too much, pour it into a jar and keep it solidified in the fridge just as you would a pat of unbrowned butter. That way, I can scoop some out when I need it, warming it through with sage and garlic to toss with ravioli, or letting a few cold nuggets drip through a bowl of piping-hot new potatoes.

One of the best things to do with it, though, is to make this shrimp toast. I love the old-fashioned glamour of this perfect one-person dinner. It has all the main components of a retro potted shrimp – namely: butter, spice, and tiny brown peeled shrimp. But rather than clarifying the butter and creating a thick, custard-yellow seal, the butter is browned and then whipped until smooth and glossy to be spread thickly on toast.

The buttered shrimp also work really well as a nibble if you spoon them on to little fried or toasted squares of soda bread or thin slices of baguette. I love making a version of this for a special brunch too, piling the shrimp on to toasted muffins and topping them with poached eggs and plenty of chopped chives.

Serves 1 (with plenty of brown butter left over)

170g salted butter
1 garlic clove, peeled and bashed
70g brown shrimp
a little grated nutmeg
a pinch of cayenne
½ lemon, juiced, plus extra wedges to serve
1–2 thick slices of bread (soda, a good brown or sourdough work well)
cracked black pepper
a few flat-leaf parsley leaves, to serve (optional)

Put the butter in a small saucepan over a low–medium heat. You'll need to cook it for about 11 minutes, maybe a bit longer, until the butter is browning and smells toffeeish. Watch it while it's cooking, checking the milk solids don't burn. When the liquid is golden and the solids pale brown, and everything smells incredible, take the pan off the heat and pour the butter into a bowl, making sure to get all the milk solids out.

Leave it to cool for 20 minutes, then put it in the fridge to firm up a little. When it's started to solidify in places (this should take about another 40 minutes), take it out of the fridge and beat it with an electric whisk until it's thick and glossy – it should be the consistency of butter icing. It's now ready to use, but you can put it back in the fridge and let it solidify further, if you like. I like to spread it on toast when it's cool but spreadable, not cold and rock solid.

To cook the shrimp, take a spoonful of the browned butter and put it back in the pan over a medium heat. When melted, add the garlic and swirl it around in the butter. Leave to cook for 1 minute.

Add the shrimp, nutmeg and cayenne and season with some black pepper. Stirring regularly, cook the shrimp in the butter for about 4 minutes, or until heated through and glossy. Add the lemon juice and cook for another 1 minute.

Meanwhile, toast the bread well.

To serve, spread the toast thickly with some of the smooth, chilled brown butter and pile the lemony shrimp on top. Finish with parsley, if using, and serve with lemon wedges for squeezing.

Burrata for one (on toast, with marinated anchovies)

Is a whole burrata for one person too much? Possibly, yes. Should that deter you? Absolutely not. Life is too short not to occasionally smother a piece of toast with an entire burrata.

If you wanted to serve something with this 'for health' (but also because it's delicious), I like a peppery watercress, endive or rocket salad tossed with a little olive oil and thick balsamic, or another kind of fruity vinegar whisked with some honey. The bitter leaves and sweet, syrupy dressing work so well with the burrata and anchovies.

Serves 1

6 really good anchovies
½ lemon, zest and juice
a few thin slices of red
　　chilli (with or without
　　seeds, as you wish)
2 teaspoons olive oil
2 thick slices of bread
　　(sourdough, ciabatta
　　or something else
　　open-textured would
　　work best)
1 garlic clove, peeled
1 small burrata

Lay the anchovies on a plate, sprinkle the lemon zest over them, scatter with chilli and drizzle over the oil. Cover and leave for at least 30 minutes for the flavours to mingle.

Set a griddle pan over a medium heat. Griddle the bread so it toasts and blackens a bit. When it's still hot, rub the garlic over each slice.

Break the burrata in half and roughly spread one half on each slice of toast, making sure you have a good distribution of the tougher outer layer and gooey centre. Lay three anchovies on top of each slice, saving the marinating oil. Pour the oil into a bowl, add the lemon juice and beat with a fork to make a dressing. Drizzle the dressing over the toasts.

Mushrooms with sherry vinegar, potatoes, soured cream and toasted buckwheat

I love the confidence of a meal that is less a complete dish than it is a few good things thrown together. No one ingredient gets centre stage – they all need and bolster each other. Often, I find, the best way to go about assembling these sorts of dinners is to think about ingredients that grow together, or at least ones that emerge at the same time of year. The French are so good at this – peaches with lavender honey and fresh goat's cheese; figs and almonds; tomatoes, courgettes and thyme; pumpkin, chestnuts and game. They could all have come from the same field, not just the same moment in the calendar. Together, they taste exactly as they should and don't require much else to make them shine.

Throughout the year, I make endless versions of this dinner, swapping things in and out depending on where the weather leads my appetite. In the summer, I'll swap the fried mushrooms for ripe tomatoes, leaving them raw but still tossing them in the sherry vinegar and a little salt. The soured cream might be replaced by aioli (see page 21), or a dollop of cold labneh or ricotta. In spring, steamed new potatoes replace the crispy chunks of Maris, I might roast a couple of beetroot in place of the mushrooms and add a mound of cucumber, peeled, sliced and dressed with crème fraîche, loosened to a dressing with lemon, vinegar and olive oil.

For this autumnal incarnation, I love adding a sprinkle of toasted buckwheat (I also find this makes a great last-minute addition to bowls of ragù and other pastas). It gives a toasty crunch that works so well – the little extra savoury bite you didn't know you needed.

Serves 1

Preheat the oven to 230°C/210°C fan/Gas 8.

2 large Maris Piper potatoes, peeled and cut into large chunks
2 tablespoons olive oil
1 rosemary sprig, leaves stripped
2 garlic cloves, skin on
3 teaspoons buckwheat (or chopped hazelnuts or pine nuts)
60g butter (use brown butter if you have some – see page 49)
170g mushrooms (ideally chanterelles, left whole; or chestnuts, halved)

Toss the potatoes in the olive oil on a baking sheet. Scatter the rosemary leaves over the potatoes along with a little salt. Add the garlic too. Roast for 45 minutes, or until the potatoes are golden and crispy.

Meanwhile, set a frying pan over a medium heat and dry fry the buckwheat (or hazelnuts or pine nuts) for 1 minute, until it smells toasty. Transfer to a plate to cool.

Turn the heat up under the pan and melt the butter. Add the mushrooms and cook until well browned – keep going until they've really reduced in size and have a good colour on them (this might take a good 20 minutes). Use a slotted spoon to transfer them from the pan to a plate.

a little sherry vinegar
1 head of little gem (or
  endive, if you fancy
  something punchier)
½ shallot, finely sliced
½ lemon, juiced
flaky salt
soured cream, to serve
a few chives, snipped,
  to serve

Sprinkle flaky salt over the mushrooms, then put your thumb over the end of the vinegar bottle and shake some vinegar over them – not so much that they go soggy.

Trim the end off the little gem and quarter it. Toss the leaves and shallot in the lemon juice and a little salt.

To serve, transfer the hot, crispy potatoes to a plate with the soft garlic cloves and top with the vinegar-y mushrooms. Put a little pile of leaves on the side and a great dollop of soured cream. Finish with a few chives and the toasted buckwheat.

Glazed broccoli with sesame noodles and a crispy egg

There are few things quite so satisfying when you're starving as a deep bowl of salty, spicy, sticky noodles. I love boiling dried, quick-cook noodles for just a couple of minutes so that they retain some chew, then tossing them in a dressing that has the perfect balance of salt, sweet, acid and heat. For this iteration, there is sweetness from maple syrup, acid from rice vinegar and umami heat from gochujang, the addictively good Korean chilli paste made from fermented soybean, chilli powder and sweet glutinous rice. Sesame oil and paste bring that essential nuttiness. You could use Chinese sesame paste or tahini, though it's worth noting that Asian sesame paste is made from toasted sesame seeds, whereas Middle Eastern tahini is made from raw, hulled grains. It also has a coarser texture than tahini and has a nuttier, more savoury flavour.

You could make this with Tenderstem broccoli, but I like how the fluffy heads of an old-fashioned broc absorb the liquid and crisp up in the oven. The fried egg isn't essential, but I do love it when the yolk drips down into the noodles, mixing with the sauce and making it instantly richer.

Often, I'll serve this with a quick pickle, or just some cucumber, peeled and cut into batons, with a little salt and rice vinegar shaken over them. This goes really well with a few of the pickled radishes on page 24. I also like to make double the recipe so that there are cold noodles to eat the next day, possibly with another hot, fried egg, and definitely with more lip-tingling crispy chilli oil.

Serves 1

1½ tablespoons sesame oil
½ broccoli head, broken into florets
1 tablespoon maple syrup
1 teaspoon gochujang
1 garlic clove, finely grated
1 tablespoon rice or white wine vinegar
1 teaspoon tahini (or other sesame paste)
1 tablespoon dark soy sauce
60g medium quick-cook dried noodles
1 egg
olive oil, for frying
flaky salt

Preheat the oven to 230°C/210°C fan/Gas 8.

Put the sesame oil in a large bowl along with the broccoli florets and a little salt. Toss them in the oil, then use tongs to transfer them to a baking sheet, leaving the excess oil in the bowl. Roast the florets for 10 minutes.

Meanwhile, add the maple syrup, gochujang, garlic and vinegar to the sesame bowl. Whisk to combine.

Take the florets out of the oven and return them to the bowl. Toss them in the maple mixture to coat well, then put them back on the sheet, leaving the excess mixture in the bowl. Roast for another 5 minutes, or until crisped up and glazed.

Meanwhile, add the sesame paste to the maple bowl and whisk to combine. Then, add the soy sauce.

Cook the noodles until just al dente (you want them a little chewy still), then drain them and add them to

To serve
2 spring onions, finely
sliced
as much crispy chilli oil as
you like (I love the Lao
Gan Ma crispy chilli)
a pinch of black sesame
seeds

the bowl with the maple and soy mixture. Toss the
hot noodles in the sauce.

While the noodles are cooking, fry the egg in plenty
of oil in a hot frying pan. I like crispy edges and a
runny yolk, but fry the egg just as you like it.

To serve, tumble the broccoli on top of the noodles,
top with the fried egg, a few spring onions, crispy
chilli oil and a sprinkle of sesame seeds.

Cheese-jar potatoes with fennel and apple salad

In my humble opinion, these are game-changing potatoes. Golden, crunchy,
blanketed in thick, Colman's-licked rarebit sauce, with a crisp, tart salad to
cut through the almost fondue-y richness. I've always loved the idea of covering
potatoes with cheese. Nigel Slater does a good line in a cheesy tattie. In fact,
I remember reading a recipe in the original *Kitchen Diaries* for what he called
'smothered potatoes'. They were to be cooked on 'a cold night' with onion, garlic,
thyme and fontina, possibly as a side dish, but more likely as the main event.
I didn't realise you could just have cheesy potatoes for tea. It seemed like
cheating, and I loved it.

This is one of those sauces that provides you with a good opportunity to use up
all those gnarly, forgotten bits of cheese in the fridge. My nanna always kept a
jar of cheese in her 1970s Electrolux. It was where all the odds and ends went to
die, only to live again in a white sauce or a delicious if extremely unorthodox
carbonara, or to be stirred through a leek and potato soup. She was born in
Wembley in 1919 and would never have heard the word umami, but that's just
what her cheese jar was for. It gave everything that funky oomph; it was her own
homemade flavour-enhancer. Almost certainly unsanitary, but a risk worth taking
for a truly exemplary cheese sauce.

This isn't just a cheese sauce though, it's a rarebit – that thick, unctuous concoction
made with stout and enough Colman's to make your eyes water. You could add
hunks of ham hock or some lardons so it becomes something more akin to a
tartiflette. Onions would be a good addition, roasted alongside the potatoes or
lightly pickled and served in a mound on the side. A little finely chopped rosemary
would be lovely in the roasting pan, or fresh parsley to finish. It's a great dish for
a crowd, but works surprisingly well for a solo dinner. It's proper Friday comfort
food, crying out for an old movie and a night under a blanket.

And, if after making it you still have a small hunk of cheddar left over, why not
start your own cheese jar?

Serves 1

For the fennel and apple salad
1 tablespoon cider vinegar
1 tablespoon good olive oil
1 teaspoon wholegrain mustard
1 teaspoon runny honey
½ fennel bulb, very finely sliced
1 very cold Granny Smith apple, finely sliced

For the potatoes
as many small waxy potatoes as you think you can eat
1 teaspoon olive oil
flaky salt
a few chives, snipped, to serve

For the rarebit
15g butter
2 teaspoons plain flour
½ teaspoon English mustard powder
60ml beer, stout or cider
100g strong cheese, grated or crumbled
1 teaspoon Colman's English mustard
a few dashes of Worcestershire sauce
1 egg yolk, lightly beaten

Preheat the oven to 210°C/190°C fan/Gas 7.

First, get started on the salad. Whisk together the cider vinegar, olive oil, mustard and honey to make a dressing and toss it together with the fennel. Leave the fennel to marinate in the dressing while the potatoes cook.

Put the potatoes in an oven dish. Drizzle them with the oil and sprinkle over a little salt. Roast the potatoes in the oven for 30 minutes, until tender and golden brown.

Meanwhile, make the rarebit. In a small saucepan, melt the butter over a medium heat. Then, add the flour and mustard powder and stir continuously so it comes together in a roux. Cook for a couple of minutes so the flour loses its raw taste, then add the beer, stout or cider and stir to combine. Add the cheese, mustard and Worcestershire sauce and keep stirring until the cheese has melted. Then, add the yolk and beat to combine.

Remove the pan from the heat and set the rarebit aside while the potatoes finish cooking. When they've had their 30 minutes, remove them from the oven and crush each one with the back of a spoon. Put the dish back in the oven for 10 minutes, until the potatoes crisp up. Meanwhile, heat your grill to high.

Remove the potatoes from the oven and cover them in the sauce. Pop the smothered potatoes under the hot grill and grill until the sauce is bubbling and browning.

Meanwhile, slice the apple and add it to the fennel salad, giving it all a quick toss together.

To serve, scatter chives over the potatoes and eat them with the salad and perhaps a few cornichons or pickled onions.

A brief word on pasta

I am incapable of cooking the correct
amount of pasta.

That, right there? That was a lie. I just lied to you. I'd apologise
but I suspect you knew it was a lie. The thing is, I do know how
to cook the correct amount of pasta. I just choose to cook more
than I need, which, coincidentally, is always exactly the amount
that I want.

Often, I'll play a little game with myself, leaving a small half
portion back in the pan. Am I going to come back and eat the
rest once I've finished this regular-sized bowlful? Of course
I am. Pigs will fly, Oasis will tour again, Huw Edwards will
start presenting events of major national importance in a unitard
before I leave pasta uneaten in a pan to be 'put in the fridge
for tomorrow's lunch'. 'Oh, I always make too much,' she cried,
daintily transferring her leftovers into a container from the
neatly stacked, totally accessible drawer of plastic food boxes.
No need to even hunt for the correct lid – there it was, ready
and waiting for her.

Unfortunately, that is not my life, and it never will be. In my
defence, I come by this refusal to cook the right amount of food
or keep a neat container drawer honestly. My mum is very much
of the 'Are-you-sure-that-will-be-enough-spaghetti?' school of
thought, and her plastic container drawer is like the seventh
circle of hell. (Sorry, Mum.)

There are some parts of ourselves that we just can't do
anything about, and nor should we try. For instance, I will
always be very bad at packing – open my suitcase on the first
day of a holiday and you will find an awful lot of, frankly,
baffling things that I definitely won't need in there. I will always
maintain that broken biscuits don't count (see also: ice cream
when eaten with a teaspoon, from the tub, while standing in
front of the freezer, with the door open). I will always secretly
want to watch *Mamma Mia! Here We Go Again* (go on, Cher)
over any of your art-house, Baumbachian, commentary-on-the-
middle-class, cult classics. And I will always, always cook too
much pasta.

Bloody Mary rigatoni

There are some pastas born entirely out of a combination of profound hunger and happy accident. This is one such pasta. A craving for something deeply, lip-smackingly savoury with a bit of a kick; tomato-y but not especially saucy; a little creamy without being heavy; a pasta that sits somewhere between sexy and ordinary. Sometimes when I'm really hungry, I find I go into a kind of trance while I cook, picking up bottles and jars without much of a game plan, shaking in a bit of this, a bit of that, tasting as I go. It's at times like these that the most delicious dinners seem to emerge. This is one of them. I call her Bloody. Mary. Rigatoni.

She follows a similar set of principles to the New York/Italian classic pasta alla vodka, but with a few notable additions: celery seeds, a healthy dash of Worcestershire sauce, and as much hot sauce as you can take. At her core she's just a pretty simple tomato sauce, the kind you've made a thousand times. But then she has the audacity to go and have all the umami, peppery thwack of a really good, hangover-beating Bloody Mary. She's a happy accident of a dinner that quickly became a failsafe I've returned to again and again.

I favour a fruity hot sauce for this, so using something like a bottle of Frank's would be perfect. You could, of course, use fresh or dried chillies, though I find the slightly sweet, vinegary tang of a bottled chilli sauce adds something. I use rigatoni, because it will really catch the sauce. Serve the pasta under a cloud of parmesan and black pepper.

Serves 1

1 tablespoon butter
2 teaspoons olive oil
1 red onion, finely sliced
1 celery stick, very finely chopped
100g rigatoni
1 large garlic clove, grated
½ teaspoon celery seeds (or 1 teaspoon celery salt and reduce the flaky salt)
3 tablespoons tomato purée
2 teaspoons Frank's hot sauce (or other, to taste)
a good few dashes of Worcestershire sauce
1 tablespoon vodka or gin
½ lemon, juiced
50ml double cream
flaky salt
grated parmesan and ground black pepper, to serve

Put the butter and olive oil in a heavy-based saucepan over a low–medium heat. When the butter has melted, add the onion and celery and a good pinch of salt. Cover the pan with the lid and cook the onion and celery for 15 minutes, or until both have turned properly soft.

Meanwhile, put the pasta on. Cook the rigatoni in plenty of well-salted boiling water, until al dente. Reserve a couple of tablespoons of cooking water when you come to drain it.

Add the garlic and celery seeds (or celery salt) to the onion and celery and cook, without the lid, for 1 minute. Turn the heat up a little and add the tomato purée, hot sauce and Worcestershire sauce. Cook, stirring, for 2 minutes, then add the vodka, lemon juice and a good pinch of salt. Cook for 2 minutes, stirring, until the sauce has come together and looks smooth and glossy. Take the pan off the heat.

Tip the pasta and the reserved cooking water into the pan with the sauce and add the cream. Put the pan back over a low heat and mix everything together, tossing it thoroughly to make sure the sauce is clinging to the pasta. Serve with plenty of parmesan and black pepper.

Bucatini with mushroom cream and crispy sage

As a general rule, I'm a more filling than cake, more custard than crumble, more sauce than pasta girl. When it comes to a coffee and walnut, I'm in it for the buttercream, and I like a bowl of pasta that I need to finish with a spoon. Not that there's anything wrong with a neat bowlful, where just enough sauce clings to just the right amount of tagliatelle. You wouldn't, for example, necessarily want your carbonara swimming in golden yolk – I tend to think you're after a level of sauciness that will have each strand of spaghetti glistening. Sometimes, though, I want a proper puddle of sauce in the base of the bowl, the kind that is going to get trapped in the grooves and crevices of the pasta and require a spoon or hunk of bread to finish the job properly. With some pastas, more is more. This is one such pasta.

The mushrooms are soaked and then fried in butter. Marmite adds to their naturally funky, savoury punch, and the cream, nutmeg and madeira give the whole thing a rich, slightly retro flavour. I love the way the bucatini catches the sauce and makes for some really exemplary slurping.

If blitzing it all feels like one step too far for a Friday night, you could absolutely skip that step and leave the mushrooms chunky. I just rather like the creamy, concentrated sauce you get from whizzing and straining it. If you're leaving the mushrooms whole, you might want to add a few fresh ones to the pan too when you're browning the dried. They'll bring a welcome bite alongside the softer rehydrated wild mushrooms. A few toasted pine nuts would be a lovely addition alongside the crispy sage. A cloud of grated parmesan is absolutely essential. Serve the pasta in a good bowl, which you should pre-warm so the sauce at the bottom holds its heat for longer, finish with a drizzle of olive oil, and sink into a generous helping of bucatini with slightly too much sauce.

(Photograph on page 31.)

Serves 1

30g dried mushrooms
1 teaspoon Marmite
200ml just-boiled water
olive oil, for frying and
   finishing
a few sage leaves
40g butter, plus an extra
   teaspoon cold from
   the fridge
1 shallot, roughly
   chopped
1 garlic clove,
   finely sliced
1 lemon, juiced

Put the mushrooms and Marmite in a large bowl. Pour over the hot water, stir and cover the bowl with a plate. Leave the mushrooms for 15 minutes to rehydrate.

Set a frying pan over a medium–high heat and add a good glug of olive oil. Fry the sage leaves until crispy, then remove them from the pan to a plate, sprinkle them with a little salt and set them aside.

Add the 40g of butter to the pan. Let it melt and foam up, then use tongs to transfer the mushrooms from the bowl to the pan, reserving the soaking liquor.

Fry the mushrooms for about 8 minutes, tossing them occasionally in the butter. Add the shallots and cook

2 tablespoons madeira
   or marsala wine
150ml double cream
a little grated nutmeg
100g bucatini
flaky salt and freshly
   cracked black pepper
grated parmesan, to
   serve

for another 3 minutes, then add the garlic and
cook for another 2 minutes. You want the mushrooms
to have browned and the shallot and garlic to have
taken on some colour and started to soften. Add a
pinch of salt and plenty of black pepper and stir.

Pour the lemon juice and madeira or marsala into the
bowl with the mushroom soaking liquor and add this
to the mushroom pan. Simmer for a minute or two,
then remove the pan from the heat. Pour everything
into the bowl of a food processor and blend until it's
very smooth.

Push the mushroom mixture through a sieve back
into the pan. You absolutely don't have to do this
step, but it does make the sauce beautifully smooth.
If you go for the sieve, discard the pulp left in it.
Add the cream and nutmeg to the pan. Cook the
sauce over a low heat for another couple of minutes,
stirring occasionally, to heat everything through.
Then remove the pan from the heat.

Boil the bucatini in plenty of well-salted water until
al dente. Reserve a good couple of tablespoons of
cooking water when you drain the pasta.

Add the pasta and cooking water to the mushroom
pan and place it back over a low heat. Stir everything
thoroughly so the sauce really sticks to the pasta.
Add the teaspoon of cold butter and keep stirring.

At this point there will probably be a fair bit more
sauce in your pan than pasta. Spoon some of it into
your bowl, so you have a good puddle going, then use
tongs to tumble the bucatini on top.

Finish with a drizzle of olive oil, the crispy sage,
more black pepper and some grated parmesan.

Good loving

Taking true pleasure from eating dinner
alone doesn't come naturally to me.

I've had to work at it, had to earn the joy that eating a meal
in companionable solitude now brings. I think perhaps my
reluctance is partly because I come from a family that lived in
the kitchen. Growing up, an empty kitchen was a rare, strange
thing; the idea of a meal alone, a foreign concept. The kitchen
wasn't just the place where the fridge and the bread bin were
– all of life happened there. There was always someone over,
always something cooking or a bottle being opened, always
someone sitting at the table. It was where we talked, laughed,
sang Carole King very loudly, and had our battles royale. My
siblings and I have friends that remember sitting around that
battered cherry-wood table at five years old who are still often
to be found sitting around it now. The legs are wonkier – we
probably are too – but the sound of chatter and bustle around
it hasn't changed in 26 years.

Kitchen tables, of course, can be symbols of loss as much as
of happy chaos. Hold on to one for long enough and it might
even weather both. There is a *Modern Love* essay that speaks to
this so poignantly. It's by Bette Ann Moskowitz, a writer from
Woodstock, NY, written after her husband of 56 years died.
'Dinners without him are terrible,' she writes, matter of factly,
having just burned her thumb pulling a bubbling casserole from
the oven. 'Practically speaking, weren't casseroles invented for
giving to widows to heat as their solitary dinners? He and I
didn't eat casseroles. We preferred steak, some fish, a chicken,
a chop. Oh, we loved our lamb chops. Like Jack Sprat and his
wife, he couldn't eat the fat along the rib, while I devoured it.
He didn't like the marrow in Osso Bucco, either. How lucky to
be married to someone who left all the good bits for me.'

In an interview with the column's accompanying podcast, Bette
reflected on the many things in her life that had changed since
her husband died, chief among them being her cooking, which
was now for one. 'We had the same taste; we both loved oysters
[...] No casseroles, except mac 'n' cheese. And when I'm in the
kitchen I'm instinctively cooking for both of us. Even when
I was cooking for the two of us, I was always cooking for four

or six, and it was his job to finish the leftovers because I don't love leftovers. So, I feel his presence at dinner time.'

I have read Bette's story over and over and it might sound strange, but it never ceases to uplift me. I think it's because however keenly she feels the loss of this great love, she seems determined to live well in its wake – not just live, but live well. She learns how to fill the car up with petrol, use a screwdriver and pay the bills. She keeps living and she keeps cooking. 'I want to see what comes next,' she writes. 'And I believe that is what a lifetime of good loving can do.'

I like to think of Bette making herself a plate of lamb chops with the fat along the rib, or buying half a dozen oysters and relishing them on her porch, knowing in her bones that it would be all too easy not to bother, but that it'll always be worth it to make the effort and cook a good dinner.

I didn't used to enjoy eating alone, but it's worth getting good at it, I think. Whether a solitary meal is a regular occurrence in your life or a once-in-a-blue-moon thing, cooking something delicious for yourself is always going to be worth it. Whether it's a fried egg and oven chips because that's exactly what you fancy, or something absurdly extravagant – let it be generous. And as often as you can, cook yourself something truly special, something you'd make for a great love.

Broad beans and peas simmered with saffron, wine and ricotta

Serves 1

a good pinch of saffron
1 lemon, juice of half and
  zest of the whole
2 tablespoons ricotta
olive oil, for frying
60g slab of pancetta, cut
  into thick chunks
1 tablespoon butter
1 rosemary sprig
1 shallot, finely chopped
2 garlic cloves, peeled
  and bashed
1 teaspoon fennel seeds
50ml rosé or white wine
90g shelled broad beans
  (with bigger ones, pop
  the green interiors out
  of their shells)
100g frozen peas
a handful of fresh herbs
  (parsley, basil, oregano
  or mint would be good,
  or a mixture), roughly
  chopped or torn
flaky salt and freshly
  cracked black pepper
good olive or cold-pressed
  rapeseed oil, to finish

In a small bowl, mix the saffron with the lemon juice and leave it to sit. In another bowl, combine the zest and ricotta with black pepper and a little salt. Leave that to sit too.

Set a casserole pan over a medium heat with a glug of oil. Add the pancetta and fry until crispy. Remove the meat from the pan with a slotted spoon and set it aside on a plate lined with kitchen paper.

Turn the heat down and add the butter and rosemary sprig. When the butter has melted, add the shallot, garlic and fennel seeds and season with salt. Cook for 10 minutes, or until the shallot and garlic are soft. Add a splash of water, and the wine, the saffron and lemon mixture and some more black pepper. Simmer for another 10 minutes, then add the beans and cook until tender (about 4 minutes, depending on the size of your beans). Then add the peas and simmer for 1–2 minutes, until just cooked.

Immediately ladle the beans and their liquor into a warmed bowl. Sprinkle with herbs, scatter the pancetta on top and add a spoonful or two of the lemony ricotta. Finish with a drizzle of oil.

Hake and soft tomatoes with chilli butter

On their own, these tomatoes make for an oddly elegant dinner, but with the fish and the chilli butter they become something really special. Cook it all for one, or up the recipe for the tomatoes and make a batch so that you can then blitz the leftovers for a sweet, fresh pasta sauce or to spread on bread with anchovies for *pan con tomate*.

Serves 1

For the tomatoes
olive oil, for frying
290g plum tomatoes,
    quartered
½ teaspoon flaky salt,
    plus extra to season
    and finish
1 garlic clove, finely
    sliced
a splash of red wine
    vinegar

For the fish
a chunky hake steak,
    skin on
35g butter
1 garlic clove, finely
    sliced
½ small red chilli,
    deseeded and finely
    chopped
a pinch of smoked
    paprika
thick slices of good bread
a few sprigs of flat-leaf
    parsley, roughly torn
a few big basil leaves
flaky salt
a lemon wedge, to serve
    (optional)

Heat a good glug of olive oil in a small frying pan or casserole pan with a lid over a very low heat. If you can, pick a pan that is going to be able to fit the tomato wedges in a single, snug layer over the bottom. Arrange the tomato quarters in concentric circles. Sprinkle over the salt and garlic. Put the lid on and leave the tomatoes to cook for 30 minutes – don't move the pan too much, just leave the tomatoes to cook slowly, until they release lots of sweet juices and slump a little. Shake over a little vinegar (don't stir the tomatoes when you do), smush the tomatoes a little with the back of a spoon, put the lid back on and cook for another 5 minutes, so the tomatoes return to a simmer.

Meanwhile, sprinkle the hake with salt. Set a small frying pan over a medium heat. Add a splash of olive oil and, when hot, fry the fish, skin side down for 3 minutes so the skin crisps up and the flesh starts to cook. Then, remove the pan from the heat and transfer the fish to the tomatoes, lowering it into the pan so the skin stays above the liquid and the flesh can continue cooking in the simmering juices. Cook for 3 minutes, until the fish is cooked through.

Meanwhile, melt the butter in a small saucepan with the sliced garlic, the chopped chilli and the paprika, plus a pinch of salt. Let it foam up and cook for a minute, swirling the pan as it does. Set the flavoured butter aside in the pan.

Toast the bread (either in a toaster or in a griddle pan if you want more of a char), then drizzle it with oil and sprinkle it with flaky salt.

Finish the tomatoes and fish with the chilli butter and herbs. Serve with a wedge of lemon, if you wish.

Chicken schnitzel tenders with crispy chilli cucumbers

When it comes to comfort food, I'll often reach for softness – the cosy embrace of a bowl of mashed potatoes; a thick, creamy sauce or plate of silky noodles; the reassuring squidge of a good sponge cake. But comfort can come in many forms, and sometimes it's crunch and crispness I crave. When that's the case, I'll often make some form of schnitzel.

I love making schnitzel ... bashing out a chicken breast or pork or veal escalope, dredging it in flour, egg and breadcrumbs, then shallow frying it so that you get a golden crust and perfectly moist meat. For a quick and extremely delicious dinner, I'll cut my bashed-out chicken breast into strips and coat them in cayenne-spiked flour and panko breadcrumbs for a kind of adult excuse for chicken tenders.

I love eating these in a soft brioche bun with a little spicy mayo and these cucumber ribbons tossed with addictive Chinese crispy chilli oil, piling them on top of the chicken for extra crunch and lip-smacking freshness.

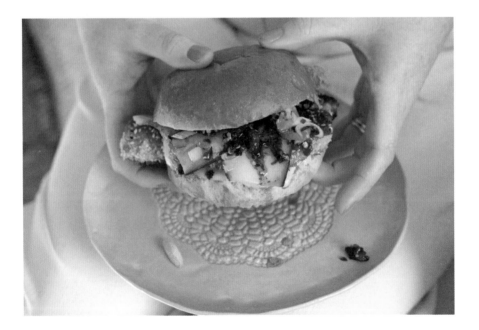

Serves 1

For the chicken
1 large chicken breast
40g plain flour
½ teaspoon smoked
  paprika
a pinch of cayenne
½ teaspoon fine salt
2 eggs, lightly beaten
40g panko breadcrumbs
2 teaspoons sesame
  seeds
plenty of rapeseed oil,
  for frying
flaky salt, for sprinkling
a slick of mayo
a shake or two of
  sriracha
a brioche bun, sliced in
  half
a lime wedge, to serve
  (optional)

For the cucumber
2 teaspoons sesame oil
2 teaspoons crispy chilli
  oil, plus extra to serve
½ lime, juiced
½ teaspoon salt
1 teaspoon maple syrup
  or runny honey
2 spring onions, finely
  sliced lengthways
⅓ chilled cucumber,
  sliced into ribbons

Put the chicken breast in a sandwich bag or between two pieces of cling film or baking paper and bash it until it's about 2.5cm thick. (I tend to use a rolling pin for the bashing.) Slice the bashed-out chicken into wide strips.

Take two large plates and a wide bowl. On one plate mix the flour with the paprika, cayenne and salt. Put the beaten eggs in the bowl. On the other plate, mix together the crumbs and sesame seeds.

One by one, dredge the chicken pieces in the flour, then the egg, then the crumbs. Really pack the crumbs on to the chicken, pressing them on with your hands to coat the strips all over.

Heat plenty of rapeseed oil in a large frying pan over a medium heat. Fry the chicken pieces for about 3 minutes on each side. Don't move them around in the pan; just leave them to really go golden and crisp up. If the crumbs are cooking too quickly, turn the heat down a little. When the chicken is cooked through, remove the strips to a plate, drain them on kitchen paper and sprinkle them with flaky salt.

While the chicken is cooking, make the cucumber. Put all the ingredients apart from the cucumber itself in a large bowl and beat them together with a fork to make a dressing.

Put the cucumber strips in a sandwich bag and bash them a little with your rolling pin. Then, toss them in the dressing. They'll happily sit in the fridge for a while before serving.

Mix the mayo with a couple of shakes of sriracha. Turn the heat back on under the chicken pan and quickly fry the cut side of each bun half, then remove the halves to a plate, toasted sides upwards. Spread a little mayo on the bottom half of the bun, then pile the hot chicken on top, then the cold, spicy cucumber. Serve with a lime wedge for squeezing into your bun just before you bite into it, if you like, and a little more crispy chilli oil.

Just the two of us

She sends me a text
She's coming home
the train emerges
from underground

I light the fire under
the pot, I pour her
a glass of wine
I fold a napkin under
a little fork

the wind blows the rain
into the windows
the emperor himself
is not this happy

'The Emperor' by Matthew Rohrer

Seafood and steaks to fall in love over

I have always felt there is as much romance to be found in sitting at a table opposite a cherished friend as there can be on a date with someone who you have just realised you might really, really like. It's probably because the most romantic relationships in my life have been with my closest girlfriends. With them, every meal is an opportunity to set the world to rights – every plate of roast chicken or carefully poached egg a reminder of the love and care those friendships hold.

In principle, I love the whole idea of the messy glamour of eating spaghetti in bed with a lover, like Rachel and Mark in *Heartburn*. In practice, though, I can't do the eating-in-bed thing. Crumbs on sheets give me the heebie-jeebies. But it's not really about the spaghetti anyway. It's about the moment they are sharing. The sapling freshness of a new relationship, when everything is fun and exciting, and every moment spent together is a story you might tell each other nostalgically at some far-off point in the future. M.F.K. Fisher perhaps put it best when she said: 'Sharing food with another human being is an intimate act that should not be indulged in lightly.' Even if it's just the other half of a Twirl on a long train journey, sharing food engenders a special kind of intimacy. Maybe that's why cooking for someone or being cooked for often feels like an act of love.

It makes sense to me that cooking is so often associated with love, because food can be such a profound conduit for joy. And joy, like a good meal, doesn't happen accidentally; it's hard won. That isn't to say it's something you have to deserve – far from it. But you do have to choose to put yourself in the way of it. You have to forge connections and then nurture them; you have to try to lean towards the good, the funny, the ridiculous, while not turning away from the harder, grittier moments that make up a full life. Because being able to feel unfettered joy is surely the greatest thing about being alive, isn't it? Sometimes I just wonder if we don't spend too much time looking for it in the wrong places. We are all different, but you probably won't find it in the office, the gym or in the contents of your phone. You might, however, find it on a dance floor or on the sofa with your family; immersed in nature or looking at some form of art; in the corner booth of a low-lit restaurant or at the kitchen table, sharing a meal with someone you love.

Sometimes we forget to prioritise joy, and sometimes it can simply feel spectacularly out of reach. All you can do, as the poet Mary Oliver says, is try to lean in to joy when it appears.

She writes: 'If you suddenly and unexpectedly feel joy, don't hesitate. Give in to it. [...] It could be anything, but very likely you notice it in the instant when love begins. Anyway, that's often the case. Anyway, whatever it is, don't be afraid of its plenty. Joy is not made to be a crumb.'

That's what it feels like when someone who loves you cooks for you – proper joy and more than just the crumbs. It feels like delicious generosity, like being taken care of and celebrated, like the most ordinary thing in the world and the most profound act of love.

Steak with persillade potatoes and too much béarnaise (see page 84)   75

Prawns with smoked cheddar polenta and burnt Scotch bonnet sauce

A well-cooked pan of polenta manages to pull off that rare trick of being as homely as it is elegant. With the right amount of butter and cheese, the gritty cornmeal becomes so gloriously silky, like the smoothest, most decadent mashed potato. There are lots of ways to make it – some cook the corn with milk or cream, you could use stock or just cook it in water and bring in flavour and seasoning from other sources – and endless ways to serve it. I often have it with meatballs cooked in a rich tomato sauce, or a ragù. But for a quick, oddly stylish Friday night dinner, I love making a version of that southern American classic 'shrimp and grits'.

For this, I tend to use raw, shell-on prawns. Cajun spice mix would give a more authentic shrimp-and-grits flavour; and chorizo, another kind of spicy sausage or pancetta would be nice additions, as would a few blistered cherry tomatoes or some sautéed pepper. I like melting smoked cheddar through the polenta to give it a savoury punch, but any strong hard cheese would do, as would a creamy blue, or you could just go heavy on the parmesan. You might want a bit of soured cream to even out the chilli sauce, though the cheesy polenta should do a good job of that.

Serves 2

For the chilli sauce
1 Scotch bonnet chilli
1 pointed red pepper
1 large garlic clove
1 teaspoon fennel seeds
1 large lime, juiced

For the prawns
1 teaspoon smoked
   paprika
1 teaspoon cumin seeds
1 teaspoon fennel seeds
⅓ teaspoon ground
   allspice
220g raw, shell-on
   prawns
olive oil, for frying
1 lime, juiced, plus extra
   wedges to serve
2 spring onions, finely
   sliced
a handful of flat-leaf
   parsley or coriander,
   leaves and stems torn

First, make the chilli sauce. If you have a gas hob, turn on the widest ring, or alternatively you could use a barbecue or pop the peppers under a hot grill. If you're using your hob, hold the Scotch bonnet over the flames with tongs. Take your time, cooking until most of the skin is blackened and the flesh has softened a little. Set aside and do the same with the red pepper.

Leave them to cool a little, then remove the stalks and seeds (you can leave the Scotch bonnet seeds in if you like it super-spicy). Roughly chop the chilli and peppers and put them in a food processor (or you can use a hand blender, a pestle and mortar, or just chop everything finely with a sharp knife). Add the garlic, fennel seeds and lime juice. Blitz to a smooth salsa. Keep the sauce covered, but out of the fridge, while you cook everything else (you don't want it fridge temperature when you come to eat).

Mix together all the spices for the prawns in a bowl, and then add the prawns. Toss them in the spice mix and leave them to sit for 20 minutes.

Meanwhile, cook the polenta. Pour the chicken stock into a deep saucepan over a medium–high heat and bring it to the boil. Then turn the hob down to

For the polenta
650ml chicken or fish
  stock
120g quick-cook polenta
½ teaspoon fine salt
75g smoked cheddar,
  grated
15g parmesan, grated
60g salted butter
a little grated nutmeg
cracked black pepper

a low–medium heat and start whisking the stock with a balloon whisk. Pour the polenta slowly into the swirling stock, whisking continuously. Keep whisking for 6 minutes, then turn the heat down low and leave the polenta to cook for 10 minutes, stirring occasionally. It'll blip a bit – be careful you don't get scorched by flying polenta.

Stir in the salt, both cheeses, butter, nutmeg and plenty of black pepper. Cook for another 5 minutes, or until the cheese has melted. It'll happily sit while you cook the prawns – it might just need a vigorous stir and the heat back under it for a minute to loosen it again.

To cook the prawns, set a large frying pan over a medium heat with a splash of oil. Fry the prawns for a couple of minutes on each side, or until cooked through. Add the lime juice and cook for 1 minute.

To serve, spoon the polenta into shallow bowls, then top with the prawns, spring onions, torn herbs, and a good spoonful of chilli sauce. Serve with lime wedges for squeezing over.

My kingdom for a themed cocktail

It's funny how cocktails go in and out
of fashion, like trainers and haircuts.

There was the Aperol spritz summer, when no barbecue was
complete without plastic cups filled with fizzy liquid the colour
of Irn Bru. They tasted like bitter Fanta, but would get you
drunker than you'd ever planned to be. Then there was the year
everyone discovered negronis and no 'small plates' restaurant
menu was complete without a new take on one. Margaritas were
big for a while (I can't hear the word margarita without thinking
of Ross from *Friends* and his 'FAJITAS!'), picklebacks had their
moment in the sun, and the reign of the espresso martini doesn't
look likely to come to an end anytime soon.

I love any cocktail that is ice cold, a little bitter and packs a
punch. I like to know I'm drinking a spirit, not half a pint of
juice and a bag of ice. At home, I'm a sucker for a theme and
like matching a cocktail to whatever dinner I'm making. A
batch of spicy frozen margs (the only reason I ever get out my
NutriBullet) for a taco party, dark vermouth with olives and
orange slices to go with tapas, boulevardiers to ease yourself
into steak night.

I think the key is to keep things simple and not too sweet. I
don't think you need all that many ingredients to mix a really
excellent drink, but I like having a few things on hand to
upgrade a cocktail when the mood takes me. Crushed pink
peppercorns to sprinkle over a gin and tonic, a jar of green
olives for martinis, some sort of citrus and a good bottle of
bitters (Fee Brothers do a huge range these days, from molasses
to cardamom, black walnut or rhubarb). It helps, also, to be the
kind of person who always remembers to buy ice, which I am
not and probably will never be.

Dark vermouth with too many olives

Serves 2

6 pitted green olives
2 salt-cured anchovies
lots of ice
2 orange wedges
250ml dark vermouth

Take two cocktail sticks and thread three olives and an anchovy on to each. Divide the ice and orange wedges between two tumblers. Pour over the vermouth, equally into each glass, and finish with a loaded cocktail stick in each.

Rosemary boulevardiers

Serves 2

For the rosemary syrup
70g granulated sugar
2 rosemary sprigs, needles stripped

For the cocktail
70ml bourbon
60ml Campari
60ml sweet vermouth
plenty of ice
2 short rosemary sprigs
2 slivers of orange peel

First, make the syrup. Put the sugar, 60ml of water and the rosemary needles in a small saucepan over a low–medium heat. Cook, stirring occasionally to help the sugar dissolve, until the mixture comes to the boil. Then, simmer for about 7 minutes, or until it becomes syrupy. This could take a little while – cook it for longer if you think it isn't quite syrupy enough. A good way to test it is to spoon a little on to a plate, leave it to cool for a minute and then touch it with your finger to see if it is of appropriate syrupiness. When it's a nice consistency, take the pan off the heat and leave the syrup to stand until cool enough to put in the fridge. Strain it through a sieve, then chill the syrup in the fridge before using it in the cocktail.

When you come to make the drink, put the bourbon, Campari and vermouth with 1 tablespoon of the syrup in a cocktail shaker with plenty of ice.

Put more ice in two tumblers (or use two of those giant negroni ice cubes), along with a sprig of rosemary and a piece of orange peel each. Strain the cocktail over the ice and serve.

Clams, salami, sherry and tomato toasts

When you want a Friday night to feel special and celebratory, it helps to make something new, something you wouldn't turn to on autopilot in the week. Shellfish is endlessly helpful in this regard, I think. It always feels novel and almost shockingly delicious. Clams are one of those things I know I love and yet don't make often enough.

Once, around Christmas, my brother (the youngest and without a doubt the best cook in the family) made something resembling these clams, with thinly sliced ribbons of salami fried off with a soffritto of shallot, celery and garlic. It was so simple and so good – one of those meals that begins with an idea you have when walking past the fishmonger, and with the help of a few things already in the fridge, becomes something properly special. I've been attempting to recreate it ever since.

This is great served in big bowls with the toasts, or in smaller portions as part of a wider tapas spread.

Serves 2

For the clams
500g small clams
olive oil, for frying
1 tablespoon butter
1 shallot, finely chopped
1 celery stick, finely
    chopped
2 garlic cloves, finely
    sliced
2 tomatoes, finely
    chopped
1 teaspoon fennel seeds
60g salami, sliced into
    thin ribbons
250ml dry sherry or
    white wine
½ lemon, juiced
a good few dashes of
    Worcestershire sauce
a handful of flat-leaf
    parsley, leaves and stems
    roughly chopped
salt

For the toasts
1 tomato
2–4 slices of sourdough
1 garlic clove, peeled
a little olive oil

First, give your clams a rinse, then fill a clean sink with cold water and dunk them in the sink while you cook everything else. It's a good way to clean the clams and it's easier to spot any with broken shells – which you should discard.

Set a large casserole pan with a lid over a low–medium heat. Add a few glugs of olive oil and the butter. Once the butter has melted, add the shallot and celery, along with a good pinch of salt. Put the lid on and cook for 10 minutes, or until the vegetables are soft. You don't particularly want them to take on too much colour – more to sweat and soften. Add the garlic and cook, uncovered, for 2 minutes, then add the tomatoes, stir, and cook for another 6 minutes, until they have slumped.

Meanwhile, coarsely grate the tomato for the toasts into a bowl. Add a pinch of salt and leave it to sit while you finish the clams.

Turn the heat up a little under the tomato mixture, then add the fennel seeds and salami. Cook for 4 minutes, or until the salami has crisped up a little and everything smells great.

Pour in the sherry or wine, and the lemon juice and Worcestershire sauce. Let the mixture bubble up, then taste it and add a little more salt if you think it needs it. Simmer for 3 minutes, then turn the heat down low and add the clams. Put the lid on and cook them for about 6 minutes, or until all the clam shells open. Now might be a good time to put your bread on to toast. When toasted, rub the bread with the peeled garlic clove.

Add the parsley to the pan with the clams and stir, then ladle it all equally into two bowls, making sure you each get plenty of bits and bobs and liquor.

Drizzle the toasts with olive oil and spoon over some of the tomato flesh to serve.

Steak with persillade potatoes and too much béarnaise

I don't know if I'm in the minority here, but I really think steak and chips is a supremely sexy meal. It might be something about the sheer messy indulgence of it. It could also be my romanticised image of those cavernous old Parisian brasseries – all filled with chintz and brass. I love how the plain white, indestructible plates, the paper tablecloths, the stocky little wine glasses with average house red, and mildly terrifying service all exist within this absurdly opulent setting. The air seems to fizz as waiters mince around you, brandishing sauce boats and dishes of piping-hot *épinards à la crème*. The menu is always sprawling. If you ate everything in sight from the entrées right down to dessert, you could start with snails, terrine, tripe or celeriac remoulade, move on to anything from a neat little *confit de canard* to great platters of *choucroute* or *chateaubriand* for six, via a pitstop at the *chariot de fromage* and on to an *île flottante* (is there a more ridiculous pudding?) or profiteroles the size of a baby's fist. Say what you like about the French, but they really know how to do glorious excess. Though I do always wonder if anyone actually orders the lone *filet de saumon*, buried somewhere in the plats.

When I was at university, I lived in Paris for a year in a tiny apartment on the Île Saint Louis with my friend James, sharing two rooms with a black-and-white tiled floor and tall, rickety shutters. One room was my bedroom – but also the galley kitchen and bathroom; the other housed James's bed, the world's smallest sofa, and the loo. I worked for a children's newspaper, he at the BBC Paris bureau. We spent weekends strolling around the city, sitting by the river and drinking cheap wine by the bucketful. We were 20 and didn't know how lucky we were. We had very little money, but occasionally on a Friday night would treat ourselves to dinner at a place near Bastille called Café de l'Industrie. It was a bustling bistro where people wandered, glass in hand, between the bar and restaurant, which sprawled across buildings on either side of the street. They came for the wine and the chatter; they stayed for the fried potatoes.

I'm not sure I've had potatoes that good before or since – crispy yet buttery, and tossed in persillade (a mixture of salt, finely chopped raw garlic and parsley). For €10 you could get an enormous plate of carpaccio de boeuf with lemon and capers, a mustardy green salad and a great mound of pommes sautées.

It's probably impossible to recreate the atmosphere of a bustling French brasserie or intimate bistro at home, but there's nothing to stop you from having a go at the food. Why not, then, pick up some steak, salad and potatoes on the way home.

When it comes to choosing something to adorn steak frites, a heavy slick of Dijon is often perfect. But there is something extremely pleasing about a sauceboat filled to the brim with béarnaise. If it's the béarnaise flavour I'm craving, but I can't quite find the time to make it, I'll steep finely chopped shallot in wine vinegar and add it to a mixture of Dijon mustard, mayonnaise and tarragon for that béarnaise tang.

I have two go-tos when it comes to steak. The first is a couple of cheap hangers, given a dusting of flaky salt and black pepper, quickly seared and sliced against

the grain (to avoid toughness). But if I'm splashing out, I'll buy a hunk of bone-in côte de boeuf with a good rib of fat on it. I'll sear it in a cast-iron frying pan (as below), then finish it off in the oven, before taking it out, quickly adding butter, garlic and rosemary and basting it. I'll leave it to rest before slicing it, sprinkling it with flaky salt and serving. Whichever route you go down with the meat, why not fry a few potatoes, make a salad (something green with a thick vinaigrette, or tomato with a little finely diced shallot splattered with red wine vinegar), and transport yourself to Paris.

Serves 2

For the béarnaise
100g butter
1 tablespoon white
  wine vinegar
1 small shallot, finely
  diced
1 egg yolk
a small handful of
  tarragon, leaves picked
  and finely chopped
salt and freshly cracked
  black pepper

For the potatoes
5 large King Edward
  potatoes, peeled and cut
  into smallish chunks
olive oil
1 tablespoon flaky salt
3 garlic cloves, finely
  chopped
a handful of flat-leaf
  parsley, leaves and
  stems finely chopped
½ lemon, zested

For the steak
790g bone-in côte de
  boeuf, about 5cm thick
  (take it out of the fridge
  30 minutes before you
  cook it)
1 heaped tablespoon
  butter
1 garlic clove, peeled
  and bashed
1 rosemary sprig

Make your béarnaise at least 1½ hours in advance. It'll benefit from sitting in the fridge for a couple of hours, both in terms of flavour and of consistency, as it'll firm up a little.

Start by clarifying the butter. Put the butter in a small saucepan over a low–medium heat. Once the butter has completely melted, take the pan off the heat. Tilt the pan slightly and use a dessert spoon to skim off the foam. Carefully pour the clear, bright yellow liquid into a bowl, leaving the milk solids behind in the pan to be discarded.

In another pan, put the white wine vinegar, 1 tablespoon of water and the shallot and season with plenty of black pepper. Cook for 2 minutes, by which point most of the liquid will have reduced. Then, remove the pan from the heat and transfer the shallots to a bowl.

Set a small pan with 2.5cm of water in it over a very low heat and place a large heatproof bowl on top. When the water is just simmering, put 1 tablespoon of water and the egg yolk in the bowl and start beating it with a balloon whisk. Keep beating for 3 minutes. It'll foam up, then go creamy and should increase in volume by about a third. If it hasn't done this after 3 minutes, keep going for another 30 seconds or so, until it does.

Remove the bowl from the heat and slowly whisk in the clarified butter. Then, add the shallot and finally the tarragon, along with a good seasoning of salt. Transfer the béarnaise into whatever receptacle you're going to serve it in, cover and pop it in the fridge for at least 1½ hours. Take it out about 40 minutes before you come to serve if you want to eat it at room temperature.

When you're ready to cook everything else, start by getting the potatoes going. Put them in a pan of well-salted cold water and bring the water to the boil.

Reduce the heat and simmer the potatoes for about 15 minutes (depending on size), until just tender. Drain well, and leave them to steam for a couple of minutes in the colander.

At this point, you might want to preheat your oven for the beef. Set it at 240°C/220°C fan/Gas 9.

Set a large heavy-based frying pan over a medium–high heat and pour in enough olive oil so that it comes about 1cm up the inside of the pan. When the oil is hot, add the potatoes in a single layer, cooking them in batches, if necessary, so that you have just a single layer each time, without piling them up. Leave them undisturbed for as long as it takes for them to start to go golden brown on the underside, then use a fish slice or a couple of spoons to flip them. Keep cooking until they are golden and crunchy all over. Remove each batch to a plate lined with kitchen paper, while you cook the remainder.

When the potatoes are just beginning to brown, sear your beef. Set a large, cast-iron frying pan (the kind that could go in the oven) over a high heat. Sprinkle salt and black pepper all over the beef. Place the beef in the dry pan and don't move it for 4 minutes, or until a good crust has formed underneath. Then flip it and cook it for another 4 minutes on the other side. Finally, stand it on the side with the rib of fat on it, holding it in place with a pair of tongs. Cook it like this for 2 minutes.

Put the beef (still in the cast-iron frying pan) in the oven and cook it for 6 minutes, then remove it and add the butter, garlic and rosemary. It'll bubble and melt instantly. Tilt the pan and use a dessert spoon to baste the melted butter over the beef. Put it back in the oven for another 2 minutes, or until the beef is cooked to your liking. Then remove the beef, set it on a plate or board and leave it to rest for 10 minutes.

While the potatoes are still browning, mix together the salt, garlic, parsley and lemon zest in a large bowl. As soon as the potatoes are cooked, toss them in the herby dressing while they're still piping hot.

Slice the rested beef, sprinkle it with flaky salt and serve it with the potatoes and plenty of béarnaise.

Tiny lamb cutlets with anchovy aioli and olives

There are two kinds of people in the world: the kind who pick up bones at the end of the meal and strip every last bit from them, and the kind who are strictly knife-and-fork eaters. I love them both equally, but I must admit to being someone who appreciates a meal that really requires you to get stuck in and use your hands. Skinny little lamb chops like these make for some of the best hands-on nibbling in the business – their crispy fat, modest medallion of meat and neat little bones practically asking you to keep going until you've had every last bit.

They're a great thing to make for just a couple of people as they cook so quickly and all at the same time under a hot grill. I like swiping them through aioli and serving them with a really punchy potato salad with plenty of grain mustard and wine vinegar in the dressing.

Serves 2

1 teaspoon coriander
  seeds
1 teaspoon fennel seeds
2 garlic cloves, peeled
1 teaspoon flaky salt
1 teaspoon dried oregano
1 tablespoon olive oil
1 lemon, juiced, plus
  extra wedges to serve
6 lamb cutlets
½ recipe quantity
  of Anchovy Aioli
  (see page 21)
1 small red onion, finely
  sliced
1 tablespoon red wine
  vinegar
a pinch of salt
a handful of black olives
  (the soft, greasy kind)
a few sprigs of oregano,
  leaves picked

First, make the marinade. Put the coriander seeds and fennel seeds in a pestle and mortar and break them down a bit. They don't need to be bashed to a powder, just pounded a bit. Add the garlic and salt and keep working it until you have a rough paste. Add the dried oregano, olive oil and lemon juice.

Put the cutlets in a plastic container and pour in the marinade, turning everything with your hands. Put the lid on the container and leave the lamb to sit in the fridge for 2 hours. Meanwhile, make the anchovy aioli and pop it in the fridge until you need it.

Take the lamb out of the fridge 20 minutes before cooking. Preheat your grill as high as it will go.

Meanwhile, sit the red onion in the red wine vinegar and salt, scrunching it with your fingers. Leave it to pickle out of the fridge while you cook the lamb.

Cook the cutlets for 3 minutes on each side, or until their fat gets really well browned. Transfer them to a warm serving plate and leave to rest for 5 minutes.

To serve, scatter the olives, pickled red onion and oregano over the cutlets. Add a couple of lemon wedges and spoon the aioli into a small bowl to serve alongside them.

Note: You could serve the cutlets with some sort of potato and a tomato or green salad dressed with more fresh oregano and a slosh of wine vinegar, if you like.

A whole roasted fish with bay, anise and clementine

A Friday night dinner needs to feel distinct from the rest of the week. You've worked hard to get here; now it's time to let it all go, put some good music on and ease into the weekend. Picking something special for dinner, something that feels truly worthy of a Friday night, is your quickest route to that end-of-the-week-bliss feeling. And there is nothing quite so celebratory as cooking a whole fish.

There are a few different ways to approach this. There's the barbecue route, where the skin will blacken and the fish will become smoky and sweet. There's the paper-parcel method, which is fantastically simple and gives you such beautifully juicy, tender fish that it always seems as if you must have done more to it than you really have. Unwrapping a package filled with aromatic steam and cooking juices is just a lovely thing. There's the slow-cook approach that can work really well with fattier fish, like if you were to cook a whole side of salmon or a large piece of tuna – almost confit-ing the fish in olive oil on a low heat. The only mark against both of these methods is that you're going to have to accept that you're not going to get crispy skin. And I tend to think that wherever possible (and frankly, this goes for so many dishes) crispy skin should be your goal.

You could start the fish in a frying pan and then transfer it to the oven as you might a steak. The only risk there is that you might find the skin sticks to the pan a bit. Simply roasting it on a high heat at the top of the oven is perhaps the simplest approach.

There are any number of aromatics and citrus you could choose. Sometimes I just keep things really simple and stuff a couple of bass, mackerel or bream with lemon slices, garlic and fennel. I've found this combination of torn bay leaves, clementine slices (or orange slices, though you might want to halve them) and star anise gets you particularly delicious, fragrant flesh. The juice of a lime, and a shake of soy and sesame oil help things along, providing a little acid, salt and nutty fat.

With it, I serve a salad of thinly sliced red onion and cucumber with whole sprigs of coriander and fresh green chilli, all tossed in more clementine juice, lime, soy, ginger and honey. Sticky or basmati rice would be great, or if you're craving a potato, I like steaming a few new potatoes and tossing them in the soy citrus juices in the roasting pan once the fish has cooked. They'll soak up the salty sweetness.

Serves 2

For the fish
2 tablespoons sesame oil
3 bay leaves, torn
2 clementines, 1 sliced,
   1 halved for juicing

Continued overleaf

Preheat the oven to 230°C/210°C fan/Gas 8.

For the fish, set a small saucepan over a medium–high heat with half the sesame oil. Add the bay leaves and clementine slices. Cook for 2 minutes, then flip the clementines and cook for another minute, until they have slightly caramelised. Transfer the slices to a plate and leave them to cool. Keep any juices from the pan to add them to the roasting tin.

1 large sea bass (about
    750g in weight)
6 star anise
1 lime, juiced
2 tablespoons dark
    soy sauce
salt

For the salad
1 clementine, juiced
1 large lime, juiced
½ red onion, finely sliced
    (use a mandoline if you
    have one)
½ cucumber, sliced
    lengthways into
    ribbons
½ small green chilli,
    finely chopped
a small chunk of root
    ginger, peeled and
    finely grated
1 tablespoon dark soy
    sauce
½ teaspoon runny honey
1 teaspoon sesame oil
a big handful of
    coriander

Put the fish in a large roasting tin lined with baking paper (so the fish doesn't stick). Use a sharp knife to score one side of the fish, making 3–4 slits and taking care not to cut too deep (you don't want to go all the way down to the bone). Push the star anise into the slits. Stuff the cavity with the cooled clementine slices and bay leaves.

Squeeze the clementine halves over the fish and put the fruit skins in the roasting tin. Sprinkle in the lime juice too, and add the soy sauce, the rest of the sesame oil and the juices from the clementine pan. Sprinkle a good seasoning of salt over everything.

Transfer the roasting tin to the top shelf of the oven and roast the fish for about 30 minutes, or until the skin has crisped up a little and the flesh is just cooked.

Meanwhile, make the salad. Mix the citrus juices with a seasoning of salt in a large bowl. Add the red onion, cucumber, chilli and ginger and mix everything together. Leave the salad to sit while the fish cooks. Mix the soy sauce, honey and sesame oil separately. When you come to serve, toss the salad in the soy dressing. Add the coriander just before you serve too, chopping off any tough ends, but mainly keeping the sprigs whole.

Crab claws, aioli and garlic butter potatoes

I love those classic Sunday supplement features that roll around every couple of years asking famous people to talk us through their last meal. They're oddly revealing. Musicians usually choose their mum's roast dinner; writers fall into two camps: it's either some sort of fresh pasta they once ate with a lover on a Tuscan hilltop, or it's a full English from the local East End caff they (claim to) have been writing in for decades; politicians offer up something their aides have message-tested and decided will appeal to the broadest possible audience, making them seem in equal parts down-to-earth and statesman like. Chefs tend to pick seafood, possibly because they don't want to have to cook it themselves, possibly because they know that some of the most delicious things you could ever hope to eat involve very little cooking at all.

A proper seafood feast is a glorious thing, and if you can persuade enough people to chip in, it's one of the best meals for a big celebration. I love the sight of a great table laden with platters of prawns, glistening oysters and whole crab, as hungry hands make a beautiful mess of everything, tearing heads and cracking shells, shaking bottles of Tabasco and squeezing lemon wedges. I firmly believe, though, that you can create some semblance of that sort of meal – the kind when you seem to keep eating and eating and never want it to end – for a quieter dinner for two.

This is a great one for a summer's evening when you are both wishing you were by the sea. Get a few crab claws or a whole dressed crab, buy a bag of new potatoes (Jerseys if you can get them), make some smoky, garlicky butter, and chop up a couple of spring onions and a lemon. Whip up a bowl of aioli and maybe make a salad. Buy a nice baguette too. It'll be one of those meals that will leave you wondering why you don't make it all the time.

Serves 2

½ recipe quantity of Aioli
   (see page 21; or make it
   all and have extra)
250g Jersey royals or other
   new potatoes
3 garlic cloves, peeled
   and bashed
80g unsalted butter
1 teaspoon sweet smoked
   paprika
1 teaspoon smoked garlic
   granules
a good pinch of flaky
   salt
2 spring onions, roughly
   chopped
6 cooked crab claws
lemon wedges, to serve

Start by making the basic aioli on page 21 and set it aside while you make the potatoes and crab.

Put the potatoes in a large saucepan of well-salted water over a high heat. Add the garlic cloves and bring the water to the boil. Cook the potatoes for 20 minutes, or until tender, then drain them and leave them to sit in the colander for a couple of minutes to steam.

Meanwhile, melt the butter in a small saucepan over a low–medium heat. Once it's melted, let it bubble for a minute, then stir in the paprika, garlic granules and salt. Remove the butter from the heat and set it aside.

When the potatoes are cooked, toss them in the butter with the spring onions. Serve them piping hot with the crab claws, aioli and lemon wedges.

Citron pressé

I love the glasses of mouth-achingly tart citron pressé you get in France, with the token sachets of sugar on the side should you be wimpy enough to need them. Non-alcoholic drinks tend to be very sweet, which always seems to me a strange way to begin a meal. A proper citron pressé, though, will wake up your taste buds while you sink a few olives and a handful of crisps. I've made it longer with fizzy water.

Serves 2

1 tablespoon caster sugar
a couple of thyme sprigs,
    leaves picked
1 teaspoon flaky salt
180ml lemon juice (about
    4 lemons, depending
    on juiciness)
4 teaspoons granulated
    sugar
plenty of ice
2 strips of lemon peel
sparkling water

Put the caster sugar, thyme leaves and salt on a small plate and combine. Dip the rim of two tall glasses in water or lemon juice, then in the sugar mixture.

Whisk the lemon juice and granulated sugar in a jug with a fork until the sugar has dissolved.

Put plenty of ice in the glasses. Add a strip of lemon peel to each too.

Split the lemon juice between the glasses, pouring it over the ice, then top up with sparkling water.

Apricot, thyme and cider vinegar spritz

Serves 2

70g granulated sugar
a small handful of thyme
    sprigs, plus a couple
    extra, leaves stripped,
    to serve
1 tablespoon cider vinegar
    or white wine vinegar
8 ripe apricots, destoned
plenty of ice
chilled soda water
a shot of tequila or
    mezcal in each glass
    (optional)

Make the syrup. Put the sugar, 60ml of water and the thyme sprigs in a small saucepan over a low heat. Cook, stirring occasionally, until the mixture comes to the boil. Then, reduce the heat and simmer for about 7 minutes, or until it becomes syrupy. A good way to test the consistency is to spoon a little syrup on to a plate, leave it to cool for a minute and then test how it feels with your finger. When it's a nice syrupy consistency, take the pan off the heat and leave it to stand until it's cool enough to put in the fridge. Chill it for at least 20 minutes, then remove the thyme sprigs.

When you're ready to make the spritz, put the syrup in a blender with the vinegar and apricots. Blitz until smooth and foamy. Fill two large glasses with ice and divide the fruity syrup between them. Top with soda, then finish with thyme leaves and maybe a couple of straws – and a shot of tequila or mezcal, if you like.

'And-I-just-don't-care' chips

Human beings are weird.

We think we're going through life with no one noticing our strange little habits and foibles – the funny thing we do with the string on a teabag, or the way we always say a particular word wrong. The best thing about being close to people is being able to pick and choose when to rib someone for one of their oddities and when to sit back and take it in, quietly, lovingly, never letting on that you see them for all their glorious strangeness, marvelling at the singular way they move through the world.

My mum is possibly my favourite person to observe from a close distance. I could honestly sit and watch her from the sitting room window just crossing the road and going into the shop opposite the house all day. I can't really explain why; she doesn't have a particularly funny walk. She's just an endless source of amusement, much to her annoyance. There are a couple of Pennyisms that rattle around my head 98 per cent of the time. For example, she has the strangest reaction whenever you ask her if she wants a cup of tea. She'll stop in her tracks and really think about it, then tell you exactly why she will or won't have one, accompanying her answer with a list of everything else she's drunk so far that day. 'Actually, I won't and I'll tell you why. When I woke up I had two big cups, and then I had a small coffee when I was out and a tea when I got in and actually if I have another one now it's sort of getting a bit too close to when I might want a glass of wine so ...' It goes on.

When you're in a restaurant with her, you can be pretty sure that at some point she's going to utter these five words: 'And I just don't care.' They might come after 'and I'm having a pudding', or 'well I'm getting another glass even if no one else is', but more often than not, it's about chips. No one was going to judge her for getting chips, and anyone who stupidly hasn't ordered a portion should know they'll get short shrift if they attempt to steal one. But still, we go through this little rigmarole every time with Penny and her 'and-I-just-don't-care' chips. She is completely, wonderfully bonkers and I wouldn't have her any other way. She also happens to make truly exceptional chips.

Ham, egg and chips

I was sceptical about love languages when they first entered the zeitgeist. I tend to think personality tests are like horoscopes – you'll read into them whatever you want to. Then I took the test, realised I absolutely consider 'acts of service' to be one of my core tenets, and proceeded to bang on about them just as much as the next millennial. I'm not quite sure who I was kidding given the best way that I know to show someone love is by making them a meal. Or, more specifically, by making them a plate of homemade chips.

Very little beats a proper chip, and though they can take a bit of time to cook, they are always worth the effort. I make them as my mum does in a big pan of sunflower oil, frying them once on a low heat until they're soft but haven't yet taken on any colour, then cooling and draining them in a colander before frying a second time on a high heat until golden brown, crispy on the outside and fluffy inside.

If you're going to the trouble of making proper chips for your Friday-night-dinner date, I think it's worth letting whatever you're serving them with be relatively simple. A great pan of mussels, steamed with a little sweated shallot and garlic and a slosh of white wine. A piece of steak or maybe a roasted chicken leg with mushrooms, mustard and cream. You can't go far wrong with this old classic (admittedly given a slight update here). I'm not a huge fan of the gammon steaks you tend to get with a ham, egg and chips. They're usually saltier than the ocean and more meat than you actually want in a dish that really is all about the chips, the condiments and the dippy yolk. Instead, I like using a couple of thin slices of velvety prosciutto or parma ham, laying the ham over the just-cooked eggs in the pan to warm through, then bringing the pan to the table with the dish of hot chips for each of you to dive into. I tend to just serve this with some pickles and condiments and a bottle of Sarson's malt vinegar. But a tomato salad would make a nice addition, with a little finely chopped red onion or shallot and a splash of red wine vinegar.

Serves 2

650g Maris Piper
    potatoes
plenty of sunflower or
    another neutral oil,
    for frying
fine salt, for the chips
2–4 eggs
3–6 slices of prosciutto or
    parma ham

To serve
malt vinegar
whatever condiments you
    like (piccalilli would be
    particularly good, or a
    sweet pickled onion)

Cut your potatoes (I keep the skins on but you can peel them if you prefer) into long, relatively thick chips, and tip them into a colander over a large bowl.

Pour your oil into a deep saucepan over a low heat, or into a deep-fat fryer. Don't fill the pan more than half way up. Take a chip and add it to the pan. Once it's bubbling, the oil is hot enough. Add the rest of the chips and fry them for 10 minutes, using a slotted spoon to occasionally turn them. After 10 minutes, turn the heat off and transfer the chips to the colander. Leave them to sit and cool completely.

Meanwhile, put your oven on low and start warming a dish for your chips.

Put the heat back on under the chip pan, turning it up higher than it was before. Carefully, return the chips to the pan. Cook them until they turn perfectly golden brown. This could take a little while. Stay with the pan and be patient.

Put a piece of kitchen paper in the colander to catch any excess oil and transfer the chips to the colander when they're done. Sprinkle over plenty of salt and give the chips a good shake. Tumble them into your warmed dish and pop the dish back in the oven to keep the chips hot.

Fry your eggs as you like them. Lay the ham over the eggs in the pan to warm through (it might curl up a little at the edges, but that's okay). Put the pan on the table, along with the chip dish and whatever condiments float your boat.

Very good brown butter mashed potatoes with crispy shallots and soured cream

I am never not pining for mashed potatoes. Like a kind of culinary weighted blanket, they are a cure for every ill, a balm for all troubles, the forever answer to the question 'What can I cook that will make everything feel less totally rubbish?' They are also somewhat contentious. Everyone's an expert when it comes to mash: more butter, less milk, no mustard, lots of mustard, velvety smooth or with a healthy number of lumps. I favour a buttery approach. I love Nora Ephron's instructions for mashed potato for one, which essentially boil down to: 'Add 1 tablespoon heavy cream and as much melted butter and salt and pepper as you feel like.' She's absolutely right – the correct amount of butter should be measured entirely by your own desire, not prescribed by a list of ingredients. I also appreciate her insistence that mashed potato is an acceptable thing to make for one. Why shouldn't you make a little personal mash?

One of the best mashed potatoes I've ever had was in a bistro somewhere in the middle of France, where the *pomme purée* came to the table in a copper pan topped with an enormous dollop of thick crème fraîche, which was beginning to melt into the potato below. I can't remember anything else about the meal, it was all about those potatoes. I've added a spoonful of something sharp and creamy to my mash ever since.

This incarnation is a bit more involved than Ephron's, but it takes a leaf out of both her book and the menu at that little French bistro: plenty of butter (which you'll brown while the potatoes are cooking for an extra toasty buttery flavour) and a dollop of soured cream or crème fraîche to finish. You'll drizzle extra browned butter on top and cut through the sweetness with three hits of onion – crispy fried shallots, finely chopped spring onions, and chives. It's a luxurious way to eat mashed potatoes, and I struggle to make them any other way now. Sometimes I don't even serve them as a side but rather as the main event, just topping a bowlful with a poached egg, and maybe some wilted greens for good measure.

Make them for your Friday night date, sure ... but also make them for a whole tableful, or do as Nora would and make them for yourself.

Serves 2

450g floury potatoes
  (like Maris Piper),
  peeled and cut into
  large chunks
70g butter (or as much
  as you feel like)
1 banana shallot, finely
  sliced
2 teaspoons plain flour
olive oil, for frying
50ml whole milk
a little grated nutmeg
2 tablespoons soured
  cream or full-fat
  crème fraîche
salt and freshly ground
  black or white
  pepper
1 spring onion, finely
  chopped, to serve
a few chives, snipped,
  to serve

Put a serving dish in the oven to warm up.

Put the potatoes in a steamer over simmering water and cook them until tender (which should take about 20 minutes, depending on the size of your potato chunks). Remove the steamer from the pan and leave the potatoes uncovered for 10 minutes so some of the moisture evaporates.

While the potatoes are cooking, make the brown butter. Put the butter in a small saucepan over a low–medium heat. You'll need to cook it for about 11 minutes, maybe a bit longer, or until the butter is browning and smells toffeeish. Watch it while it's cooking, checking the milk solids don't burn. When the liquid is golden, the solids pale brown, and everything smells incredible, take the pan off the heat and pour the butter into a bowl, making sure to get all the milk solids out.

Make the crispy shallots while you're waiting for the potatoes to cook too. Put the sliced shallots and the flour in a bowl and toss them together so the shallots are coated in flour. Set a large frying pan over a medium–high heat with plenty of olive oil. Fry the shallots until crispy, turning them occasionally and watching to make sure they don't burn. Then, transfer the onions from the pan to a plate lined with kitchen paper. Sprinkle with salt to season.

Mash the potatoes using a ricer if you have one, or just a masher and a bit of elbow grease. Pour in most of the browned butter (reserve a dessertspoonful) and the milk, and add a good pinch of salt, black or white pepper and a little grated nutmeg. Keep mixing until you have a smooth, creamy mash.

Spoon the mash into the warmed serving dish. Spoon over the reserved browned butter, dollop soured cream on top, scatter over the crispy onions and spring onions and finish with a few snipped chives.

Barbecued lamb rump with griddled apricots, tahini sauce and garlicky labneh

This recipe will make too much labneh for two, but it's one of those things you may as well make in a decent-sized batch. It keeps for a few days in the fridge (especially if you pour a good layer of olive oil over the top), and you can use it on toast with honey or apricot jam, or for lunch with pitta, olives and raw veg.

Serves 2, with labneh left over

For the labneh
300g full-fat natural yoghurt
1 garlic clove, grated
1 teaspoon coarse salt
1 teaspoon za'atar
olive oil, for drizzling

For the lamb and apricots
1 tablespoon fennel seeds
1 tablespoon dried oregano
2 garlic cloves, grated
2 tablespoons olive oil
2 teaspoons flaky salt, plus extra for the tahini and apricots
600g lamb rump or leg steaks
4–6 apricots, halved and destoned
3 teaspoons runny honey
1 lemon, zest and juice
1 teaspoon chilli flakes
a few mint leaves, torn
1 tablespoon pine nuts, toasted
1 teaspoon sumac
½ recipe quantity of Tahini Sauce (see page 21)

Make the labneh the day before you want to serve. Line a sieve with a piece of muslin (or just use a clean tea towel) and set it over a bowl. Pour the yoghurt into the cloth and add the garlic and salt. Tie the cloth up and suspend the yoghurt over the bowl. I often tie the cloth to a wooden spoon and hang it over a deep bowl or jug. Refrigerate for 24 hours. The yoghurt will lose its moisture, and become thick and cream-cheese-like in consistency. Help it along by giving it a squeeze every so often.

A couple of hours before you're ready to cook, marinate the lamb. Mix together the fennel seeds, oregano, garlic, olive oil and salt and pour them over the meat. Leave to marinate for 2 hours in the fridge.

If you haven't made it already, use this time to make the tahini sauce (see page 21).

Get the barbecue or griddle pan piping hot and cook the lamb, depending on how you like it. I like a good crust on the outside but a blush in the middle, which takes about 3 minutes on each side for a chunky piece of lamb rump. Don't move the lamb around while it cooks, just leave it to seal on one side before flipping it. When the lamb is done, take it off the grill and leave it to rest on a warm plate. Meanwhile, griddle the apricots. Cook them, cut side down, for 2 minutes. Then, flip them and drizzle over half the honey. Cook for another minute or two, until they are charred and caramelised.

Mix the lemon juice, the rest of the honey and the chilli flakes in a bowl with a pinch of flaky salt. Add the griddled apricots and baste them with the lemon and chilli. Leave them to sit like this for a few minutes.

To serve, spread a spoonful of labneh on the plate, drizzle with oil and sprinkle over a little za'atar. Slice the lamb and divide it between two plates with a couple of apricot halves and a spoonful of the lemon and chilli marinade. Add a few mint leaves, and sprinkle over the pine nuts, lemon zest and sumac. Finally drizzle with tahini sauce and any lamb juices.

Serve this with some pitta, or make a couple of griddled flatbreads, like the ones on page 108. This would also go really well with the aubergine below.

Smoky aubergine and mozzarella

Serves 2

1 garlic bulb
2 aubergines
½ lemon, zest and juice
½ teaspoon chilli flakes
½ teaspoon flaky salt
1 tablespoon olive oil, plus extra for serving
a handful of coriander, roughly chopped, plus extra to serve
a few basil leaves, torn
1 large ball of mozzarella, torn
a couple of pinches of sumac
freshly cracked black pepper

Preheat the oven to 200°C/180°C fan/Gas 6.

Wrap the garlic in foil and pop it in the oven to roast for about 40 minutes, until soft, then set aside.

Place the aubergines directly on the flames of your hob, or on the barbecue. Use tongs to turn them occasionally, letting them char and soften for about 15 minutes. You can leave them on there to soften completely, or once the skin is burnt and flaky, pop them on a tray in the oven for 15 minutes, until soft.

Allow the aubergines to cool down slightly and peel the skins off. Pull the flesh into strips and put the strips in a sieve over a bowl. Drain them for about 1 hour, so the aubergines lose some water.

Push the soft garlic flesh out of the skins into a bowl and mix it with the lemon zest and juice, then the chilli, salt, olive oil and plenty of black pepper. Add the strained aubergines, and the coriander and basil, stir and leave to sit for about an hour.

To serve, pile the aubergine mixture on to a warm dish with extra coriander and the torn mozzarella and sprinkle with sumac.

This is lovely tossed through pasta, and great as part of a kind of mezze, or just eaten with flatbreads.

Frying pan flatbreads with Extremely. Addictive. Butter.

These would work brilliantly with the lamb and the aubergines on the previous pages, but you could serve them alongside all manner of things. I sometimes make them for brunch, wrapping them around merguez sausages with labneh, pickled red onions and coriander.

Makes 6 large flatbreads

7g fast-action dried
   yeast
1 teaspoon runny honey
300ml lukewarm water
100g rye flour
150g plain flour, plus extra
   for dusting
250g strong white bread
   flour
½ teaspoon fine salt,
   plus extra to season
   the butter
2 tablespoons natural
   yoghurt
olive oil, for greasing
½ recipe quantity of
   Extremely. Addictive.
   Butter. (see page 20)

First, make the dough. Put the yeast and honey into a measuring jug and top it up with the lukewarm water. Stir and leave for 5 minutes. It should go slightly frothy if the yeast is active.

Put the flours and fine salt in a large bowl and mix to combine. Make a well in the middle and pour in the liquid. Use a fork to bring the flour in from the sides to begin mixing it into the liquid. Before the dough is completely combined, add the yoghurt and keep mixing until it all comes together. Tip the dough out on to a floured surface and knead it with floured hands until you have a smooth, springy ball. Place it in a large, lightly oiled bowl. Cover with a damp tea towel and leave in a warm spot for an hour, or until the ball has doubled in size.

If you haven't already made it, now's the time to make the butter. If you have made it, and it's in the freezer or fridge, take it out: you want it to be room temperature when you brush it on to the hot flatbreads.

To make the breads, tip the proved dough out on to a floured surface and knead it a bit to knock the air out of it. Use a knife to divide the dough into six pieces, roll each piece into a ball and either use them immediately or pop them into the fridge until you're ready to cook and eat.

If using immediately, roll each ball out roughly into a disc a little less than 1cm thick. Don't worry about making a perfect circle. It's meant to be craggy.

To cook, you can either set a cast-iron frying pan or a griddle over a medium flame or griddle these directly on the grills of a barbecue. Either way, once your cooking surface is piping hot, lay a disc of dough over it, leave the dough without moving it for about 2½ minutes, and once the flatbread is browned underneath and puffing up, flip it and cook it for another 2–3 minutes, until nicely charred and cooked through. Remove and set aside, sprinkling over some salt. Repeat with the remaining dough.

Brush the breads with the butter while they're still hot, then serve.

White beans with fennel, anchovy crumbs and soft chorizo

Often when you're cooking, paying attention to time is important. There's no getting around it, there are just some things that really will be at their best when cooked for exactly the right number of minutes, like a steak seared for precisely as long as it wants to be, or a batch of scones pulled from the oven just at the correct moment so that each round of dough is perfectly light and fluffy. There is nothing quite as satisfying as cooking a piece of fish to perfection or nailing the cook time on a cake; that moment when you plunge a kebab stick through the middle of a sponge and it comes out mixture-free first time – it feels like such a win that I almost expect a round of applause to ripple through the kitchen.

There are some dishes, however, that are fantastically forgiving. You seem to be able to cook them for as long or as little as you like and they'll still come up trumps. As much as I love the kind of cooking that requires you to watch a pot (or at least to keep a timer close by), I do love a dish that you can leave on a low heat on the hob and forget all about, like a ragù, a tomato sauce, or a pan of gently braising beans.

I make a big pot of beans at least once a fortnight. I keep them relatively plain, usually just with salt and garlic, maybe a little rosemary or lemon. Then I use them as the base for a million other meals, loosening them with stock or water and adding a handful of pasta and some greens, blitzing them for a thick soup or serving them alongside meat or fish. Sometimes I'll add a few sautéed prawns and chorizo, or sweat a handful of cavolo nero with garlic and pile it on top of the beans with a boiled egg and a few shavings of some sort of hard cheese. My mum often makes a pan of beans like this to go alongside a roast lamb on a Sunday and they truly make for some of the best leftovers around.

I love the fennel and splash of dry sherry in this – it smells special, somehow, and a bit of holidays. Sometimes I'll fry off a few greens in the leftover chorizo cooking oil. For the beans, I love using jarred cannellini, haricot or butter beans. Jarred beans tend to be softer and require less cooking to become creamy, but they are more expensive than the tinned kind. You could absolutely use tinned beans instead; you'll just find you need to cook them for a little longer.

If you can, make these beans the day before you want to eat them. They're only going to develop more flavour if left to muddle and meld first. Take the recipe as a set of guidelines, and know that you can't go too far wrong. Let them cook for longer if you like, or get the beans on and the sausages sizzling simultaneously.

Serves 2

olive oil, for frying
1 banana shallot or small
 onion, finely chopped
1 celery stick, finely
 chopped
1 small fennel bulb,
 finely chopped (keep
 the fronds to use at
 the end)
1 garlic clove, sliced
1 bay leaf
1 teaspoon fennel seeds
½ teaspoon caraway
 seeds
a small orange, juiced,
 and a strip of its peel
200ml dry sherry
150ml chicken stock
350g jarred red peppers,
 drained, then sliced into
 1cm strips
1 x 600g jar white beans
 with their water
1 tablespoon sherry
 vinegar
4 chorizo sausages
a big handful of flat-leaf
 parsley, leaves and stems
 roughly torn
salt and freshly cracked
 black pepper
2 lemon wedges,
 to serve

For the crumbs
olive oil, for frying
1 salt-cured anchovy
1 garlic clove, bashed
60g fresh breadcrumbs

Set a stock pot or large casserole pan with a lid over a low heat with a good glug of olive oil. Add the shallot, celery and fennel with a big pinch of salt. Cook with the lid on for about 15 minutes, stirring occasionally, or until all the veg is soft and translucent.

Add the garlic, bay leaf, fennel seeds, caraway and strip of orange peel to the pan. Cook for another 3 minutes, then turn up the heat a little, pour in the sherry and let it bubble up. Add the chicken stock, the orange juice, a pinch of salt and a little black pepper. Bring the liquid to a simmer and cook for 5 minutes over a low–medium heat, until bubbling.

Turn the heat down as low as it'll go and add the red peppers and beans. Stir, then bring the liquid back to a simmer. Pop the lid on and cook the beans for at least 25 minutes, longer if you like, until they're soft and the liquid is thickening nicely, mashing some of the beans a little with the back of your wooden spoon.

When you're close to serving, add the sherry vinegar and a little more salt if the beans need it. Leave the beans to sit for 10 minutes with the lid half off before serving – the sauce will thicken a bit as it cools.

Meanwhile, cook the chorizo. Set a large frying pan (or two, depending on how big your pan is) over a medium heat. Drizzle in a little oil, and when the pan is hot, add the sausages. Cook for about 20 minutes, turning occasionally, until the sausages are well browned and cooked through. You can have them like that, or do what I do and slice them down the middle, and frying the flat edges too before serving. Reserve some of the rust-red chorizo oil that will leak out – you can spoon a little over each bowl of beans.

For the crumbs, set a large frying pan over a medium heat with plenty of olive oil. When the oil is piping hot, add the anchovy and the garlic. Break up the anchovy with a wooden spoon so it starts to melt into the oil. Add the crumbs. Watch them, tossing them in the oil occasionally, leaving them to cook until golden brown and crispy (about 2 minutes). Transfer them to a plate lined with kitchen paper.

Ladle the beans into four shallow bowls. Top with equal amounts of the chorizo, a scattering of crumbs, a little torn parsley and the leftover fennel fronds. Finish with a wedge of lemon for squeezing over, too.

Squid rolls with smoky lime butter sauce

There are some meals that live on in your memory. They get filed like photos in an album, for you to return to whenever you need them: the fish and chips that you ate with someone special at golden hour on a beach years ago; the first dinner you ever made your partner; the oozing pizza slice devoured hungrily on the street on a hot night on a long-forgotten holiday. Among the meals I return to again and again is a dinner I ate by the sea in Maine in the summer of 2016. I was on a road trip with my best friend Rosie, making our way around northeast USA with Vote Hillary bumper stickers on our hire car (oh the adorable pre-November '16 optimism), pretending we were Lorelai Gilmore and stopping at every lobster roll shack, every donut stall, and every bar selling oysters and local beer. One day, we went for a hike in Acadia National Park and by the evening, having survived all day in the heat on nothing but a couple of cheese sarnies, we were famished. We drove around the island as night fell, looking for somewhere to eat. I can still remember seeing twinkling lights in the distance down by the water. We pulled up to Thurston's Lobster Pound, suspended on wooden stilts on the shore, and joined the queue of people waiting patiently to pick a lobster to be cooked in front of them.

We sat at a table, drank cold beers, wore plastic bibs (at least one of which I think I still have somewhere) and tucked into a pair of lobsters with soft rolls, potato salad, corn-on-the-cob and coleslaw. The best bit? Dipping sweet lobster flesh into a pot of melted butter. It just doesn't get better than that.

This bun – dripping with smoky lime-flecked butter, filled with sweet, sharp, ketchup-like sauce and crispy fried squid – attempts to recreate something like the buttery seafood we ate on that trip. I could eat three of these given half the chance. They are ridiculously, messily delicious – reminiscent of those sweet rolls you can buy from beachside stalls up and down America's northeastern coastline. They're a great one to make on holiday, when (depending on where you live) you might have more access to good seafood. But if you can't get squid, you could apply the same principles to chunks of white fish, dusting them in semolina and deep-frying them. Or you could give this the full Maine makeover and buy a couple of lobster tails.

Serves 2

For the butter sauce
80g unsalted butter
a splash of olive oil
1 red onion, roughly
   chopped
270g tomatoes, roughly
   chopped
2 teaspoons chipotle
   chilli flakes

Continued on page 114

First, make the sauce. Set a large heavy-based pan over a low–medium heat with the butter and olive oil. Add the onion, tomatoes, and a good pinch of salt to season. Cook for about 10 minutes, or until the onions are soft and the tomatoes have slumped.

Sprinkle over the chipotle flakes and paprika, stir and cook for another 1 minute. Turn the heat up a little, add the purée, caster sugar and lime juice, stir and cook for 3 minutes, until thick and bubbling.

Turn the heat off, and then either pour the mixture into a measuring jug and use a hand blender or pour

1 teaspoon sweet smoked
  paprika
1 tablespoon tomato
  purée
1 dessertspoon caster
  sugar
1 lime, juiced
salt

For the squid
60g unsalted butter
1 lime, zest and juice, plus
  extra wedges to serve
plenty of neutral cooking
  oil, for frying
60g semolina
½ teaspoon sweet smoked
  paprika
160g squid, thickly sliced
  into ribbons flaky salt,
  for sprinkling
2 brioche hotdog buns,
  split in half (but not
  cut through)
a handful of coriander,
  leaves and stems

it into a food processor and blitz it until smooth.
You're going to use the pan again once you've
blended the sauce.

Set a sieve over the pan and push the sauce through
it, scraping the smooth sauce from the underside
of the sieve as you go. You'll be left with lots of pulp
in the sieve. Keep it, as you'll use it in a moment.

For the squid, set a small saucepan over a medium
heat with the butter. Add the lime zest and juice
and the pulp from the sieve. Stir and cook it for
2 minutes, just to melt the butter and bring
everything together. It'll sit while you do the rest.

Pour your frying oil into a deep pan over a medium
heat, or into a deep-fat fryer. Don't fill the pan or
fryer more than half the way up. Put something like
a nugget of bread or potato in the pan. When it rises
to the surface and is bubbling and clearly frying, the
oil is hot enough.

Meanwhile, put the semolina and paprika in a
shallow bowl along with a good pinch of salt.
Toss the squid in the semolina until well coated.

Fry the squid for about 3 minutes, or until the
coating is crispy and pale golden. Remove it from
the pan with a slotted spoon and transfer it to a
plate lined with kitchen paper. Sprinkle the squid
with flaky salt.

Spoon a little flavoured melted butter on each plate.
Dip the cut side of the buns in any excess butter left
in the pan. Spoon the warm tomato and lime sauce on
to the bottom half of the buns, then top each with a
mound of crispy squid and a few sprigs of coriander.
Squeeze over a lime wedge, fold the buns together
and eat immediately, dunking the bun in the butter
on your plate and any extra sauce.

Pork chops with quince butter and orange and endive salad

There is an old Jamie Oliver pork-chop recipe that I have made a hundred times. You make a flavoured butter with dried apricots and prosciutto, cut careful slits in thick chops and stuff them with the butter. They are lip-smackingly delicious and I've made various versions over the years. These chops are a kind of Spanish riff on them, and make a great Friday night dinner for two as they feel a bit special but are pretty easy to rustle up.

I love membrillo, that dusky terracotta quince paste that is so good with sharp, salty hard cheeses. Here, it's blitzed with chorizo, sage and butter and stuffed into pork chops, where it oozes out and on to the potatoes cooking underneath. Then, while the chops rest, you'll give the potatoes a dousing of sherry vinegar and crisp them up in the oven. I like how the bitter freshness and citrus in the salad cuts through the richness of the chops. Some roasted wedges of cabbage would be great too, or another kind of green, with a little lemon squeezed over them.

Serves 2

*For the potatoes
  and pork*
6 large potatoes
  (something that'll crisp
  up well like Maris
  Pipers), cut into chunks
  (no need to peel)
4 garlic cloves, skin on
olive oil, for roasting
  and frying
60g membrillo
70g unsalted butter
100g cooking chorizo,
  skins removed
8 sage leaves
2 thick-cut pork chops
  (they should be about
  5cm thick)
a few shakes of sherry
  vinegar
salt

Continued on page 117

Preheat the oven to 220°C/200°C fan/Gas 7.

Put the potatoes in a large roasting tin with the garlic, a good seasoning of salt and plenty of olive oil. Toss everything together, then roast the potatoes in the oven for 30 minutes, until soft and golden.

Meanwhile, make the butter. Blitz the membrillo, butter, chorizo and sage with a good pinch of salt. You want a relatively smooth paste.

Use a small sharp knife to make a pocket in the meat. You should make a wide slice at a 45° angle in the bit between the fat and the bone. Don't cut all the way through to the bottom or to the other side. You want a pocket to stuff the butter into.

Use your fingers to stuff the chops with the butter. Don't worry about them being messy. You'll have excess butter, which you're going to add to the potatoes. Seal the flap of pork back over the butter with your fingers.

Set a medium frying pan over a medium–high heat with a splash of oil. When the pan is hot, fry the chops for 3 minutes on each side, starting with the side that doesn't have the pocket). You're aiming to seal them and give the fat a chance to start browning. Don't move them around while they're cooking.

For the salad
1 orange, juiced
1 teaspoon runny honey
1 tablespoon sherry
 vinegar
½ lemon, juiced
1 teaspoon wholegrain
 mustard
3 teaspoons good
 olive oil
½ red onion, finely
 sliced
1 tablespoon capers in
 vinegar, drained
2 endives, tailed, leaves
 separated
a handful of watercress
 or another bitter leaf

Take the potatoes out of the oven and turn the heat up to 230°C/210°C fan/Gas 8. Place the chops, along with any melted butter that has escaped during the frying, on top of the potatoes, cut side up. Blob the leftover butter over the potatoes. Put everything back in the oven for 10 minutes. Then, remove the chops from the oven and set aside. Shake a little sherry vinegar over the potatoes and return them to the oven for about 10 minutes to crisp up.

Meanwhile, make the salad. Put the orange juice, honey, vinegar, lemon juice, mustard, olive oil and a good seasoning of salt in a large bowl and whisk everything together with a fork. Put the red onion in the bowl and toss everything around. Leave it to sit for a few minutes.

When you're ready to serve, add the capers and all the salad leaves and toss them in the dressing too. Serve plated with a few potatoes, a juicy pork chop and the cooking juices.

'Come over, I'll cook'

Let me cook you some dinner.
Sit down and take off your shoes
and socks and in fact the rest
of your clothes, have a daquiri,
turn on some music and dance
around the house, inside and out,
it's night and the neighbors
are sleeping, those dolts, and
the stars are shining bright,
and I've got the burners lit
for you, you hungry thing. ⸱

'The Love Cook' by Ron Padgett

Fried things and fizz, birthday vongole and going the whole hog

Sometimes, dinner parties can go a bit Bridget Jones; from
'already a legend' to blue soup in the space of an evening.
The key to enjoying yourself while hosting is to remember this
simple truth – no one is really there for the food. I have wasted
so many great evenings faffing about chopping and stirring
when I should have been at the table, not worrying about what
was happening on the hob. I've grown (marginally) better at
realising when I need to admit defeat and order a takeaway
rather than attempt to cook for the eight people who on
Tuesday I invited over not realising that by Friday I'd have
nothing in the fridge and little inclination to rustle up a feast.
(NB: Remember, when time isn't on your side, pizza always
will be.) But whenever I can, I pull out all the stops. I really,
dearly love dedicating a few hours to making a meal. Given
the chance, I'd happily spend a whole day cooking for my friends.
I love planning menus, going shopping for food, making lists
and ticking things off. I love picking a theme and then planning
everything from the cocktails to the music and the pudding
around it – a late summer dinner of balsamic roasted cherries
and soft goat's cheese on toast, a roast chicken with fennel,
lemon and aioli, an apricot cake with thick cream; a French
seaside night with mussels and chips and cider, followed by
lacy crêpes with salted caramel sauce and vanilla ice cream.

Judi Dench once said in an interview she is at her happiest when
anticipating someone arriving. I know exactly what she means.
I love that fizzy feeling that builds as you get ready for a bunch
of your nearest and dearest coming over – lighting candles,
getting glasses down, putting crisps in bowls.

I have a natural tendency to go overboard when it comes to
hosting, but I have learned that you can help yourself by keeping
some aspects of the meal as simple as can be. I like to let people
pick at some good nibbly bits while chatting, before sitting
down to something hearty. I'll load the table with nice things
for people to munch on. Sometimes it's little more than tortilla
chips and a big bowl of guac; sometimes I'll assemble a full

spread. The great Diana Henry says it's worth remembering that people appreciate you assembling delicious shop-bought things just as much as if you'd cooked every element yourself, and I completely agree. The most I'll do is assemble a salad of sorts for people to pile on to hunks of bread and eat with their fingers – sliced oranges and mozzarella, dressed with torn mint and good oil, roasted figs with torn basil and parma ham, or a plate of silvery anchovies scattered with lemon zest, chilli and finely chopped parsley. I quite like a hunk of hard cheese for people to hack away at too – a nutty, salt crystal-y parmesan or a comté – and usually there has to be some sort of dip.

I'll then tend to pick a big crowd-pleasing main, and I'll often just get ice cream, cheese or chocolate for afters. Sometimes, though, I'll get a hankering to make a proper pud, the kind that makes everyone feel like a child again (I'm talking ice cream sundaes, a tower of meringues and cream, or a great bowl of chocolate mousse).

If I had to draw up a list of hosting commandments it would boil down to this:

1   You don't need to actually cook more than one course.
2   Sprinkly, dippy bits are key.
3   Everyone is in it for the carb.
4   Cheese is better than pud.
5   But if you're going to do pudding, really do pudding.

If you send everyone away full, happy and having lost their voice screaming along to Stevie Nicks at 2am, you should consider the evening a roaring success.

Fried things and fizz

I love deep-frying things.

Partly because I love eating deep-fried things, but also
because passing round a platter of piping-hot fritters is
always guaranteed to make everyone happy. Whether it's
a mound of pakoras, tempura prawns with sweet chilli sauce,
arancini, croquetas or deep-fried pickles, nothing generates
oohs and aahs quite so successfully as a stack of crispy,
reassuringly beige bits and bobs.

I remember ordering a little plate of *fritti* in a trattoria in
Rome once while Interrailing. From memory, there was a
large olive, an artichoke and a zucchini flower, all fried in the
lightest possible batter and served with a lemon wedge. They
were among the best things we'd eaten the whole trip, though
that might have been because we were 20 and had just been in
Sweden where we'd run out of krone and had to resort to eating
cheese cubes for dinner on a park bench. For a masterclass
in proper Roman *fritti*, look no further than the great Rachel
Roddy. Here, you'll find an arancini and a stuffed olive recipe
in the next pages alongside a few other deep-fried delights.

I'm not convinced there are all that many things you can't
deep fry. People are often, understandably, trepidatious about
frying, but if you've never done it before, it isn't nearly as
much of a faff as you might imagine. You don't need a fryer,
just a deep saucepan, plenty of neutral oil, and a bit of
concentration to make sure you don't have any accidents.
I tend to put my pan on the back ring of the hob because it
feels safest there; I don't pour the oil more than half the way
up; I start it over a low heat, and as I don't have a thermometer,
I use a little piece of bread or potato to test whether the oil is
hot enough to start frying – when it floats to the surface and
fizzes, it's time to get down to business.

I like a gram flour and water-based batter for coating vegetables,
and follow the brilliant Felicity Cloake's lead when it comes
to arancini, first dipping the balls of rice in a mixture of plain
flour, water and egg, then rolling them in panko breadcrumbs.

Some sort of bitter or tart cocktail tends to work well with a fried nibble. So does a glass of very cold, not-too-sweet fizz. Think about it – a piping hot, molten-middle croqueta, and an ice-cold glass of cava. It's just guaranteed to be a good way to kick off an evening.

Is your hair and kitchen going to smell like a chippie? Yes. Is it worth it? Also, yes. So, chill a couple of bottles of fizz and whip up some deep-fried bits.

'Come over, I'll cook'

Green herb and taleggio arancini

*Makes 14 large
(clementine-sized)
or about 20 small*

For the risotto
1 tablespoon butter
olive oil, for frying
1 small onion, finely
    chopped
1 garlic clove, finely
    chopped
125g risotto rice
150ml white wine or
    dry sherry
30g grated parmesan,
    plus a parmesan rind
600ml hot chicken stock
a very large handful of
    soft herbs (I like a
    mixture of mint, basil
    and chives)
2 tablespoons double
    cream
1 lemon, zest and juice,
    plus extra wedges
    to serve
salt and freshly cracked
    black pepper

For the arancini
100g taleggio, broken
    into small, pea-sized
    nuggets
100g plain flour
1 large egg
60g panko breadcrumbs
plenty of neutral cooking
    oil, for deep-frying
flaky salt, to serve

First, make the risotto (or if you already have some leftover risotto, just use that and follow the final steps to make the arancini). Set a large pan with a lid over a low–medium heat. Add the butter and oil and, once the butter has melted, add the onion and a good seasoning of salt. Cook for 12 minutes, or until the onion has softened. Add the garlic and cook for another 3 minutes, until softened but not coloured.

Turn the heat up and pour in the rice. Stir well so the rice becomes coated in the oil and butter. Cook for a few minutes until the grains turn translucent, brown a bit and smell toasty.

Pour in the wine or sherry and stir until it becomes entirely absorbed. Add the parmesan rind (but not the grated cheese – that's for later). Then, add the stock a ladleful at a time, stirring continuously, and only adding more stock once the ladleful before has been absorbed. Keep going until the rice is tender and creamy.

In a food processor (or using a hand blender), blitz the herbs with the double cream and a little salt.

Turn the heat off under the risotto and stir through the grated cheese, then season with black pepper and salt. Add the herb mixture and the lemon zest and juice and stir well, pop the lid on and leave it to sit for a couple of minutes. Then give it one final stir and spoon the risotto into a large flat dish to cool quickly. Once cool enough, fully chill it in the fridge.

When you come to make the arancini, get your taleggio nuggets ready. Take a tablespoonful of chilled risotto in one hand, press a piece of taleggio in the centre, and smush the rice around it, rolling it into a tight ball. Place the ball on a baking tray. Repeat until you've used up all your mixture. Put the baking tray in the fridge so the balls of rice can firm up for 30 minutes.

Beat the flour with the egg, then slowly pour in about 50ml of water – or enough to get it to a thick batter, roughly the consistency of American pancake mixture. Put the breadcrumbs in a shallow bowl.

Dunk the rice balls in the batter, then the crumbs, fully coating them in each. Lay the arancini on a baking tray and put them in the fridge for 30 minutes to firm up.

Pour your frying oil into a deep pan over a medium heat, or into a deep-fat fryer. Don't fill the pan or fryer more than half the way up. Put something like a nugget of bread or a blob of leftover risotto in the pan. When it rises to the surface and is bubbling and frying, the oil is hot enough.

Fry the arancini in batches. You want them to be cooked through and golden brown on the outside, and you don't want the crumbs to cook before the arancini have heated through – so turn the heat down under your oil if you need to. I tend to cook one tester, break it open and check it's piping hot in the middle before I fry the rest. It's usually about 3 minutes for larger arancini or 2 minutes for smaller ones.

Sit the fried arancini on a baking tray lined with kitchen paper, sprinkle with flaky salt and serve with a couple of lemon wedges for people to squeeze over.

Deep-fried olives stuffed with anchovy and goat's cheese

Makes roughly 40

210g soft goat's cheese
8 salt-cured anchovies, finely chopped
40 very large pitted olives
120g plain flour
1 large egg
80g panko breadcrumbs
plenty of neutral cooking oil, for deep-frying
freshly cracked black pepper
flaky salt, to serve (optional)

Put the goat's cheese, anchovies and plenty of black pepper in a bowl and mash them together with a fork. Use your fingers (or a combination of your fingers and a teaspoon) to cram as much goat's cheese as you can get into the olives. It's a bit fiddly but just pack in as much as you can. Don't worry about neatness – the olives will get covered in batter and crumbs.

Beat the flour with the egg, then slowly pour in about 60ml of water – or enough to get a thick batter, roughly the consistency of American pancake mix. Put the breadcrumbs in a shallow bowl.

Dunk the olives in the batter, then the crumbs, fully coating them in each. Lay the stuffed olives on a baking tray and put them in the fridge for 1 hour to firm up.

Pour your frying oil into a deep pan over a medium heat, or into a deep-fat fryer. Don't fill the pan or fryer more than half the way up. Put something like a nugget of bread or potato in the pan. When it rises to the surface and is bubbling and clearly frying, the oil is hot enough.

Fry the olives in batches, lowering them into the oil with a slotted spoon so the oil doesn't splash back at you. When golden brown (about 2 minutes), transfer them to a baking tray or plate lined with kitchen paper. Sprinkle with flaky salt, if you like, and serve with cocktail sticks for people to spear them with.

Crab and 'nduja croquettes

Makes roughly 30

75g butter
40g 'nduja
3 tablespoons plain flour
568ml whole milk (a pint,
    in old money)
3 tablespoons grated
    parmesan
200g mixed white and
    brown crab meat
2 lemons, zested, then cut
    into wedges to serve
2 eggs, beaten
90g panko breadcrumbs
plenty of neutral cooking
    oil, for deep-frying
flaky salt, to serve

Set a large saucepan over a medium heat and add the butter. Once it's melted, add the 'nduja. Cook for about 10 minutes, letting the 'nduja fry off in the butter and leak its rust-red fat. Stir it occasionally and break up any bigger chunks with your wooden spoon. Then, add the flour and stir. It'll come together as a paste. Turn the heat down and keep cooking for about 5 minutes, stirring as you go.

Slowly pour the milk into the pan, adding a little at a time and stirring as you go. It'll thicken up at first and then slacken as you add more milk. Keep going until you have added all the milk and you have a thick béchamel.

Keeping a low heat under the pan, stir in a good seasoning of salt, the parmesan, the white and brown crab meat and the lemon zest. Cook for 10 minutes, stirring regularly. You want the mixture to be piping hot and bubbling. It might splatter a bit, so be careful you don't get burnt.

Scrape the mixture into a bowl, leave it to cool, then refrigerate it for at least 1 hour, or until chilled and firm.

Get out two shallow bowls, put the egg in one and the breadcrumbs in the other.

Take a dessertspoonful of mixture and use your hands to form it roughly into a short sausage shape. You might want to flour your hands when you do this, so they don't get quite so sticky with mixture.

Dip the croquettes in the egg, then the crumbs, making sure they're well coated. Then put them on a baking tray lined with baking paper. Put them back in the fridge for 30 minutes to firm up.

Pour your frying oil into a deep pan over a medium heat, or into a deep-fat fryer. Don't fill the pan or fryer more than half the way up. Put something like a nugget of bread or potato in the pan. When it rises to the surface and is bubbling and clearly frying, the oil is hot enough.

Fry the croquettes in batches, using a slotted spoon to lower them carefully into the pan so the oil doesn't splatter. You want them to be cooked through and golden brown on the outside, so turn the heat down under your oil if you need to. It'll take about 3 minutes per batch.

Lay the cooked croquettes on a baking tray lined with kitchen paper and sprinkle them with flaky salt. Serve with a couple of lemon wedges for squeezing over.

Shrimp fritters with chillies and nuoc cham

Makes roughly 12

1 recipe quantity of Nuoc Cham (see page 26)
90g gram flour
120ml cold sparkling water
3 spring onions, finely sliced
1 small red chilli, seeds removed, finely sliced
2 large garlic cloves, finely sliced
140g brown shrimp
plenty of neutral cooking oil, for deep-frying
1 teaspoon sesame seeds
flaky salt
1 lime, cut into wedges, to serve

If you haven't already, start by making your nuoc cham (see page 26) and set it aside.

For the fritters, put the gram flour in a large bowl with a good seasoning of salt. Trickle in the sparkling water, beating continuously with a balloon whisk. Keep going until you get a mixture slightly thicker than crêpe batter. Add the spring onions, chilli, garlic and shrimp. Stir well, making sure everything is well distributed and coated in batter.

Pour your frying oil into a deep pan over a low–medium heat, or into a deep-fat fryer. Don't fill the pan or fryer more than half the way up. Put something like a nugget of bread or potato in the pan. When it rises to the surface and is bubbling and clearly frying, the oil is hot enough.

Fry the fritters in batches. Use two dessert spoons, scooping a spoonful of mixture in one and carefully guiding it into the pan with the other. Be really careful when you do this as the oil may bubble up.

Fry the fritters until they're really well browned (about 3 minutes per batch). Then, remove them from the pan with a slotted spoon, transferring them to a plate lined with kitchen paper. Sprinkle with sesame seeds and flaky salt. Serve hot, with the nuoc cham for dipping and lime wedges on the side.

Aubergine fritters with honey and dipping vinegar

Makes roughly 22

1 recipe quantity of
  Coriander Dipping
  Vinegar (see page 25)
90g gram flour
1 large aubergine, cut into
  batons roughly the size
  of a chunky chip
plenty of neutral cooking
  oil, for deep frying
runny honey, for
  drizzling
1 teaspoon nigella seeds
flaky salt

Make the dipping vinegar according to the method on page 25. Leave it to sit while you make the fritters.

Put the gram flour and a good pinch of salt in a large bowl and trickle in about 130ml of water, beating continuously with a balloon whisk as you do. Keep going until you get a mixture slightly thicker than crêpe batter.

Dip the aubergines in the batter, making sure they're well coated.

Pour your frying oil into a deep pan over a low–medium heat, or into a deep-fat fryer. Don't fill the pan or fryer more than half the way up. Put something like a nugget of bread or potato in the pan. When it rises to the surface and is bubbling and clearly frying, the oil is hot enough.

Fry the fritters in batches, using tongs to carefully lower the aubergines into the oil. Be cautious when you do this as the oil may bubble up.

Cook the aubergines until they're really well browned (about 3 minutes). You want the aubergines to be super-soft and the batter crispy. Then remove them from the pan with a slotted spoon, transferring them to a plate lined with kitchen paper.

Drizzle a little honey over the fritters from a height, sprinkle them with flaky salt and nigella seeds, and serve them alongside the dipping vinegar.

Blackberry rum party punch

There is something so enticing about the idea of a big glass bowl filled with punch, a ladle with a looped handle resting against its lip ready to slosh ruby-red liquor into cups. It feels instantly celebratory and also makes you feel a bit like you're in *Mad Men*, which is a bonus. Though, I don't have a proper a punch bowl, so I tend to use a trifle bowl or my biggest pan.

The punch itself can be a good way to use up odds and ends of bottles. I often keep the actual punch quite strong and treat it as a kind of base that people can then drink neat over ice or top up with soda water or tonic themselves (it runs the risk of losing some of its fizz if you pour it straight into the punch bowl). This incarnation with blackberries and rum is just the right side of sweet. The blackberry syrup would make a lovely non-alcoholic cocktail too, with a wedge of lime and some soda water or ginger beer.

Keep a bag of ice on hand (I often stick one in the sink if it's going to be needed constantly) for people to add to their glasses, as the punch will be at its best when very cold.

(Photograph on pages 124–5.)

Serves at least 16, depending on how strong a drink everyone pours

960g blackberries, plus a few extra to serve
220g granulated sugar
4 limes, plus extra wedges or slices to serve
plenty of ice
750ml dark rum
a couple of large bottles of cold tonic water

Put the blackberries and sugar in a saucepan. Add the zest and juice of two of the limes. Bring everything to a simmer over a low heat, stirring, and cook the blackberries for about 20 minutes, or until the juices have reduced and started to turn a little syrupy. It's fine if they're still a bit loose. Push the mixture through a sieve into a large bowl and discard the pulp. You should have about 460ml of blackberry syrup liquid. Leave it to cool, then chill it before using it.

Put lots of ice in your punch bowl. Pour over the blackberry syrup and the rum. Add the juice of the two remaining limes. Leave your guests to top up their glasses with tonic water as they wish, and drop in a slice or wedge of lime.

Fizz and bitters

Serves 6–7, depending
on how generously
you pour

4 sugar cubes or
  3 teaspoons caster
  sugar
a few dashes of bitters
a very cold bottle of fizz
  (a dry cava, sparkling
  wine or champagne –
  prosecco might be a
  bit sweet)

If you're using sugar cubes rather than caster sugar, break them up a bit. I tend to use a rolling pin to give them a bash so that they split into chunks. Better to have chunks than pound it to a powder, but it's no biggie if you're planning to use caster sugar. If you're using chunks, distribute them evenly between the glasses. If you're using caster sugar, each glass should get slightly less than ½ teaspoon.

Shake the bitters over the sugar in each glass.

Carefully pour fizz over the sugar and bitters. The sugar will make it froth up so go slowly, going back to top the glasses up. Serve straight away.

Frozen jalapeño margs

For someone who lives in a pretty small flat, I have an unwieldy amount of glassware. Tucked away in a cupboard are big bowl-like gin glasses, sturdy tumblers, little bistro wine glasses and a few ropy plastic cups from festivals. On the shelf where all the Nice Bits go are my flatmate's granny's pale pink champagne coupes, which we tend to use for puddings more often than fizz. There are two tiny cranberry sherry glasses my friend Martha gave me, an even tinier gold cup (which would be good for little more than a thimbleful of something), and the cut-glass flutes and whisky tumblers I swiped from my godson's christening (I was permitted to steal them, I should just clarify; I'm not that ungodly). Balanced on top of the Billy bookshelves in the living room is the rest of the ever-growing haul. I don't use any of them enough to justify keeping them all, but I do hold on to some distant vision of a fabulous cocktail cabinet to one day house them in.

Among my favourites has got to be a set of four vintage margarita glasses decorated with big painted daisies. They're ridiculously kitsch and sturdy and I love their undulating sides. They are perfect for a round of frozen margaritas.

Serves 4

300ml tequila
150ml triple sec
200ml freshly squeezed
  lime juice (about
  8–10 limes)
2 tablespoons simple
  sugar syrup
lots of ice
20g brined jalapeños,
  finely chopped

Put the tequila, triple sec, lime juice and sugar in a blender. Top with ice and blend to a smooth slush.

Add the jalapeños and use a long spoon to mix them through the slushy. Pour straight into glasses and serve immediately.

Oven face

I have a face that gives me away.

It's why I could never be a spy and why I shouldn't play poker.
The nonsense rattling around my head is always inevitably going
to end up plastered across my face. I'm a terrible blusher, and if
I shed a single tear, I'll look like I've been stung on the eyelids
by a swarm of bees for the rest of the day. I blame the red hair.
Or maybe it's something to do with being a Leo. Suffice to say,
enigmatic I am not. I'm not sure there's much to be done about
it, but if I could, I'd perhaps at least do something to fix what
my friends call my 'oven face'.

It's about as attractive as it sounds. Essentially, if I do any
cooking that requires me to spend a lot of time opening and
closing the door to the oven, my face goes bright red and it'll
stay the shade of an underripe tomato for longer than seems
decent. There's also often an expression of grim concentration
that I'm told really completes the look. It means I have to accept
that if I'm having a dinner party, I'm going to look like a sweaty
mess for the vast majority of the evening, and every time I turn
from the oven back to the table you can guarantee someone is
going to let out a cry of, 'Alright oven face?'

I suspect it doesn't help that I'm such a haphazard host. I always
imagine myself gracefully, calmly finishing things off as people
start arriving, but I'm almost always still shoving all the mess
that has accumulated around the flat into my bedroom when
everyone gets here. When it comes to the food, I tend to bite
off more than I can chew. I start off planning a menu that sounds
simple and effortless, but somehow I end up overcomplicating
things, adding nibbles, courses and sides that no one needs,
or suddenly deciding I absolutely have to make a seven-hour
lamb shoulder that in all likelihood will still be stubbornly
slow-roasting at 10pm. I suppose I could fight my natural bent
towards a touch of chaos. Then again, does it really matter if
there's clutter everywhere if everyone has a great time and leaves
so full, they practically have to roll home? If you need a plan,
make a plan; if you're more of a fly-by-the-seat-of-your-pants
cook, don't beat yourself up about it. Pour yourself a cocktail
and remember – when in doubt, just roast a chicken, and wear
your oven face with pride.

Party potatoes with za'atar salt and soured cream and onion dip

Party food is tricky. Do you go full canapé or assemble some sort of Instagrammable grazing board, or is it just a crisps and dip situation? Whether I'm pulling out all the stops or relying on bags of tortilla chips to do the heavy lifting, I have never hosted a party without at least making a tray of potatoes.

I truly think party potatoes are going to solve all your problems. For a start, I remain convinced that when it comes to party food, all anyone really wants is some good carb. My sister made a tower of focaccia for my 30th birthday party, stacking them on top of each other and spearing a bread knife through the middle as if it were King Arthur's sword. The bread was completely delicious and gone in moments. Bring out a platter of potatoes and you'll see everyone's eyes widen and find yourself swarmed by hungry hands within seconds.

The great thing about these potatoes is that you can mainly cook them in advance and just have them crisping up in the oven as people are sinking their first couple of drinks, wondering what smells so good. You could even make them entirely in advance if you wanted, though you might lose a bit of crunch in a reheat.

Party potatoes bring all the fluffiness of a really good roast potato (you'll pre-steam and then chuff them just as you would for a roastie), but you're going to leave the skins on to ensure extra craggy edges, all the better for crisping up. You'll roast them in olive oil and make a flavoured salt to shake them in too, with za'atar and smoked paprika. When they're golden brown and have been given a dusting of sweet, smoky, sesame-flecked salt, you'll tumble them on to a platter around a deep bowl of soured cream, packed with lots of finely chopped red onion, soft sautéed spring onions, lemon and chives.

Will all your guests burn their mouths on them? Possibly. But it'll be one of the greatest potato 'moments' they've ever experienced.

Serves 8 as a side, more as a party nibble

For the potatoes
2.5kg King Edward potatoes, skin on
plenty of olive oil
5 heaped teaspoons za'atar
3 teaspoons flaky salt
2 teaspoons smoked paprika

Continued overleaf

Preheat the oven to 230°C/210°C fan/Gas 8.

Set a steamer pan over a low heat with about a 5cm-depth of water. Cut the potatoes into rough chunks. I tend to think you want them smaller than roast potatoes but not quite bitesized. The more uneven the chunks the better – irregular edges mean more crunch. Steam the potatoes over simmering water for 15 minutes. Then remove the steamer tray from the pan and sit it on the side with the lid off for 5 minutes to allow some of the moisture to evaporate.

In the meantime, pour enough oil on to a large baking tray that it's about 1cm deep. You don't want

For the dip
1 tablespoon good
  olive oil
12 spring onions, chopped
  into 5cm pieces
1½ lemons
650ml soured cream
1 red onion, very finely
  chopped
2 handfuls of chives,
  snipped
salt

to over-crowd the potatoes while they cook, so if you need to, use two trays. Put the tray(s) in the oven for 5 minutes so the oil has a chance to get nice and hot.

Put the lid on the potatoes in the steamer tray and give it a shake to chuff them up. Get them nice and craggy. Then take the baking tray(s) out of the oven and carefully tumble the potatoes on to it (them), bailing hot oil over the top of each tattie. Put the potatoes in the oven and roast them for 40 minutes, turning half way through so they crisp up evenly. You want them as golden and crunchy as possible.

While they're are cooking, mix together the za'atar, salt and paprika and set aside. Then, make the dip. Heat the oil in a small frying pan over a medium heat. Fry the spring onions with a pinch of salt for 2 minutes, then squeeze over the lemon half and set aside.

Mix the soured cream with the finely chopped red onion, the juice of the remaining lemon, and the chives, half the fried spring onions and a good seasoning of salt. Spoon the dip into whatever bowl you're serving it in and scatter the remaining soft, lemony spring onions on top.

When the potatoes are cooked, leave them to cool for a couple of minutes when they come out of the oven. Drain the oil from the baking tray (getting as much as you can out of the tray). Scatter the spiced salt over the potatoes and shake the tray, tossing the potatoes in the salt. Scatter the potatoes on to a large serving dish or into a serving bowl and serve them piping hot with the bowl of dip easily accessible for dunking.

Beef shin ragù

This is the definition of get-ahead hosting. You can either make it the day before (the flavour will improve with time) or just get going early on in the day and let the beef shins cook away slowly, generally sorting themselves out in the heat of the oven, and requiring little more of you than to boil a tangle of pasta when it comes to serving. I love making this for a wintry dinner when you can sense everyone just needs to sit and tuck into a hearty bowlful and nurse a big glass of red wine.

I'm not sure you need to serve anything with this, though I'll sometimes make a gremolata (see page 21), or toast a few buckwheat grains to sprinkle on top. Their nutty crunch makes a lovely addition to the soft, comforting pasta. A winter salad might be a nice way to kick off the meal – something fresh with apple or pear and blue cheese perhaps, or an earthy beetroot and goat's cheese number. To finish, I'd go tiramisù (a recipe for which you'll find on page 232). You can make that ahead too, and though everyone will groan they're too full after the ragù, there's no way they're going to turn down a helping of perfectly creamy, boozy pud.

Serves 6

2kg beef shin on
 the bone
olive oil, for frying
3 onions, chopped
3 rosemary sprigs
2 bay leaves, torn down
 the stem
1 whole garlic bulb,
 sliced in half through
 the middle
2 tablespoons tomato
 purée
350ml red wine
2 x 400g tins of chopped
 tomatoes
a fair bit of nutmeg,
 grated (I grate about
 ½ nutmeg into a ragù
 of this size)
1 parmesan rind, plus
 grated parmesan
 to serve
1 tablespoon red wine
 vinegar
600g pasta (something big
 that will hold the sauce
 well, like pappardelle or
 paccheri)
salt and freshly cracked
 black pepper

Preheat the oven to 160°C/140°C fan/Gas 3.

Dust the beef shin with salt and black pepper.

Set a large casserole pan with a lid (the kind that can go in the oven) over a medium–high heat with a splash of oil. Brown the beef all over, using tongs to turn the meat as it browns. Be bold and leave it to brown properly before turning. Then remove the meat from the pan and set it aside.

Turn the heat down and add another splash of oil to the pan. Add the onions and a good pinch of salt. Cook for 10 minutes, until softened, then add the rosemary and bay leaves and cook for another 3 minutes.

Add the two halves of the garlic bulb, cut side down, to the pan and cook for a couple of minutes, stirring regularly. Add the tomato purée and stir everything to really coat all the onions.

Pour in the wine and let it bubble up, then add the tomatoes and nutmeg. Season with salt and pepper and add the parmesan rind.

Bring the sauce to a simmer, put the meat back in the pan, then cover the pan and put it in the oven. Cook, covered, for 3 hours, then remove the lid and cook for another 30 minutes.

Remove the sauce from the oven and check how the meat is doing. By now, it should be super-soft and you should be able to pull it from the bone easily with a spoon (if not, pop it back in for 5 minutes and check again). Remove the meat from the pan and set it aside.

Add the vinegar (and more salt if you think it needs it) to the sauce. Set the pan over a medium heat on the hob and simmer it for about 10 minutes so that the sauce reduces a little.

Shred the meat from the bone and stir it through the sauce, removing any sinewy bits. Shred the rosemary needles from the stalks and push the garlic from its skins. Stir all that through too. It'll happily sit while you cook your pasta.

Put some well-salted water on to boil. Cook the pasta until al dente, reserving a little cooking water when you come to drain it. Tumble the pasta into the pan of sauce along with the reserved water. Stir well so the sauce really clings to the pasta.

Serve in warmed bowls with grated parmesan.

Thank God for sausage pasta

There are some recipes that you carry with you through the years like a pair of really good jeans. You know those magic ones that seem to expand and contract with you and get softer with every wash? They might need the occasional alteration or update; they might even be sporting an unseemly hole in the gusset. But somehow, even after a decade, after pieces of your life have become embedded in the denim, they still fit, still make you feel reassuringly yourself every time you wear them.

If I could track my twenties against one item of clothing it would be a pair of buttery soft, pale blue, ripped Anthropologie jeans. If I could track them by meals, it would be this sausage pasta.

It was born on a cold, rainy night in Devon, cobbled together roughly based on something I'd read in the *Good Housekeeping* cookbook (a tome of a thing) that I'd been sent off to university with. I shoved it in a plastic container to take on a train to Plymouth, where my friend Rosie and I were to interview the (extremely kind) comedian Mark Watson for our (extremely haphazard) student newspaper, for which we were the 'Arts Editors'. After the show, we drank a lot of cheap rosé in the Wetherspoons by the station and on the last train back to Exeter remembered the tub of pasta. I can still recall messily spearing conchiglie in the back seats of the carriage, probably annoying everyone as we warbled on.

That pasta became a mainstay, and in the years since, there is no other meal I have made as often as this one. I firmly believe a bowl of sausage pasta and the prospect of a night watching films with your best people should be prescribed as a cure for all ills.

There are no hard-and-fast rules with sausage pasta. You could add a few peas to the sauce, use crème fraîche rather than cream, omit the chilli and use any kind of soss you fancy, from a proper Italian fennel-flecked number to a pack of Sainsbury's Cumberland. The only thing you must do is to properly brown the nuggets of meat, and go heavy on the lemon. The pasta shape is your choice and yours alone, though I'd make a case for something that is going to catch the sauce – finding a bit of sausage in a pasta tube or shell is a very good thing.

My final suggestion is that you should do yourself an enormous favour and buy a garlic baguette to eat with it. And when I say garlic baguette I mean (and I cannot stress this enough) the supermarket kind that will probably burn your fingers and the roof of your mouth. There are some things in life – like French service station salad bars and cheap cheddar – that are better than their more gastronomic cousins. Somehow, a homemade garlic bread just doesn't do it in the way that a £1.60 twin pack from Tesco will. At one point Rosie actually suggested this book be called *The Many Garlic Breads of Our Lives*, which tells you all you need to know about the number of times one of us has said those two little words: 'Sausage pasta?'

Serves 4

8 sausages
olive oil, for frying
2 banana shallots, finely
  sliced
2 garlic cloves, finely
  sliced
2 teaspoons fennel seeds
½ teaspoon chilli flakes
350ml white wine
a little grated nutmeg
2 lemons, the zest of
  1 and the juice of both
200ml double cream
400g dried pasta of
  choice
a good handful of grated
  parmesan, plus extra
  to serve
a big handful of flat-leaf
  parsley, leaves and stems
  roughly chopped
salt and freshly cracked
  black pepper

Optional, to serve
1 supermarket garlic
  bread. (Go on. It'll be
  the best decision you
  make all week.)

First, set a large pan of salted water on to boil for
the pasta.

Remove the sausagemeat from its skins and break
the meat into nuggets.

Set a large frying pan over a medium–high heat.
Add a splash of oil, and once the pan and oil are
hot, add the sausage nuggets. Fry them until well
browned and gnarly all over. Transfer them from the
pan with a slotted spoon to a plate. Don't pile them
on top of each other too much or they'll go soggy.

Turn the heat down low under the pan. There should
be a good bit of sausage fat in the pan, but add a
splash more oil. Fry the shallots with a pinch of salt
for 8 minutes, or until softened and golden. Then,
add the garlic and cook for another 2 minutes. Thanks
to your sausage-y pan, this is all going to go pretty
gnarly as opposed to leaving you with perfectly
translucent softened shallots and garlic. But that's
okay. Gnarliness = flavour.

Add the fennel seeds and chilli flakes and cook for
1 minute, then return the sausage nuggets to the pan.

Pour in the wine and let it bubble up. Add the grated
nutmeg to taste and the lemon zest and juice. Simmer
for 1 minute, then turn the heat off and add the cream.
Stir everything together and leave it all to sit while the
pasta cooks.

Cook the pasta in the water, which is by now at a rolling
boil, until al dente. Reserve a little cooking water when
you drain it.

Turn the heat back on low under the sauce. Add the
pasta and cooking water to the sausage pan along with
the handful of grated parmesan and some black pepper.
Use tongs to toss everything together, making sure all
the pasta is coated in sauce. Then add the parsley and
toss again.

Serve in warm bowls with extra parmesan to grate over
each bowl.

Roast chicken with chicken juice rice and orange and onion salad

'I'm roasting a chicken.' There is surely nothing nicer than getting that text when you're on your way over to someone's house for dinner. All the best people I know make a really good roast chicken. And when it's good, it's pretty much unbeatable. It doesn't need to be complicated; the simplest bird smeared with butter and salt and roasted until golden and juicy is one of the best things in the world. I love making a rub with salt and spices to ensure really crispy, golden skin and lip-smacking juices, or spatchcocking a bird and sitting it in buttermilk, lemon, garlic and fresh chillies for a few hours before roasting it.

It's one of the few things I think you can eat on any night of the week. My family has weirdly strict rules about what you can have for dinner depending on what day it is. You couldn't, for instance, have lasagne on a Sunday. You could make your way through a batch of soup from Monday to Thursday, but don't even think about suggesting a bowl of leek and potato for dinner from Friday onwards. Fish is a total minefield – my mum actually refers to salmon as a 'midweek fish'. Sausage and mash is a tricky one. It's deemed a midweek meal in general, but has been known to slip through the net unnoticed Friday to Sunday.

For reasons known only to the mad people I have the privilege of sharing DNA with, roast chicken gets an oddly free reign. It's the only roast you could have during the week, though it would have to be served with some sort of salad and skin-on potatoes or mash in lieu of roasties and gravy (woe betide anyone who proposes gravy on a weeknight).

This chicken takes a bit of time, but it's very much worth the wait. First, you'll make a thick, sweet marinade with Dijon and wholegrain mustard, orange juice and brown sugar, as well as a few fennel seeds and some grated garlic. You'll sit it in the marinade for about four hours (or longer if you want to), then slow roast it with onions, bay leaves and a cinnamon stick. Slow roasting will ensure the sweet marinade doesn't catch too early and the bird stays juicy and very tender. Then, while the bird is resting, you'll cook basmati in all the buttery juices and a slosh of white wine to make a kind of pilau. It's one of the most satisfying things to make and comforting things to eat. A little tangy pomegranate molasses and a salad with more orange, mint and soused onion brings it all together.

If you're in more of a potato mood, you could halve new potatoes and cook them alongside the chicken rather than the rice; you could make an oniony potato salad, or even fry up a few crispy tatties. The mustardy, peppery radish remoulade on page 152 might also be a nice addition.

Serves 4, with leftovers

For the chicken
1 tablespoon wholegrain
    mustard
1 tablespoon Dijon
    mustard
1 tablespoon light brown
    soft sugar
1 teaspoon fennel seeds
2 large garlic cloves,
    grated
1 teaspoon coarse salt
2 oranges, zest and juice
1 medium chicken (about
    1.3kg)
80g butter, softened
2 red onions, peeled
    and cut into wedges
1 large cinnamon stick
4 bay leaves, torn down
    the stem
600ml white wine or
    dry sherry
370g basmati rice
135g currants
a little pomegranate
    molasses, for drizzling
a small bowl of seasoned
    natural or Greek
    yoghurt, to serve

For the salad
1 red onion, finely sliced
2 tablespoons red wine
    vinegar
3 oranges
1 tablespoon olive oil
1 teaspoon runny honey
a big handful of mint,
    leaves picked
a pinch of sumac
salt

First, make the marinade. Put both mustards, the brown sugar, and the fennel seeds, garlic and salt in a bowl. Use a large fork to mash everything together. Add the orange zest and finally the juice.

Put the chicken breast-side up in a roasting tin. Pour over the mustard mixture, rubbing it into the crevices and into the chicken's cavity. Cover the tin and put it in the fridge for at least 4 hours. When you're closer to roasting, leave the chicken to sit out for 40 minutes. Preheat the oven to 220°C/200°C fan/Gas 7.

Uncover the chicken and use your fingers to smear the softened butter on to the chicken skin. It'll be messy because of the marinade and may fall off in places but don't worry about that – just try and cram as much butter between the wings and on top of the bird as you can. Add the red onion wedges to the tin along with the cinnamon stick and the bay leaves.

Put the chicken in the oven and immediately turn the heat down to 150°C/130°C fan/Gas 2. Roast the chicken for 1 hour, then remove it and add 150ml of the white wine. Return the chicken to the oven for another 1 hour, basting occasionally with the juices. Then, take the roasting tin out again and add another 150ml of wine. Return it to the oven and roast the chicken for a final 30 minutes, until it's cooked through. Test this by sticking a small knife between one of the legs and the breast – the leg should easily pull away at the join and the juices should run clear – and the skin will be beautifully browned.

At some point while the chicken is cooking, start the salad. Put the red onion slices in a bowl with the red wine vinegar and a good seasoning of salt. Scrunch the onion with your fingers, cover and leave it to sit for 30 minutes. Put the rice in to soak in cold water.

Transfer the chicken to a warm serving dish, first tipping it on its end to pour all the juices in the bird into the roasting tin. Leave the onions, cinnamon, bay and juices in the tin. Turn the oven heat down and start warming a deep serving dish for the rice.

Put the roasting tin on the hob over a low heat (you might want to turn two hob rings on, so the heat is relatively evenly distributed). Pour in the remaining wine and let it simmer for 1 minute. Pour in 750ml of water and add a really good seasoning of salt and let the liquid bubble up for a minute. Drain the rice and add it to the tin, along with the currants. Stir – the rice should be completely covered with liquid. Cover the roasting tin tightly with foil and turn the heat under the tin down as low as you can. Cook the rice for 25 minutes, then turn the heat off and leave the rice to sit, covered, for 5 minutes, until completely tender. Take off the foil and fluff up the rice with a fork. Transfer it to your warm serving dish and drizzle over a little pomegranate molasses.

While the rice is cooking, finish the salad. Using a small knife, slice the top and bottom off each of the oranges. Then carefully slice the peel and pith off from end to end. Thinly slice the oranges and lay them on a serving plate. Scatter over the onions, leaving the vinegar back in the bowl. Whisk the olive oil and honey into the vinegar to make a dressing and pour this over the oranges and onion. Scatter over the mint leaves and sprinkle over the sumac.

Carve the chicken and let everyone help themselves to rice and salad, and a dollop of yoghurt too.

Radish remoulade

I truly believe celeriac remoulade from a French supermarket to be one of the greatest things on this Earth. I've tried to recreate it so many times and never quite nailed that very particular tang. This incarnation, however, made with bright peppery radishes, is a lovely little side dish or starter in its own right, and has just a touch of that French supermarket remoulade about it. I like serving it with roast chicken or thick-cut pork chops.

Serves 4 as a side

240g radishes
2 tablespoons white wine vinegar
1 lemon, juiced
1 teaspoon flaky salt
1 tablespoon Dijon mustard
2 tablespoons full-fat mayonnaise
a few chives, snipped
freshly cracked black pepper

Cut the top off the radishes and use a mandoline to slice them as thinly as you can get them, then cut the slices into matchsticks. You could also just use a very sharp knife, or coarsely grate them (though if they're small, grating can be a bit fiddly). Put the radish matchsticks in a bowl.

Put the vinegar, lemon juice and salt in a small saucepan over a medium heat and bring the liquid to the boil. Simmer for 1 minute, then pour the vinegar mixture over the radishes. Leave the radishes in the vinegar, turning them over occasionally, until they are completely cool.

Drain all but about a dessertspoonful of the vinegar mixture from the radishes and discard it (or keep it and use it in a salad dressing).

Add the mustard, mayonnaise, chives and plenty of black pepper to the bowl with the radishes and mix everything together well.

Eat the remoulade immediately or leave it for later. It'll keep for a couple of days in the fridge.

Very fresh courgette, lemon, basil salad

This salad is my ultimate catch-all. It's so satisfyingly fresh and tangy and can be adapted in any number of ways. You can swap the basil for any other soft herb, add a little fresh chilli or some crumbled feta, and switch out the lemon for a lime. It works really well when made into a dip by stirring it through lots of natural yoghurt for a kind of tzatziki. It's good as a side with all manner of things from lamb kebabs to garlicky chicken thighs, barbecued mackerel or fresh tuna. I like it tossed through pasta or orzo too. You can make it in advance or on the night, and if you have leftovers, they'll keep nicely in the fridge for a couple of days, just needing a good stir every time you return to them.

Serves 4 as a side dish

2 courgettes, finely grated
1 teaspoon fine salt
1 large lemon, zested and juiced
2 small garlic cloves, crushed
2 handfuls of basil, leaves and stems roughly chopped

Put the grated courgettes in a large bowl with the salt. Toss them together and leave them for 30 minutes. Then, put them in a sieve to drain over a bowl or the sink. Press the courgettes a little to squeeze out more liquid but don't overdo it. You don't want to mash them.

Mix the courgettes with the lemon zest and juice and garlic and leave them for another 20 minutes. Finally, toss everything with the basil.

Boozy potatoes

'Gubbins' was a much used word in our house growing up. The gubbins were the crispy, oozy, gnarly bits that got welded to the edges of an oven dish. 'Good gubbins with this one', someone would usually proclaim as we dived into the shepherd's pie or lasagne, wolfing down our portions so we could get to the good stuff, booting each other's forks out of the way as we made light work of the leftovers. Perhaps it's because I rarely cook those big, gutsy, feed-the-whole-family-with-one-dish oven bakes, but I don't have enough gubbins in my life these days. Every time I do rustle up something nostalgic that gives good gnarly bits, I wonder why I don't cook like that more often.

One thing I do make a lot is some version of these potatoes. They start roughly the same: peeled and thinly sliced as you would for a gratin, then layered, sometimes as they are here with finely chopped red onion, rosemary, bay leaves and garlic. Occasionally, I'll make more of a boulangère, cooking them with chicken stock and a bit of butter, but they're really at their best with a bottle (yes, an entire bottle) of white wine poured over them. The floury potatoes (make sure you don't use waxy ones) soak up the wine and lemon juice, leaving them soft and tender. A little butter will help the top layer crisp up beautifully.

I find these potatoes work particularly well when cooked underneath a slow-roasting piece of meat or a whole fish. You could get the potatoes started in the oven, then stick a grill or a metal cooling rack over the baking dish and roast a couple of duck legs over them, letting the fat drip down into the tatties below. Or, when they only have about half an hour to go, sit a couple of fat bream stuffed with fennel and citrus on top. Whatever you do with them, they're sure to leave you with some seriously good gubbins.

Serves 6

Preheat the oven to 200°C/180°C fan/Gas 6.

1.25kg King Edward potatoes, peeled and sliced very thinly with a mandoline or very sharp knife
1 tablespoon flaky salt
2 teaspoons freshly cracked black pepper
3 tablespoons olive oil
6 rosemary sprigs, leaves stripped & finely chopped
3 garlic cloves, finely sliced
2 red onions, finely chopped
6 bay leaves
2 lemons, juiced
1 bottle of white wine (nothing too sweet)
20g butter, cut into small chunks

Put the potatoes in a large bowl with the salt, pepper and olive oil. Add the rosemary, garlic and red onion. Use your hands to mix everything together really well. You want everything to be evenly distributed.

Tumble the potatoes into a large baking dish. They don't need to be arranged neatly, just pile them in – an uneven top layer will make for good crunchy bits. Tuck the bay leaves into the top layer of potatoes. Pour the lemon juice and the whole bottle of wine into the dish. Cover the dish with foil and put it in the oven.

Bake the potatoes for 1 hour, then remove the foil and turn the heat up to 220°C/200° C fan/Gas 7. Top the potatoes with the knobs of butter and put the dish back in the oven for 30 minutes, or until the potatoes are cooked through and well browned on top. Leave them to cool for a few minutes before serving – they're going to be hotter than the sun.

'Come over, I'll cook'

Birthday vongole

A birthday meal is always going to feel special just by dint of the fact that you're celebrating someone. You're already most of the way there because you've assembled some people around a table to make someone's day. You can cook the thing you know is their favourite, or something guaranteed to feel celebratory and bring cheer – like a spread of really great curries, a barbecue or a lamb shawarma. It helps, I think, if it's something you wouldn't make on any old night. It just needs to somehow say: let's celebrate another year of wonderful you. The dish that hits the spot most frequently in my book for a simple but special supper (possibly because so many of my favourite people seem to count this as their favourite) is spaghetti vongole.

A couple of very cold bottles of rosé or some sort of fizz, and a great platter of vongole (with extra parmesan cheese because, with apologies, on this point and this point alone I really do have to go against the Italians). It's easy, festive, delicious birthday fare.

Serves 6

5 tomatoes, finely
    chopped
3 garlic cloves, finely
    sliced
olive oil
720g dried spaghetti
½ teaspoon dried chilli
    flakes
420ml dry white wine
    or vermouth
about 1.5kg little clams in
    their shells
a big handful of flat-leaf
    parsley, leaves and stems
    finely chopped
fine salt
grated parmesan
    (optional), to serve

Put the tomatoes in a bowl with the garlic, a good pinch of salt and a glug of olive oil. Leave to marinate for 10 minutes.

Set a large pot of well-salted water on to boil. Cook the spaghetti until al dente, reserving a little cooking water when you come to drain it.

Meanwhile, put a large pan with a lid over a low–medium heat. Add the tomatoes and garlic along with the chilli flakes and fry for 6 minutes, or until the tomatoes have softened. Take care not to let the garlic brown.

Pour in the wine and bring it to a simmer. Then tip in the clams, pop the lid on and leave them for about 2 minutes, or until all the shells have opened.

Tumble the pasta and reserved water into the clam pan, along with half the parsley, and use tongs to toss everything together and really coat the pasta in the sauce. Discard any clams that haven't opened.

Serve the pasta in warmed bowls, sprinkled with the remaining parsley, and with grated parmesan, too, if you like.

Dad's paella

We all have a few meals that crop up at roughly the same moment every year, marking the passage of time. They're usually the meals we make to celebrate something, be it a religious festival, a birthday or just one of those big annual family get-togethers, but they can be smaller moments too. The first barbecue of the summer can feel momentous, or the first crumble when the weather turns at some point in October. December 22nd is very important in our house because it's Ham Night, when the gammon is cooked and first eaten hot with champ and sticky sauce before it's rolled out again and again in the days that follow as cold cuts. Honestly, Ham Night has become so sacred it's almost more important than the main event.

At some moveable point near the start of every summer, for as long as I can remember, my dad has cooked paella for friends in a huge pan on the barbecue. I think if I ever had a wedding, I'd probably have to serve paella. It just looks so beautiful and always feels like the perfect thing for a big celebration. I love those giant paellas you find cooking away at festivals and in markets in Spain and southern France, the smell so enticing it's impossible to walk past without buying a portion.

For this version – Dad's version – you'll roast the chicken thighs separately with thyme and garlic while you cook everything else, you'll fry the rice in chorizo oil and cook until it's super sticky with plenty of lemon, hot stock and saffron, then lay shell-on prawns and squid on top of everything, cover with foil and let them cook through. You could add a couple of handfuls of clams or mussels too. Lots of lemon wedges and parsley are crucial when it comes to serving. And, if you wanted, you could make the aioli on page 21 and serve a bowl of that alongside the paella too.

Serves 10

10 chicken thighs
plenty of olive oil
a few thyme sprigs
10 garlic cloves (4 left whole and in their skins, 6 finely chopped)
380g cooking chorizo, cut into large chunks, or – even better – about 20 of those small, almost bitesized chorizo sausages
3 large onions, finely chopped
1kg bomba rice
400ml white wine
1.5 litres hot chicken or fish stock

First, get your chicken on to roast. Preheat the oven to 220°C/200°C fan/Gas 7. Lay the chicken thighs in a roasting tin, drizzle over oil, sprinkle with plenty of salt, then add the thyme sprigs and the whole garlic cloves. Cook for 35 minutes, or until the skin is crispy and the meat tender and cooked through. Set aside, covered with foil, until the rice is nearly done.

While the chicken is cooking, put your paella pan (or a very large casserole pan) on the hob over a medium heat with a good glug of oil. Add the chorizo and fry until well browned all over. Then remove it from the pan with a slotted spoon and set aside.

Turn the heat down, add a little more oil to the pan, which should have a fair bit of rust-red paprika oil from the chorizo. Add the onions and a little salt. Fry for about 12 minutes, or until the onions have softened. Add the chopped garlic and cook for 4 minutes to soften.

3 lemons, juiced, plus lots
of extra wedges to
serve
a large pinch of saffron
strands
1 x 465g jar of roasted red
peppers, sliced into
ribbons
20–30 shell-on prawns
500g squid, cut into
rings
salt

To serve
2 handfuls of flat-leaf
parsley, leaves and
stems roughly
chopped
flaky salt

Turn the heat up and add the rice, stirring as you
fry it for a couple of minutes. You want the rice to
be really well coated in the oil and to start browning
a little and turning translucent.

Pour in the wine and let it bubble up. When it's all
absorbed, start adding the stock. Turn the heat down
a bit and keep stirring and ladling in stock slowly
until the rice is really sticky and tender. You're
going to add the lemon before the rice is completely
done, so while the rice is cooking, mix the lemon
juice with the saffron and leave it to infuse for a few
minutes. Then add it to the pan when you've nearly
run out of stock.

When the rice is almost done (try it and see if it
still has a little bite to it), put the chorizo back in
the pan and stir it through the rice. Lay the chicken
pieces, peppers and roasted garlic cloves on top.
Finally, scatter over the prawns and squid. If you're
using a paella pan, turn the heat down low and cover
the pan with large sheets of silver foil. If you're
using another kind of pan, either do the same or
if there's a lid, put it on. Cook for 25 minutes, or
until the prawns and squid have cooked through and
everything is piping hot.

Scatter a little flaky salt and lots of parsley over
the pan and serve with extra lemon wedges.

Osso buco with saffron risotto and gremolata

This is one of those meals that packs a huge flavour punch. A meaty braise made with a not overly expensive cut; little bones filled with marrow, some of which will melt into the sauce as it cooks; bright, fragrant saffron risotto and a punchy lemony gremolata to cut through the sticky rice and rich gravy. It's a lovely thing to cook, with the meat just blipping away gently in the oven in a big roasting tin, smelling more and more enticing as it cooks. Meanwhile, you can get on with the soothing business of making a great pan of risotto.

It's a good one for a crowd but the meat freezes really well too, so you can always make a big batch and box up the leftovers, or make extra risotto for arancini. Future you will be extremely grateful for a forgotten freezer bag of osso buco, and tomorrow night you can fry up a couple of hot, crispy arancini.

Serves 8

For the osso buco
1 tablespoon plain flour
8 beef shins, bone in
olive oil, for frying
2 onions, finely chopped
2 carrots, finely
  chopped
2 celery sticks, finely
  chopped
3 garlic cloves, finely
  chopped
4 bay leaves
1 tablespoon tomato
  purée
450ml red wine
1 x 400g tin of chopped
  tomatoes
650ml hot chicken stock
a little grated nutmeg
2 x recipe quantities
  of Gremolata (see
  page 21)
salt and freshly cracked
  black pepper

Continued on page 162

Preheat the oven to 170°C/150°C fan/Gas 3.

Make the osso buco. Mix the flour in a large bowl with a good seasoning of salt and plenty of black pepper. Add the beef shins one at a time, turning them over in the flour and setting them aside on a plate as you go.

Set a large stock pot on a high heat with a splash of olive oil. When the oil is piping hot, start frying off the beef shins. Cook them in batches, letting them get nice and brown all over before frying the next one. Set them aside in a large roasting tin.

When the beef shins are all browned, turn the heat down and add another glug of oil to the stock pot, along with the onions, carrots, celery and a good seasoning of salt. Stir, top with a lid and leave to sweat for 18 minutes, or until the vegetables are really soft. Add the garlic and bay leaves and cook for another 5 minutes, then add the tomato purée, stir and cook for another 2 minutes.

Turn the heat up and pour in the wine. Let it bubble up, scraping the bottom of the pan with your wooden spoon. Add the chopped tomatoes, chicken stock and nutmeg. Bring the mixture to a simmer and cook it for 5 minutes, then ladle it over the beef in the roasting tin. Cover with foil and place the beef in the oven. Immediately turn the heat down to 150°C/130°C fan/Gas 2. Cook for 1½ hours, or until

For the risotto

2 tablespoons butter, plus an extra knob of cold butter for the end
1 tablespoon olive oil
2 onions, finely chopped
3 garlic cloves, finely chopped
1 bay leaf
a large pinch of saffron strands
1 lemon, juiced
700g arborio rice
450ml dry white wine
1 parmesan rind, plus a handful of grated parmesan
1.25 litres hot chicken stock (or good vegetable stock)

the meat is soft and falling away from the bones and the sauce is thick and smelling incredible.

Just before you make the risotto, mix all the ingredients for the gremolata together (see page 21). It's worth making it a little while ahead of serving so that the flavours have a chance to meld.

For the risotto, set a large pan with a lid over a low–medium heat with the butter and oil. Once the butter has melted, add the onions and a good seasoning of salt. Cook for 12 minutes, or until the onion has softened. Add the garlic and bay leaf and cook for another 3 minutes to soften the garlic.

Meanwhile, put the saffron and lemon juice in a little bowl. Mix with a teaspoon and leave it to sit for a bit.

Turn the heat up under the veg and pour in the rice. Stir well so that the rice becomes coated in the oil and butter. Cook for a few minutes until the grains turn translucent and smell toasty.

Pour in the wine and stir. Keep stirring until the wine becomes entirely absorbed. Add the parmesan rind (but not the grated cheese – that's for later) and the saffron. Then ladle in some stock. Add the stock one ladleful at a time, stirring continuously, and adding more stock only once the previous ladleful has been absorbed. Keep going until you have used all the stock and the rice is tender and creamy.

Turn off the heat and stir through the handful of grated parmesan and a little salt to taste. Add the knob of cold butter, pop the lid on and leave the risotto to sit for a couple of minutes. Then give it one final stir.

To serve, warm your bowls and add a ladleful of rice to each. Top with a beef shin (making sure everyone gets a bone with a good bit of marrow still quivering in the centre) and a puddle of sauce. Finish by spooning over some gremolata.

The whole hog

My store cupboard doesn't fully close. A metal IKEA shelving unit that was meant to keep things vaguely organised has never properly fitted inside, meaning the door stays permanently ajar. It doesn't help that every tray is overflowing... all the usual suspects are there – tins of chickpeas, chopped tomatoes, tuna in olive oil, and a good supply of emergency Heinz. There are bottles of passata too, and a jar of anchovies and one of green olives. There are half packets of basmati rice, brown rice, risotto rice, polenta and dried lentils. There are some old jars of jam that are still slightly sticky from the time a tin of treacle leaked on to the tray below. And a whole section of the rackety shelf of doom is devoted to pasta.

Occasionally, a couple of fancier jarred beans or chickpeas make it into the cupboard – the kind you find in delis that cost a lot more than common or garden tins but contain the softest, creamiest pulses. When one turns up in my stores, it rarely stays in there for long; I tend to use it straight away. And for something like this dish, where the chickpeas have a starring role but are going to cook quickly in the pork fat and juices, using the creamier jarred kind makes all the difference.

This is a project pork – a slow-roasted shoulder that'll need to sit in the dry rub for a few hours before you roast it. The cook itself is long and low for the meat to get so soft you could pull it away from the bone with a spoon. Occasionally, I like to play long ball with dinner, to start making it hours before we're going to eat, knowing that as time ticks by it's only getting better in the heat of the oven. It might take a bit of care and attention, but sometimes it's nice to go the whole hog.

This is great as it is with the saucy chickpeas, feta and yoghurt, but if you wanted to serve something green with it you could make a very lemony chopped salad, or sauté some chard, cavolo nero or another kind of leafy green with a little garlic.

Serves 8–10

For the pork
3 teaspoons smoked
  paprika
2 teaspoons ground
  cinnamon
2 teaspoons fennel seeds
2 teaspoons cumin seeds
2 teaspoons caraway
  seeds
2 teaspoons garlic
  granules
3 teaspoons flaky salt
2.5kg bone-in pork
  shoulder (ask your
  butcher to score the
  skin)

Continued overleaf

Put greaseproof paper at the bottom of a large roasting tin. In a small bowl, mix together all the spices, along with the garlic granules and salt. Rub the spice mixture all over the pork. Cover, then refrigerate the meat for at least 4 hours. The longer you can leave it with the rub on the better – overnight if you have time. When it comes to cooking, take the pork out of the fridge 40 minutes before you're going to put it in the oven, so you're not roasting from fridge temperature.

Preheat the oven to 220°C/200°C fan/Gas 7. Uncover the pork, add the onions and garlic to the tin, and pop it in the oven for 20 minutes. Then, take the tin out of the oven, cover with foil and reduce the heat to 150°C/130°C fan/Gas 2. Put the pork back in the oven and cook it for 4½ hours, or until it is super-soft and you can pull it off the bone with a spoon.

3 red onions, peeled and
    cut into wedges
1 garlic bulb, sliced down
    the middle
500g cherry tomatoes
300ml red wine
3 tablespoons tomato purée
1 teaspoon dried chilli
    flakes
2 x 700g jar of chickpeas
    with their liquid
450ml chicken stock
1 tablespoon red wine
    vinegar or sherry
    vinegar
1 lemon, juiced
salt

To serve
350g feta, crumbled
2 big handfuls of flat-leaf
    parsley, leaves and stems
    finely chopped
a big handful of oregano,
    leaves picked
1 lemon
8–10 tablespoons natural
    yoghurt
a good pinch of sumac

At some point while the pork is in the oven, make
the feta crumble and the seasoned yoghurt to serve.
Pat the feta dry with some kitchen paper, then use
your hands to crumble it into a large bowl. You want
fairly small pieces, so crumble it thoroughly. Add the
herbs and stir to combine. Zest the lemon and add
the zest to the bowl. Mix it with the feta and parsley.
Then cut each end off the lemon and, using a small
knife, carefully remove the skin and pith. Roughly
chop the flesh, taking care to discard any pips. Set
the lemon flesh aside to add it to the feta mixture
just before you're about to serve. (This is to avoid the
lemon making the feta wet and creamy, which would
make everything stick together.) Set the feta aside
in whatever bowl you're going to serve it in. Put the
yoghurt in a bowl and mix it with a pinch of salt.
Top with a sprinkle of sumac. Set aside in the fridge.

Transfer the cooked pork to a large, warm serving
dish. Loosely cover it with foil and leave to sit
for at least 30 minutes. If you want to crisp up the
crackling, remove the skin and pop it under a hot
grill for a few minutes just before serving.

While the pork is resting, remove the greaseproof
paper from the tin. Take out any really gnarly bits
of onion and squeeze the garlic from their skins,
but make sure you're leaving behind all the cooking
juices. Put the tin with all the juices on the hob over
a medium heat. You might want to put it over two
rings so the heat is more evenly distributed. Add the
tomatoes and cook them in the hot fat for 2 minutes
so that they start to soften. Pour in the wine and
scrape the bottom of the pan so you get all the fat
and gnarly bits up while it simmers. Add the purée
and chilli flakes, beating the purée into the wine.
Then add the chickpeas and their liquid, a seasoning
of salt and the stock. Bring the liquid to a simmer and
cook for 15 minutes, smushing the tomatoes with the
back of a spoon as they soften. Then, add the vinegar
and lemon juice and cook for another 1 minute.

Use two forks to shred the pork from the bone.
Add it to the roasting tin of chickpeas and juices
and toss it all together.

Add the reserved lemon flesh to the feta mixture.

To serve, spoon the pork, chickpeas and cooking
liquor into deep, wide bowls and top with a piece
of crackling (if you made it) and some feta crumble.
Let everyone help themselves to a dollop of yoghurt.

Chicken Milanese and spaghetti with 4-hour tomato sauce

Sometimes I think the other ingredient in every recipe, the one you won't find written in the ingredients list, is your own mood. I bake terrible cakes when I'm angry, scones come out right only if I'm whistling a happy tune (not literally – I can't whistle), a roast chicken will end up tough if I'm anxious. Our mood runs through our cooking – and it can also shift at any intangible point as we chop and stir. If I'm in a bad mood when I start making tomato sauce, I'm rarely grumpy by the end. It might be because it's so reassuringly reliable: onion, garlic, olive oil, salt, tomatoes, wine and time. Lots of time. It's all in the pan in a few minutes, but leave it long enough, blipping away over a low heat, and it becomes the silkiest, most comforting liquor – tangy yet sweet; buttery yet fresh. It's my favourite thing to eat on any day of the week, and my favourite thing to cook when there's time.

It might also be because it's the food that most reminds me of childhood. This sauce is called PPS in our family – Penny's Pasta Sauce. We grew up on it, and all have friends who still remember coming round for PPS as children. The scent of a huge pan of tomato sauce cooking is enough to make me feel a deep sense of calm, as only nostalgic food can – from the moment the onions hit the hot oil, their harshness mellowing as they soften, to the rich sweetness that used to float up the stairs as the sauce cooked down and down. It's the thing I most want when I'm under the weather or feeling low. Remembering there is tomato sauce in the freezer that I can quickly defrost for dinner is like finding a £10 note in an old coat pocket. Often, I'll just have the sauce as it is with spaghetti, but a brilliant way to make it feel that bit more special, more worthy of a Friday night, is to serve it with a platter of golden, crispy chicken (or veal) escalopes and plenty of lemon wedges.

Serves 6

For the tomato sauce
olive oil
3 onions, chopped
4 garlic cloves, chopped
2 tablespoons tomato purée
3 bay leaves
2 small glasses of red wine
2 x 400g tins of chopped tomatoes
400g passata
2 teaspoons sugar
480g dried spaghetti
flaky salt and freshly cracked black pepper

Continued overleaf

Set a large pan with a lid over a low–medium heat with a good glug of oil. Add the onions, along with a pinch of salt, pop the lid on and sweat the onions until they are very soft (about 10 minutes). Then, add the garlic and sweat for another couple of minutes. Turn up the heat, add the tomato purée and stir well. Then, add the bay leaves and red wine and bring the mixture to a simmer.

Add the chopped tomatoes, passata, sugar and a little more salt and black pepper. Pop the lid on and leave the sauce to simmer on a very low heat for about 4 hours. Then, remove the bay leaves and use a hand blender to blitz the sauce until smooth.

When you're ready to eat, cook the spaghetti in a big pan of well-salted boiling water until al dente.

Dip the chicken escalopes or bashed breasts in the flour, then the egg and finally the breadcrumbs to

For the chicken
6 chicken escalopes or
  breasts (for breasts,
  pop them in a freezer
  bag one at a time and
  bash them out with a
  rolling pin)
4 tablespoons plain flour
2 eggs, lightly beaten
2 handfuls of panko
  breadcrumbs
2 tablespoons butter
2 rosemary sprigs
1–2 lemons, cut into
  wedges

coat. Set a large frying pan over a medium heat and add the butter and rosemary. Fry the escalopes in batches (take care not to overcrowd the pan), for about 4 minutes on the first side, until the underside is golden and crispy, then flip them and fry for a further 3–4 minutes, until cooked through and golden and crispy all over. Set each batch aside on kitchen paper while you fry the remainder.

To serve, stir plenty of sauce through the drained spaghetti, sprinkle flaky salt over the escalopes and squeeze over a couple of lemon wedges.

Lillet Rosé and tonic with pink peppercorns

I love beautiful bottles – looking at them, displaying them, using them for flowers or making retro Italian trattoria candlesticks from them and, of course, pouring from them. A line-up of gorgeous labels on bottles of all different heights and colours is a happy-making sight. I use a Habitat bedside table to store my liquor, regularly rearranging the bottles so the most attractive ones are at the front while the failsafe gins and cheap cooking booze bring up the rear.

One of the prettiest bottles in regular rotation is a white or pink Lillet. It's a wine-based apéritif that is much lighter and slightly floral. It's great mixed with something sparkling, and I like topping it with a sprinkle of crushed pink peppercorns, which are handy to have around for pepping up a common or garden G&T.

Serves 1

plenty of ice
a ribbon of cold
  cucumber
60ml Lillet Rosé
  or Blanc
a little tonic water
a pinch of pink
  peppercorns,
  crushed between
  your fingertips

Put plenty of ice in a tall glass along with the cucumber. Pour over the Lillet Rosé or Blanc, top up with tonic water and finish with the pinch of crushed pink peppercorns.

More bread than salad with tapenade dressing

I like a salad that is hefty enough to hold its own, and this is a game-day salad. It's main-meal-worthy, as substantial as it is fresh and zingy, and with lots of different textures, which I tend to think is what makes a dish so satisfying – our palates want that contrast of crunch and softness.

This recipe sits somewhere between a panzanella, a Greek salad and a fattoush. You can make it vegetarian by leaving out the anchovies. It would be great served alongside barbecued meat or fish, or as part of a kind of Mediterranean mezze, perhaps with some griddled aubergines and courgettes, a bowl of olives and a whole halloumi baked with honey. It's perfect for a summer evening when you want dinner to be a table covered in good things for people to dive into messily.

Serves 6

8 large tomatoes, quartered (use different coloured toms if you can, because it looks beautiful)
2 teaspoons flaky salt
2 red onions, finely sliced
½ teaspoon caster sugar
4 tablespoons red wine vinegar
olive oil, for frying
roughly 350g stale white bread, torn into chunks (or tear up as much bread as you think you'll want)
3 spring onions, finely sliced
400g thick Greek yoghurt
1 lemon, zest and juice
200g feta, broken into large chunks
a few oregano leaves
a good pinch of sumac

Put the tomatoes in the serving bowl or dish you're going to use. Sprinkle over half the salt and leave them to release some of their juices while you fry the bread.

Toss the red onion in a bowl with the sugar and the remaining salt. Pour over the red wine vinegar and leave to steep.

Set a large frying pan over a medium heat with a good glug of oil (the bread will soak it up, so you'll need more than you think). Fry the bread in batches, turning until golden all over. Set aside on a baking tray lined with kitchen paper and sprinkle with a little salt. You could also griddle the bread on a barbecue, if you prefer.

To make the dressing, roughly chop the olive flesh. In a bowl, mix the olive flesh with the parsley, oregano, anchovies and garlic and season with black pepper. Add the lemon and capers, and lastly beat in the olive oil with a fork.

Pour the juices that the tomatoes have released into the dressing bowl and do the same with the vinegar that the onions have been sitting in (tip the onions themselves into the bowl of tomatoes). Give everything a really good whisk so it comes together nicely as a loose dressing.

Add the spring onions and most of the bread (reserve a few pieces) to the bowl of tomatoes and toss

For the dressing
100g black olives (I use
   dry salt-cured), pitted
a handful of flat-leaf
   parsley, leaves and stems
   roughly chopped
a big handful of oregano,
   leaves and stems torn
6 salt-cured anchovies,
   finely chopped
1 garlic clove, finely
   grated
1 lemon, juiced
2 tablespoons capers
2 tablespoons good
   olive oil
salt and freshly cracked
   black pepper

everything together with the dressing. (You'll add the reserved pieces of bread only when you're ready to serve so you can be sure to have a couple of super-crunchy bits in there.) Leave the salad for about 15 minutes before tossing again.

Meanwhile, mix the yoghurt with the lemon juice and a good pinch of salt. Use a tablespoon to spread the thick yoghurt on a big serving dish, almost to the edges. Pile the salad on top, adding your remaining chunks of crunchy bread and scattering over the feta and oregano leaves. Finally, sprinkle over lemon zest and sumac, and serve.

Big summer pasta

Spontaneous dinner parties belong to the summer. Those few weeks when the days are long enough that you don't want them to end, you just want to sit outside enjoying your friends until the last candle burns down, you're using three iPhone torches to see and someone is working out how to order wine on Deliveroo.

On nights like these, when dinner needs to feel festive and summery and not take too much planning, I reach for a great big pasta with lots of soft herbs and lemon. There are so many ways to go with this kind of pasta, but I think a good rule of thumb is to include a mixture of textures and go heavy on the olive oil.

I like thinly slicing courgettes and frying them on a high heat so you get these nice crispy-edged sheets, half of which you toss through the pasta, the rest you scatter on top so they don't go soggy. I like charring little gem and blanching peas so they stay bright green (for a quick midweek pasta I'm more likely to just chuck a handful of frozen peas in the sauce at the end for speed, but it usually means some of them will end up overcooking a little), and tend to make something more akin to a dressing than a sauce to toss the pasta in. You could add cream or crème fraîche, but to keep things light and tangy, I like mashing soft goat's cheese and lemon zest together and dolloping it on top of the dish for everyone to stir and melt through their own bowlfuls.

Tumble everything on to a warmed serving dish and make sure your bowls or plates are warm too. Pass round a block of parmesan and a grater, and a pepper grinder.

Serves 6

3 little gem lettuces
8 tablespoons olive oil,
    for frying, plus extra
    for drizzling
3 large courgettes, halved
    lengthways and very
    thinly sliced with a
    mandoline or a very
    sharp knife
375g frozen peas
600g dried pasta
    (something like
    casarecce or rigatoni)
3 garlic cloves, finely
    grated
3 lemons, zest and juice
a big handful of mint,
    leaves stripped from
    the stalks and finely
    chopped
a big handful of oregano,
    leaves stripped from the
    stalks
250g soft goat's cheese
1 tablespoon butter
a big handful of chives,
    snipped
salt and freshly cracked
    black pepper

To serve (optional)
1 teaspoon of smoked
    chilli flakes
grated parmesan

Cut the little gem into quarters lengthways so the leaves are still attached at the root. Give them a wash and then lay them on kitchen paper. Leave them to dry fully before you cook them.

Meanwhile, set a large frying pan over a high heat with half of the olive oil. Fry the courgettes in batches, one handful at a time. Cook each batch for about 4 minutes, or until the ribbons have started to brown. Remove the courgettes from the pan with a slotted spoon to a plate lined with kitchen paper and sprinkle with salt. Add oil to the pan if it needs it.

Set a saucepan of salted water on to boil. Cook the peas for 2 minutes, or until just cooked, then drain them and run them under very cold water to stop them cooking. Set the peas aside.

Meanwhile, put the heat back on under the frying pan. Sear the little gem, using tongs to turn the wedges in the pan. Set them aside on a plate and sprinkle with a little salt.

Put a large saucepan of well-salted water on to boil. Cook the pasta once the water is at a rolling boil, until it's al dente. Reserve a couple of tablespoonfuls of cooking water when you drain the pasta.

Mix the garlic with the remaining olive oil, and the lemon juice, mint, oregano and a good seasoning of salt and plenty of black pepper.

Mix the goat's cheese with the lemon zest and some black pepper.

When the pasta is ready, put it back in the pan over a low heat. Add the reserved cooking water, the lemon and garlic mixture, the butter, the peas and half the courgette ribbons. Stir well to melt the butter and make sure all the pasta is dressed in the lemon mixture.

Tumble the pasta on to a large, warmed serving dish. Tuck the little gem into the pasta here and there, scatter over the remaining courgettes and top with at least six dollops of goat's cheese. Finish by sprinkling chives over everything, the smoked chilli flakes if you're using them and a final drizzle of olive oil. When everyone serves themselves, make sure they get a helping of goat's cheese and a couple of wedges of lettuce.

Buttermilk spatchcocked chicken with very tangy sauce & pickle relish

I love cooking with buttermilk. It's one of those magical ingredients that seems to make so many things better, from cakes to pancake batter, to roast chicken. There is some alchemy that minds greater than mine could explain within that sour funkiness that means everything it comes into contact with ends up more tender. Your scones will be lighter, your chicken more juicy, your sponge will get a softer crumb. Clever, really, given it's essentially a glass of sour milk you're pouring in and hoping for the best.

I particularly love a buttermilk marinade if I'm roasting a spatchcocked chicken (though you could also use the same marinade for legs or supremes). Get a butcher to do the spatchcocking for you, or teach yourself using one of many YouTube videos. I tend to serve this with some sort of potato, often parboiling a few Maris Pipers cut into chunks, siphoning off some of the marinade and roasting them in the buttermilk.

Serves 5

For the chicken
500ml buttermilk (or
    500ml whole milk and
    the juice of ½ lemon,
    left to sit for 20 mins)
4 garlic cloves, grated
1 teaspoon smoked
    paprika
4 dried bird's eye chillies,
    finely chopped
1 lemon, juice and peel
1 heaped teaspoon salt
1 large chicken (about
    2kg), spatchcocked
1 recipe quantity of Pickle
    Relish (see page 24)

Mix the buttermilk with the garlic, paprika, chillies, lemon juice and a few strips of peel, and the salt. Place a piece of baking paper in the bottom of your roasting tin (this will stop the sauce cooking off too quickly when you roast the chicken later) and place the chicken on top. Pour the buttermilk over the top. Cover the chicken and refrigerate it for at least 5 hours, more if you can. Take the chicken out of the fridge 45 minutes before you want to cook it.

Preheat the oven to 220°C/200°C fan/Gas 7. Put the chicken in the oven and immediately reduce the temperature to 190°C/170°C fan/Gas 5. Roast the chicken in its marinade for 1 hour, basting occasionally. Then, increase the heat to 240°C/220°C fan/Gas 9 and brown the chicken for 15 minutes. You want the chicken to be cooked through and moist, but the skin nicely browned.

Once the chicken is cooked, remove it from the roasting tin and set it aside on a warm plate to rest for 10 minutes. Meanwhile, pour the liquid from the tin into a small saucepan and place the pan over a high heat. Bring the liquid to the boil and cook it for 5–10 minutes to reduce it a little.

Mix the ingredients for the relish according to the method on page 24. When you serve, carve the chicken up and put it on a large, warm serving dish. Spoon the cooking juices over the chicken and let everyone help themselves to relish.

Upside-down aubergine and cous cous cake

There is something extremely satisfying about successfully upturning a pan to reveal a glistening tarte tatin, an upside-down skillet cake, or a Persian rice with a perfect *tahdig*. If you nail that flip there's an almost cartoon-like flourish to the whole thing – though five times out of ten you're going to mess it up and the bottom is going to stick to the pan. When it does come out perfectly, I allow myself a moment to feel a bit smug and take in everyone's oohs and aahs.

This upside-down cous cous cake looks far more complicated than it is and makes such a beautiful centrepiece. I serve it with a bowl of yoghurt, seasoned with salt and maybe a pinch of sumac or smoked paprika, sometimes with a little grated garlic stirred through it. The marinated feta on page 24 works really well too. And some sort of chopped salad or fattoush brings crunch – try chopped cucumber, sliced red onion, plenty of mint and a handful of dried sour cherries, all tossed in a dressing of lemon juice, dried oregano, a little honey and olive oil. The sweet and sour in the salad works brilliantly with the gentle, warming cous cous. Any leftover cake keeps brilliantly in the fridge to eat cold the next day, or to refry.

Serves 8

2 large aubergines, sliced about 1cm thick
olive oil
1 onion, finely sliced
2 garlic cloves, finely sliced
2 teaspoons fennel seeds
2 teaspoons cumin seeds
1 cinnamon stick
1 tablespoon tomato purée
1 x 400g tin of chopped tomatoes
2 teaspoons harissa, plus extra to serve
350g cous cous
500ml hot vegetable stock
a handful of pine nuts
a handful of coriander, leaves and stems roughly chopped
salt and freshly cracked black pepper
lemon wedges, to serve

Preheat the oven to 220°C/200°C fan/Gas 7.

Put the aubergines in a bowl and drizzle them with plenty of oil, turning them to coat them well. Spread them out on a baking tray and sprinkle with salt. Bake for about 40 minutes, until browned and soft.

Meanwhile, start the cous cous. Set a large, relatively deep frying pan over a low–medium heat and add a good lug of oil. Add the onion and a big seasoning of salt and cook until soft (at least 10 minutes), then add the garlic and cook for 2 minutes. Add the fennel and cumin seeds and the cinnamon stick and cook for another 1–2 minutes, until fragrant. Stir through the tomato purée, then add the chopped tomatoes and harissa. Let it all simmer for 15 minutes without a lid so that it has a chance to reduce a little. Taste and add a little more salt if you think it needs it.

Pour the cous cous into a bowl and cover it with the hot stock. Season with salt and black pepper. Cover the bowl with a plate and leave for 15 minutes, or until it has absorbed the stock. Fluff it up with a fork.

Transfer the cous cous to the tomato pan and (off the heat) mix everything together well. Transfer the mixture to a bowl and leave it to sit while the aubergines are cooking.

Toast the pine nuts in a small saucepan and set aside.

When you're nearly ready to serve, add a little more oil to the pan and lay the aubergines tightly in the base and up the sides. Tumble the cous cous on top and flatten it with the back of a spoon. Put a lid on and leave the cake to cook over a low flame for about 15 minutes, then to sit off the heat for 5 minutes. Take the lid off, place a plate on top of the pan and carefully turn out your cake with its aubergine lid. Sprinkle the cake with the pine nuts and coriander, and serve it straight away with lemon wedges, extra harissa and a bowl of seasoned yoghurt.

'Come over, I'll cook'

Treacle short ribs with sweet potatoes and soured cream

This is such a nice way to cook short ribs. Bittersweet black treacle, coffee and soy sauce make a fantastic dark, sticky coating. There's gochujang, garlic, cinnamon and anise for sweet spice and heat. And a mound of lightly soused red onion cuts through the richness. I'm not a huge sweet potato girl as a rule – I can't really get behind sweet potato fries (possibly controversial; I just sort of think life is too short not to have a proper chip), but when served with something gutsy like these ribs and a nice thwack of freshness from the soured cream, onions and coriander, a salt-crusted sweet potato is exactly what you want.

A quick note: you can make these for more people or fewer, but if you're reducing the amounts, I wouldn't make much less marinade as you want the ribs to cook in plenty of liquid. You can always reduce the sauce once the meat is cooked. The ribs would be great with the slaw on the following page.

Serves 4

200ml cold strong coffee
200ml red wine
2 tablespoons black treacle
2 tablespoons soy sauce
1 teaspoon gochujang (or 1 teaspoon miso paste and a few dashes of chilli sauce)
6 star anise
4 garlic cloves, peeled and bashed
1 cinnamon stick
4 fat beef short ribs
2 red onions (1 cut into wedges, 1 finely sliced)
4 sweet potatoes
2 tablespoons rice vinegar
4 tablespoons soured cream
a big handful of coriander
flaky salt
2 limes, cut into wedges, to serve

Mix the coffee, wine, treacle, soy sauce, gochujang (or alternative), star anise, garlic and cinnamon together in a jug to make a marinade. Pour the marinade over the short ribs and leave it in the fridge for at least 4 hours, or overnight if you can.

Preheat the oven to 170°C/150°C fan/Gas 3.

Put the short ribs and the onion wedges in a small roasting tin and pour over a third of the marinating liquid. Reserve the rest for the sauce later. Cover with foil and cook the ribs for 2½ hours, occasionally basting, and adding a little more marinating liquid if needs be.

Meanwhile, rinse the sweet potatoes under cold water and sprinkle them with salt, then once the ribs have been cooking for about 1 hour 50 minutes, put the sweet potatoes in the oven too. They'll need 1 hour to cook at that temperature.

While the ribs and potatoes are cooking, make the pickles. Put the onion slices in a plastic container with the vinegar. Put the lid on, give it a shake and leave the onions to sit while everything is cooking.

Once the ribs have had their time in the oven, remove the foil, baste them and cook for another 30 minutes. After that, the meat should be soft and falling away from the bone. Remove from the oven and set aside to rest for 20 minutes.

Meanwhile, pour the juices from the roasting tin into a small saucepan along with the remaining marinating liquid, skimming off some of the excess fat as you go. Bring to a simmer over a medium heat and reduce until you have a sticky, glossy sauce.

Serve a short rib each, with plenty of sauce spooned over the top, a handful of pickles, and a baked sweet potato split down the middle and filled with a dollop of soured cream and a handful of coriander sprigs. Finish with a couple of wedges of lime.

Gochujang coriander slaw

Serve this fresh, nutty, slightly spicy slaw with the short ribs on the previous page or with slow-roasted pork; pile it into fried chicken burgers; or place a big bowl of it in among a heaving table of barbecued food.

Serves about 8

½ small white cabbage
½ small red cabbage
1 large red onion, finely sliced
6–7cm piece of root ginger, peeled and coarsely grated
2 teaspoons flaky salt
1 tablespoon soured cream
1 tablespoon full-fat mayonnaise
1 heaped teaspoon gochujang
3 limes, juiced
1 tablespoon soy sauce
2 tablespoons sesame oil
a big handful of coriander, leaves and stems finely chopped

Shred both cabbages, either just using a sharp knife or the coarse grater blade on a food processor. Put it in a bowl with the onion and ginger. Add half the salt and mix everything together with your hands. Cover and leave to sit for 1 hour. Give it the occasional turn over with your hands or a pair of tongs. After an hour, drain off the liquid, squeezing the cabbage a bit to get rid of any excess moisture.

Mix the rest of the ingredients, including the rest of the salt, well in a large bowl. Add the cabbage and onion to the bowl of dressing and mix well with your hands or tongs. Cover and put the slaw in the fridge for an hour – or more – before serving. It'll only benefit from more time sitting in the dressing. You could even make it the day before.

Rooftop pizza

I would have outdoor pizza parties all year round if my friends let me. I once made them stand under umbrellas in the November drizzle as I stoked my little tabletop pizza oven, trying to get it hot enough to cook with in the face of some pretty strong winds. They humoured me for a while – they know there's always going to be a certain amount of faffery on pizza night – but when I looked up and realised I was outside on my own in socks and sandals in the cold while everyone desperately foraged for more crisps inside, I had to admit defeat and bake the pizzas in the oven. Did it matter? Of course not. As soon as everyone is standing around a board, grabbing the first slices and burning their mouths on molten cheese, how it got there ceases to be important.

Everyone loves a pizza party. It's always a little chaotic and messy, there's always going to be flour everywhere, there'll always be a moment when you think the dough isn't proving properly or you realise you've forgotten the mozzarella and have to send someone to the shop. But it'll be one of the best meals you've cooked all year. There is such a sense of satisfaction to be found in making your own dough and producing rounds of haphazard, incredibly delicious pizzas. I'm lucky enough to have an Ooni that I keep on my roof, but quite often I'll just use a baking sheet and a hot oven. My only real rules of thumb are to start early – it always takes longer than you think it will to cook all the pizzas – so stick to two or three toppings variations, and to have someone else sort out drinks and ice. You will have to field pleas for rogue add-ons – stand your ground, this is your pizza party, and if you don't want anchovies or mushrooms or pineapple anywhere near your pies, don't let anyone persuade you otherwise. Equally, if an anchovy pineapple pizza sounds like manna from heaven to you, go crazy. Whatever floats your boat.

I like making mainly tomato-based pizzas, but always make at least one white one to add to the mix, usually with some thin slices of potato, a little caramelised red onion and some blue cheese. Some sort of aubergine number is non-negotiable for me, preferably with goat's cheese (in the iteration overleaf I've also added chillies, honey and fresh basil), and I'll always make at least one with some sort of spicy sausage, sometimes tearing burrata over the finished pizza when it comes out of the oven.

It helps to use a pizza stone or a big tile to cook it on if you can, as it'll help get some really direct heat on the crust. But really you can use a baking tray, a cast-iron frying pan, whatever works for you. You'll have your own ideas about perfect pizza toppings. My Uncle Jon (an Italian New Yorker who makes some of the best pizza I've ever tasted) swears by using a mixture of dry and fresh mozzarella, reasoning that the dry cheese melts well and the fresh stuff brings the flavour.

Over the page is a recipe for a good basic dough, a simple tomato sauce and three topping suggestions.

Makes 6 large pizzas

For the dough
14g dry yeast
1 tablespoon caster sugar
4 tablespoons olive oil
600ml lukewarm water
750g tipo 00 flour
250g strong white bread
   flour, plus extra for
   dusting
1 teaspoon salt
a handful of fine semolina
   flour, for dusting

*A basic tomato base (for
   6 pizzas – probably
   more, depending on how
   saucy you like them)*
700g passata
3 garlic cloves, peeled
1 red onion, cut into
   wedges
1 bay leaf
1 tablespoon olive oil
½ teaspoon salt, plus extra
   for seasoning the
   toppings

*Topping 1: aubergine,
   goat's cheese, chilli and
   honey (for 2 pizzas)*
1 large aubergine, thickly
   sliced
good olive oil
80g dry mozzarella,
   roughly chopped
40g fresh mozzarella,
   roughly torn
150g goat's cheese
   (the chalky log kind),
   sliced
1 small red chilli, finely
   sliced (with or without
   seeds, according your
   preference for heat)
2 teaspoons runny honey
a few basil leaves

Continued on page 185

For the dough, mix the yeast, sugar and olive oil with the lukewarm water. Leave the mixture for 5 minutes for the yeast to activate.

Put the flours and salt in a large mixing bowl and make a well in the middle. Pour the liquid into the well. Use a fork to bring the flour in from the sides and gradually mix it together with the liquid. Keep going until it all comes together. Dust your hands with flour and use them to bring in the remaining flour from the edges of the bowl. Tip out the dough on to a floured surface and knead it until you have a smooth, springy ball.

Place the dough in a large bowl dusted with more flour. Cover it with a damp cloth and put it in a warm spot. Leave it for 1 hour, or until the dough has doubled in size. If you're not going to use the dough immediately, at this point put it in the fridge – it will slow the rising.

Meanwhile, get on with your sauce and toppings. If you're using tomato sauce, pour the passata into a saucepan and add the garlic, onion, bay leaf, olive oil and salt. Put the pan over a low–medium heat and bring the mixture to a simmer. Part-cover the pan with a lid and leave the sauce to bubble gently for 30 minutes. Then, remove it from the heat and leave it to cool. You'll discard the onion, garlic and bay leaf when it comes to spooning the tomato sauce on to the pizza bases.

If you're going to use your oven to bake the pizzas, preheat it to 250°C/230°C fan/Gas 9. If you have a pizza stone, put it in the oven or barbecue to preheat. Prepare your toppings so they're all ready to go.

For the aubergine... Roast the aubergine slices with plenty of oil and season with salt at 250°C/230°C fan/Gas 9 for 15–20 minutes, or until soft and well browned. Leave them to cool.

For the potato... Set a small frying pan over a medium heat with a good glug of olive oil. Add the onion with a little salt. Fry the onion for 10 minutes, or until well softened, then add the garlic and cook for another 2 minutes. Finally, add the splash of balsamic, stir and cook for another 1 minute or so. Leave to cool.

Now prepare the bases...

'Come over, I'll cook'

*Topping 2: 'Nduja, red
   pepper and burrata
   (for 2 pizzas)*
80g dry mozzarella,
   roughly chopped
40g fresh mozzarella,
   roughly torn
60g 'nduja, broken into
   small pieces
1 jarred chargrilled red
   pepper, thinly sliced
good olive oil, for
   drizzling
a few oregano leaves
1 large burrata

*Topping 3: Potato,
   balsamic onion,
   rosemary and
   gorgonzola
   (for 2 pizzas)*
olive oil, for frying
1 red onion, finely sliced
1 garlic clove, finely
   sliced
a splash of thick balsamic
   vinegar
100g mascarpone
½ lemon, zest and juice
a few steamed new
   potatoes, thinly sliced
90g gorgonzola,
   crumbled
a little parmesan, grated
a little rosemary, leaves
   picked and finely
   chopped
good olive oil, for
   drizzling

When you return to the dough, tip it out on to a
floured surface and knead it for a couple of minutes
to knock the air out of it. Use a knife to divide the
dough into six equal pieces and use floured hands
to form each piece into a ball.

Stretch, top and bake the pizzas one by one. Each
time: flatten a ball of dough with your hands, then
pick up the edge and let it hang out of your hand,
allowing gravity to stretch it. Keep turning the dough
in your hands, as if you're turning a steering wheel.
Keep going until the dough has stretched to roughly
the size and shape you want it, depending on what
you're cooking it on and in. Carefully pick up your
dough and either lay it on a flat, rimless baking tray
sprinkled with semolina, or on a pizza peel to be
transferred to the oven (or barbecue – but see the
tips at the end for how to cook on a barbie).

For the aubergine pizza ... Spoon 1–2 spoonfuls
   of tomato sauce on to the stretched pizza base
   and spread it out with the back of a spoon.
   (Don't overdo it on the sauce or it'll make
   it harder for the base to crisp up.) Top with
   aubergine slices, both mozzarellas and goat's
   cheese. Scatter over the chilli and put the pizza
   in to cook for 8–10 minutes, until the base is
   puffed up and the cheese is golden and bubbling.
   Remove the pizza from the oven, drizzle
   over the honey and scatter over the basil to
   serve. Repeat for another ball of dough.

For the 'nduja pizza ... Spoon 1–2 spoonfuls of
   tomato sauce on to the pizza base and spread it
   out with the back of a spoon. Scatter over half
   each of both mozzarellas and the 'nduja, and lay
   over a few slices of pepper. Drizzle over a little
   olive oil and scatter on a few oregano leaves. Put
   the pizza in to cook for 8–10 minutes, until the
   base is puffed up and the cheese is golden and
   bubbling. Remove the pizza from the oven, tear
   the burrata over the top and drizzle over a little
   more oil to serve. Repeat for another ball
   of dough.

For the potato pizza ... This is a white pizza – no
   tomato sauce. Mix the mascarpone with the
   lemon zest and juice. Spread half the mixture
   over the stretched pizza base and top with half
   the balsamic onions, potato slices, gorgonzola,
   parmesan and rosemary and a drizzle of olive oil.

Put the pizza in to cook for 8–10 minutes, until the base is puffed up and the cheese is golden and bubbling. Remove the pizza from the oven and serve. Repeat for the final ball of dough.

A few cooking tips... If you like, you can get the pizzas started in a large cast-iron frying pan over a high heat, cook for about 4 minutes on the hob, and finish them off in the oven – this will get you a very puffy frying-pan pizza rather than a thinner crispy number.

If you're using a barbecue, just make sure it's superhot before you start cooking the pizzas, and watch them – it's all too easy to burn the base. They're likely to take a bit less time on a hot barbecue than in the oven, maybe 3–4 minutes.

And if you have a little tabletop pizza oven or something similar, you sort of have to get to know your oven and find out what works through trial and error. If you're doing lots of pizzas, just remember to maintain the temperature, as you'll lose some heat every time you open and close the door.

The midnight
frying pan

I've fallen in love or imagine that I have;
went to a party and lost my head. Bought
a horse which I don't need at all.

from Leo Tolstoy's diary
(January 25, 1851)

A tuna melt hill I will die on, and other stories

I think some of the best food I've ever eaten was from a chip van on a high street in Devon. At kicking-out time at the end of a rainy Friday night out at university – all of about 2am, so booming was Exeter's nightlife 'scene' – Mr Chips on Sidwell Street was like a beacon of warmth and promise. There were burgers and kebabs and chicken nuggets, and a dozen bottles of highly suspect sauces. All I ever wanted was cheesy chips, doused in vinegar, with an unholy amount of ketchup (in a pool on the side, not splodged all over the place, I'm not an animal). We'd eat them while they were still hotter than the sun, the

apple sourz we'd finished off moments before masking the fact that we were burning the roofs of our mouths. Full and shivering, we'd stagger home in our black plimsolls and body-con skirts. It was 2009, I'll take no further comments on the sartorial choices.

Occasionally, we'd save our pennies and make a huge vat of pesto pasta at home (recipe: boil penne, drain, mix with entire jar of Sacla, cover in cheddar). We'd bring the pan to someone's bed and wash it down with mugs of tea in front of *Brothers and Sisters* or *Grey's Anatomy*. It was pre-Deliveroo, and in deepest darkest Devon, your options didn't extend much beyond Domino's – which practically cost a week's rent – when it came to late-night food. Chip vans, pesto pasta and Marmite toast were our mainstays.

More than a decade on, I'm not sure my after-midnight palate has evolved much. I stand by pasta as an effective foil for a post-pub appetite, though these days I might reach for the ingredients for carbonara over a jar of pesto. The Marmite toast might get a supplementary seven-minute boiled egg smushed on top, and an elaborate fried sandwich is now often a go-to. I also don't have to be three sheets to justify a late dinner. I often find myself doing a frantic fridge forage to fill a hole after a particularly long day at work. And you know what? Sometimes you just need a second dinner.

When it comes to what to make, I find I am led by cravings. No one wants a balanced meal post-9pm. If you are the sort of person who reaches for the bag of carrots to satisfy your late-night appetite, I salute and admire you. I tend to want something quick, hot and salty. I think the key with this sort of cooking is to channel the deep satisfaction that the hot, cheesy chips from a van in a student town once gave you, back when you still possessed the ability to bounce back from a hangover without looking like Bette Midler in *Hocus Pocus*.

The main thing is to make exactly what you fancy, and at all costs, avoid going to bed on an empty stomach.

Lifesaving carbonara

I feel I owe a debt of gratitude to whomever it was in early 20th-century Lazio that invented carbonara. It has saved me more times than I can count. I almost always have the ingredients in stock (pancetta seems to keep for ages in the fridge, and there are always eggs, garlic and parmesan), but most importantly, it never fails to hit the spot. It is so often the best and most obvious answer to the question 'What shall I make for dinner?' that I have to ration the number of times I'm allowed to make it for fear I'll overdo it and it'll lose some of its spooky magic. I'm like that with songs too. If I fall in love with one, I'll listen to it on repeat, feeling my way through every inch of it and singing it constantly, until eventually I realise I've gone too far and might never be able to listen to it again. Carbonara, then, like Joni Mitchell's 'A Case of You', has to be kept in a box marked 'Break Open in Case of Emergency'. It's to be reached for only when I really need it, when nothing but a bowl of porky, eggy spaghetti will do.

Everyone seems to have strong opinions on the best way to make carbonara. We're all loyal to a particular method and could debate every aspect, from the introduction of cream (I'm afraid I'm in the camp that considers this unacceptable; I can only apologise), to the merits of sourcing proper guanciale rather than plumping for pancetta or bacon. This is merely my interpretation. I like the pasta to be properly bitey, I like a lot of barely cooked egg yolk, and I like for there to be enough black pepper that it makes you sneeze.

Serves 2

1 tablespoon olive oil
180g cubed pancetta or
    very thin slices of
    guanciale
2 garlic cloves, finely
    sliced
3 eggs plus an extra yolk,
    beaten together
70g parmesan or pecorino,
    finely grated, plus extra
    to serve
200g dried spaghetti
freshly cracked black
    pepper

Set a large frying pan over a medium heat with the oil. When it's hot, fry the pancetta or guanciale until every piece is golden. Turn the heat off and add the garlic – it'll cook just the right amount in the residual heat of the pan while you do everything else.

Beat the eggs with the parmesan and plenty of black pepper.

Cook the spaghetti in plenty of well-salted boiling water until al dente. Reserve a couple of spoonfuls of cooking water when you drain it, then add the pasta to the pancetta pan. Use tongs to turn the spaghetti over in the oil. Add the reserved cooking water and mix that through too.

Mix in the egg mixture, stirring continuously for a minute or two off the heat. You want the egg to stay silky and liquid and cling to the strands of spaghetti, not to curdle. When the sauce has emulsified, you should serve up immediately, and top with more black pepper and parmesan.

The midnight frying pan

Smoked cheddar cacio e pepe

Often, a late-night meal is a solitary event. A quick plateful meant to fill a hole before you fall into bed. The toast devoured hungrily at the kitchen counter, the regrettable Deliveroo order, the leftovers eaten in the light of an open fridge door. But sometimes it's only as you're boiling water for pasta, happily chopping, grating and chatting at midnight that the evening really starts.

I love that feeling that the night is yours, that it could still go wherever you want it to. Just one more song, one more glass of something, and let's make some food – did we even have dinner? I often think of something the comedian Micky Flanagan said when talking about the album he and his wife always used to put on when they were first together and got in from a party: 'We had a lot of late nights together and we could sort of feel time running out. This album always reminds me of getting in at four or five in the morning, chinking the last glass of wine.' If there was ever a dish made to satisfy a craving and see you through that last glass of wine, it's this.

A good cacio e pepe is, I think we can all agree, God-tier pasta. This version, using smoked cheddar rather than parmesan, tastes a bit like a cross between a cacio e pepe and the absurdly delicious Marmite spaghetti that I've always known as a Nigella recipe but I believe was originally an Anna del Conte invention. It doesn't actually contain any Marmite, but something about the smoked mature cheddar gives it that same satisfying savouriness. It's three ingredients and comes together in minutes, perfect for two generous bowlfuls.

Serves 2

200g dried spaghetti
90g smoked cheddar,
    finely grated, plus extra
    to serve (or you could
    serve it with grated
    parmesan)
1½ teaspoons freshly
    cracked black pepper,
    plus extra for serving

Set a large pan of salted water on to boil. Cook the spaghetti until al dente. When the pasta is cooked, reserve 75ml of the starchy cooking water before you drain it.

Meanwhile, combine the cheese and the black pepper in a large bowl. Then, when the pasta is ready, add the hot cooking water to the bowl and beat it vigorously so the cheese melts. Add the pasta to the bowl and use tongs to toss it in the sauce. Return everything to the pan over a low heat and cook for about 2 minutes, stirring continuously, until the cheese sauce sticks to every strand of spaghetti.

Serve in warm bowls with extra cheese and black pepper.

Fridge-forage fried rice

The undisputed queen of the fridge-forage meals has to be fried rice. I love it so much I always make extra rice just so that I can have fried rice the next day. I do the same with potatoes. Truly – having cooked carb in your fridge to be refried has to be one of the most useful byproducts of being a cook who makes too much food. Fried rice is also one of the best meals to satisfy that kind of hunger that is only going to be sated by something salty and a little spicy and properly filling. I like making a quick warm sauce to go with this, bringing a dish of just simmered garlicky soy and shaoxing to the table to be poured over my bowl of piping hot rice.

Serves 1

For the rice
1 tablespoon neutral cooking oil
4 spring onions, roughly chopped
5–6cm piece of root ginger, peeled and finely chopped
1 large garlic clove, finely sliced
a little finely chopped chilli
2 eggs, beaten
1 teaspoon soy sauce
225g cold cooked rice
a large handful of cold cooked green veg (broccoli and any kind of cabbage or kale work well), chopped small
a small handful of roughly chopped cold leftover meat, like roast pork, duck or bacon (optional)
salt
a few coriander sprigs and a pinch of black sesame seeds, to serve

For the sauce
1 tablespoon sesame oil
1 tablespoon soy sauce
1 tablespoon shaoxing wine
1 garlic clove, finely chopped

Set a large frying pan or (even better) a wok over a high heat with the oil. Fry the spring onions and the ginger with a pinch of salt for 4 minutes, then add the garlic and chilli and cook for another 2 minutes to soften.

Mix the eggs with the soy sauce. Turn the heat down low and pour the eggs into the pan. Swirl the pan as it cooks, gently moving the egg with a spatula. Cook until the eggs firm up a bit but not quite to a stiff omelette consistency. Then remove the eggs from the pan and set aside.

Add a little more oil, then tumble in the rice. Pat it down to a roughly even layer and leave it for 3–4 minutes so the grains have a chance to crisp up on the bottom. Turn the rice over with a spatula. Keep cooking and occasionally turning until the rice is piping hot and some of the grains have crisped up.

Add the vegetables as well the meat if you're including any. Cook, turning everything over regularly, until it's all superhot. It's best not to put a lid on it – you want everything to fry not steam.

Meanwhile, mix all the ingredients for the sauce together and pour them into a small saucepan. Bring the sauce just to a simmer, then pour it straight into a little bowl.

Roughly break up the egg and spring onion mixture and stir this through the pan of rice.

To serve, pile everything into a warm bowl, top with coriander leaves and sesame seeds and bring your little side dish of sauce with you to the table to spoon over every mouthful as you like.

Green rice and crispy bacon

Every year, I attempt to grow herbs in the ramshackle pots on my roof terrace, and every year they are luscious and perky for about six weeks before tragically wilting and disintegrating. I'm not sure why I can't seem to keep them alive, but as they either have to put up with severe neglect or overwatering, it's hardly surprising. It's problematic because herbs are among my most used ingredients in the kitchen, and I love the idea of being able to snip some of my own rather than rely on the piddly packets from the supermarket that seem to be on the turn about three minutes after you've opened them. I'm lucky that my local grocer usually has big bunches of parsley, dill and mint and try to buy from them as much as possible. But inevitably, at the bottom of the veg drawer, there is often a little stash of tired greenery. Sometimes I'll freshen them up in ice-cold water, then blitz them with oil, garlic and salt and pop them in a jar in the fridge. Often, the tired herb haul (along with a bag of spinach and plenty of spring onions) finds its way into this barnstormer of a rice dish.

I love making a pan of buttery rice when it's late. I fry off the grains first with garlic, before simmering them with stock and plenty of salt. A great mound of greens and soft herbs (whatever you have knocking about, all roughly chopped) goes in right at the end, as does butter, lemon and a few dashes of hot sauce. It makes a great accompaniment to lots of things (it would be particularly good with a spiced roast chicken), but if I'm having it for a late dinner, I'll eat it as it is, often crumbling a couple of rashers of very crispy bacon on top. A dollop of thick soured cream makes this the best kind of moreish comfort food. A hug of a dinner at the end of a long week.

Serves 4

1 tablespoon butter,
  plus an extra knob
1 garlic clove, peeled
  and bashed
300g basmati rice
600ml hot chicken
  or vegetable stock
12 rashers of smoked
  streaky bacon
6 spring onions,
  finely sliced
2 lemons, juiced
a few dashes of hot sauce,
  plus extra for adding to
  each bowl
250g spinach (or another
  soft green), chopped
a big handful of flat-leaf
  parsley, leaves and stems
  roughly chopped

Set a large, deep, frying pan with a lid or a casserole pan over a medium heat and add the butter and garlic. Once the butter has melted, add the rice, stir and fry for 1 minute as you would for a risotto.

Pour in the stock and season with a good amount of salt. Bring the stock to a simmer and cook the rice uncovered for 15 minutes or until most of the liquid has evaporated and the rice is almost cooked. Turn the heat off, add the extra knob of butter, lay a tea towel over the top of the pan and put the lid on top of the towel. Leave the rice like this for 6 minutes for it to become perfectly tender.

Meanwhile, fry the bacon in a dry frying pan until very crispy, then remove it from the pan and set it aside. Turn the heat off under the pan and add the spring onions. Toss them in the hot bacon fat so they start to cook a little. You want them to retain their colour and a little bite rather than softening.

Take the lid and tea towel off the rice pan and run a fork through the rice to separate the grains. Turn

a big handful of coriander, leaves and stems roughly chopped

a big handful of dill, leaves and tender stems roughly chopped

4 tablespoons soured cream

salt

the heat back on low and stir through the lemon juice, hot sauce and spring onions. Then add all the greens. Stir them all through and cook for a couple of minutes just so everything is steaming hot.

Serve the rice straight away while the greens are still vibrant and the rice is piping hot. Chop or crumble the crispy bacon and sprinkle it on top of each bowlful. Give everyone a good dollop of soured cream and a little extra hot sauce to add as they like.

7-minute eggs on fried bread with Marmite, cream cheese and pickled shallots

A midnight meal often goes a little like this. First, I'll pull whatever loaf is on the go from the corner of the kitchen counter (oddly, I keep bread on an old wooden cake stand, squeezed between the side of the fridge and the toaster, covered with my friend Maddy's late granny's wire cloche ... not particularly out of a dedication to kitsch home furnishings, I just really need to buy a bread bin). I'll tear off a hunk of 'holding bread' to eat with butter while I ponder what I actually want to eat. Then to the fridge where I take out a usually fairly random array of ingredients – cheese, leftover tuna and bean salad, pasta or roasted veg, a punnet of olives, one of the many pickle jars, a foil parcel containing Wednesday night's potatoes. Sometimes I'll take a pan out of the cupboard too and make a meal, but more often than not I'll stand over my fridge hoard, topping squares of toast with whatever I've managed to scavenge. It never ceases to amaze me how the idiosyncratic mouthful I might cobble together late one night is likely to be one of the best meals I'll eat all week. I think maybe it's something to do with very quickly and greedily satisfying a hunger.

I realised far too late in life that cream cheese and Marmite are a match made in heaven. If it has also taken you this long to realise, then consider this recipe an important turning point in your toast game. The thing is, cold cream cheese on hot toast is already brilliant, but it does need something to pep up the flavour. Getting a slick of Marmite on the end of a butter knife and swirling it over the cream cheese is, I'm here to either inform or remind you, the answer.

When it comes to boiled eggs, I love them when they're at the point where the yolks have just begun to turn from being entirely runny to slightly set and gooey, all the better for smushing on to toast. In my mind, the perfect boiled egg should still have a bit of ooze to it, but not so much that it's going to immediately escape whatever you're piling it on to.

And while we're on bread ... listen, nobody actually needs fried bread, but isn't it just one of the best things? There's nothing better than ordering a cooked breakfast and finding it comes with a slice of fried bread. You could absolutely plump for toast here (a muffin or even a couple of crumpets would also be good, I feel). But you could also go the whole hog and treat yourself to a perfect slice of golden, crunchy fried bread.

Serves 1

½ shallot, very finely
  sliced
a pinch of flaky salt, plus
  extra to serve
2 tablespoons red wine
  vinegar
2 large eggs
olive oil, for frying
1–2 slices of white bread,
  relatively thinly sliced
1 garlic clove, peeled
1 tablespoon full-fat
  cream cheese
a slick of Marmite
a few chives, snipped
  (optional)
freshly cracked black
  pepper

First, do the shallots. Put them in a bowl with the flaky salt and scrunch them with your fingers. Heat the vinegar in a small saucepan and when it comes to a simmer, pour it over the shallots. Leave them to sit while you do everything else.

Put a pan of water on for the eggs. Lower them carefully into water, which is at a rolling boil, and cook for 7 minutes, or as long as you prefer, until hard boiled to your liking. Plunge the cooked eggs into a bowl of cold water for a minute to stop them cooking, then peel them.

To fry the bread, heat plenty of olive oil (about 1cm deep) in a small frying pan over a low–medium heat. Rub the bread with the garlic clove. When the oil is hot, fry the bread for about 2 minutes on each side, or until golden. Transfer the fried slices to a plate and spread them thickly with cream cheese. Then, swipe a slick of Marmite through the cream cheese.

Cut the peeled eggs in half and smash them on top of the fried bread. Top with a little flaky salt and black pepper, a few pickled shallots, and a sprinkling of chives if you're using them. Eat messily.

Pillowy omelette with soft goat's cheese and all the herbs

An omelette is such a good late-night failsafe. One pan, a couple of beaten eggs, a few bits and bobs from the fridge – guaranteed satisfaction. This is a little more involved than a regular omelette (or, you could just cook the eggs as you usually would and use this filling) but it's extremely satisfying to make as the whipped egg white means you get this kind of pillowy, lighter-than-air, omelette cloud. It's lovely on its own but it's also nice with a little salad, perhaps using parsley as you would leaves and tossing it with some finely chopped shallot and a few capers.

Serves 1

3 egg whites
2 egg yolks
a pinch of salt
a pinch of white pepper
2 teaspoons butter
a handful of herbs (I like some combination of tarragon, chives, dill or mint), leaves and tender stems finely chopped
60g soft goat's cheese (the kind without a rind)
a lemon wedge, to serve

Using an electric whisk, whisk the egg whites in a large, clean, dry bowl. Keep going until you're almost at the stiff-peaks stage but not quite – so a little looser than the whites would be for a meringue.

In a separate bowl, whisk the egg yolks with the salt and white pepper until they turn pale and a little frothy and mousse-like.

Using a big metal spoon, fold the egg yolks into the whites. Keep gently folding until everything is well combined.

Set a small frying pan over a low heat and add the butter.

While it's melting, gently fold a third of the herbs through the egg mixture.

Add the egg to the pan and cook it for 3 minutes. It'll puff up a little. Pinch the goat's cheese into nuggets and scatter the nuggets over the egg, followed by the rest of the herbs. Use a spatula to flip one half of the omelette on to the other. Don't worry – it isn't as fragile as it looks, you can do this with a bit of confidence.

By now it should be nice and golden on the bottom. Put a lid on the pan and leave the omelette for 2 minutes. Then carefully flip it over, cover and cook it for another 1 minute. You might need to flip it over a couple more times before it's ready, as some egg will inevitably escape whenever you turn it. When it's ready, turn the omelette out of the pan on to your plate. Serve with the lemon wedge for squeezing over.

Fried sandwiches almost (almost) make up for truly terrible dates

It is a Friday night in August, a week before my 30th birthday.

I'm walking from the tube to a brewery in south London to meet a man called Harry who I matched with on a dating app two days ago. We'd chatted for a bit. He'd suggested a drink. He's tall, into food, has a good beard. If Hinge worked in the same way as the Netflix home page, he'd be firmly in the 'Familiar Favourites' category. Possibly 'Added in the Past Year'. Definitely not critically acclaimed.

Do I think he might be the love of my life? No. Do I want to get in a snog before my birthday after a run of useless dates? Yes, yes I do. I am a woman on a mission [read: in the midst of a major milestone birthday meltdown, gritting my teeth and refusing to acknowledge it].

You know when you go to an exercise class and immediately realise you're going to have to leave? By minute seven you're wondering what fresh hell you've stumbled into. From then on, you're mentally taking a run up at getting up and walking out.

Well, safe to say, it's one of those.

For a start, he is drunk. Not frothing-at-the-mouth drunk, but red-faced and shouty. I order a beer and ask how his day had been: 'Good! I've been drinking!' Strap in, lads, we've got a live one.

I ask where he's from. 'Good question!' he yelps with a mischievous glint in his eye. 'I'll tell you in a minute. But first, I need to tell you about some other things.' Oh good. I sense a pre-prepared spiel.

What proceeds is the first of many lengthy explanations of his 'personal philosophies'. First up, it's dating: 'I like to meet interesting women and if you come away with recommendations and I come away with recommendations, then it's been a successful evening.'

'Right, so you're going to give me some recommendations?'

'Yes, two. One YouTube channel, one podcast. Not now, later.'

Fantastic.

He explains he doesn't like to tell women much about himself before a date (including, it transpires, his real name, which is not Harry). Instead, he prefers to have girls ask him questions and 'uncover the truth'. 'It's more fun like that.'

I can think of more fun ways to spend a Friday evening than embarking on a round of 20 questions with a man who is so drunk he is struggling to stay on his bar stool.

Next up, it's the economy. Prompted, by the way, by my second question, which he still hasn't answered: 'What do you do?'

He starts ranting about decentralised money, crypto currency and blockchain, becoming more upset by the minute. He is literally winding himself up in his quest to tell me why I need to totally rethink my investments (no need, pal, don't have any).

'Do you want me to explain to you what's happening with the banks?'

Reader, I do not.

'Sure.'

(*For God's sake why haven't you left yet.*)

He's really agitated now. People are staring and he keeps apologising and then diving straight back in. It's like he's recently joined a cult and been allowed out of the commune for the night on the understanding he brings back a new recruit.

I begin to count myself in: *'Right, in five minutes you're going to get up and walk out.'*

Fifteen minutes go by.

'OK. In three minutes you're sinking this pint, shaking his hand (formal) and going to get the bus.'

Nope, still haven't left.

I give myself a pep talk in the loo. *'Okay, so you're not sitting back down at the table. It's coat on, smile, the old one hand in the air that says: "Nice to meet you mate, I've actually got to run because, well, you're really quite intense, this has stopped being A Good Story and frankly I've got too much to do in the morning to let this become a classic no-dinner, one-pint-too-many, Friday-night disaster, but anyway, best of luck, cheers, bye."'*

Back at the table, he's ordered us another round. Time to leave.

I say I need to get going. 'Oh but I haven't given you my recommendations!'

'Go on then.'

'Right, so have you heard of Joe Rogan ... ?'

The thing is, I've been on some really bad first dates. Among the conglomerate of arseholes and numpties that is my Hinge back catalogue, there are some real humdingers. There was the man who had a breakdown after the first drink. There was the guy who booked an outdoor table at a restaurant, immediately had a tantrum when it rained, then became emasculated and completely silent when I suggested we moved to a pub I knew round the corner. There was the man who, ten minutes into a walk around Brockwell Park, started telling me all about the ex he'd been with for a decade and broken up with two weeks before. 'Yeah so she was basically like "shall we have a baby or shall we break up?" And yeah turns out she wanted a kid so we broke up but yeah it's really easy we're just really good mates now and talk every day, it's fine.'

There was no-chat Jack; Sustainability Fred, who went on and on about his homemade linen shirts; and an awful lot of men with 'ambitions to start a podcast'.

There have been good ones too, with men who know how to lay on a good date and then ghost you (almost worse than the genuinely bad ones) and some with men who were lovely, funny, charming, just not for me. The trouble is, I suspect, that I want a great love story. One for the ages. One I'm unlikely to find on a Friday night at a brewery in Brixton with a man who may or may not be called Harry.

I can track most of my worst dates in fried-cheese sandwiches. On the way home from another hopeless evening – tipsy, annoyed and ravenously hungry – my mind wanders to what I might make to eat. Will it be eggs, or yesterday's rice refried with whatever I can forage from the fridge? Is a late-night carbonara required (only brought out in truly dire cases), or is it just a Marmite toast situation? More often than not, though, only hot cheese will do.

The tuna melt hill I will die on

Tuna melts are one of those things that I'll never not be in the mood for. But it does need to be just right. There are any number of ways to make one. Do you add capers or pickles? What's your policy on onion – red, spring or none at all? Do you like a bit of chilli, or do you insist on mustard? Is this a greenery-free zone, or would some finely chopped dill be welcomed? What cheese do you plump for, and how melted should it be?

Personally, I need the crunch and hum of red onion. I like the tuna to be packed in olive oil (it tends to be much softer and less salty this way), and enough finely chopped dill pickles and celery that the whole thing has a slightly retro American diner feel about it. I like the cheddar to be mainly melted and bubbling, but with a bit of it still retaining some bite. And I'm quite particular about the bread. Julia Child always served her tuna salad (which included finely chopped cornichons, capers, and slices of Vidalia onion) on a toasted English muffin. I like something grain-flecked and sturdy but with a close texture, not an airy sourdough that is going to let filling escape through the holes. An American-style rye with a few caraway seeds works particularly well (or, I often just use a loaf of Kelderman, which you can get in Sainsbury's). I find the best shaped loaf is round or oval and not too risen so that you get long, relatively narrow slices.

The ingredients list is, as always, yours to tweak. This is merely my personal tuna-melt line-up of choice.

Serves 1

½ small red onion, finely sliced
½ lemon, juiced
1 x 200g tin tuna in olive oil
1 tablespoon full-fat mayonnaise, plus a little more for the bread
a few dashes of a chilli sauce, to taste
1 tablespoon roughly chopped dill pickles, well drained on kitchen paper
½ celery stick, finely chopped
a little Dijon mustard
2 slices of bread
50g extra-mature cheddar, coarsely grated
salt and freshly cracked black pepper

Put the onion in a small bowl with the lemon juice and a little salt. Mix with a fork, cover with a plate and leave it to sit while you do everything else.

Drain most of the oil off the tuna (don't worry about getting it all off) and put the fish in a bowl. Add the mayonnaise, chilli sauce, plenty of black pepper and a small pinch of salt. Add the well-drained pickles and the celery and mix everything together.

Now set your frying pan over a medium heat and get it nice and hot but not smoking.

Spread one side of each slice of bread lightly with mustard. On one slice, spread the other side of the bread with a light but thorough slick of mayonnaise. Pile the tuna mixture on the mustard side of this slice of bread. Carefully lay the onion slices on top (discard the excess lemon juice, or use it in a salad dressing) followed by the grated cheese. Don't worry about it being messy, just try and pile it high with as much as you can.

Slide a fish slice underneath this slice of bread and transfer it to the pan. Pop on the second slice and squash the sandwich down. Lay a piece of greaseproof paper on it, then place a heavy pan on top. Make sure it's weighing the sandwich down evenly. Cook for 3 minutes, or until the bread is golden and crispy and the filling beginning to bubble.

Take the pan and greaseproof off, spread a little mayo on the top slice, then use the fish slice to flip the sandwich. Put the greaseproof back on, followed by the pan, pressing it down slightly. Leave it for another 3 minutes. It's ready when the cheese is melted and bubbling and the bread golden.

Fried mort 'n' mozz sandwich with honey butter

Some of the best hot sandwiches in London are in the old Italian cafés there aren't enough of anymore – the kind where you're just as likely to get a full English or a jacket potato as you are a plate of pasta or a hefty, perfect panini. They're the best places to while away an afternoon, drinking mug after mug of coffee and zig-zagging your way across the sprawling menu. You could quite easily go from a cheese and ham omelette to liver and onions to penne arrabbiata, with a pitstop at the tower of sfogliatelle on the counter. There is a particularly brilliant one on Wardour Street in Soho called Bar Bruno with emerald leather banquettes, warm lighting and reassuring staff who will make you a piping-hot mozzarella, tomato and basil panino and a pint of tea, and let you sit and while away a couple of hours.

I love a toastie that forces you to contend with foot-long strings of molten mozzarella every time you take a bite. If you need to brace and hold on to the bread to make sure the filling doesn't all come out in your first bite, something is going right. I love the simplicity of these toasties too – often just two or three ingredients piled generously into a roll. They are the inspiration for this mortadella and mozzarella fried sandwich. You'll toast a ciabatta roll, then fill it with a couple of sheets of silky salami and dry mozzarella, drizzled with a little olive oil, fried and flattened in a hot pan. For a touch of sweetness, sometimes I'll just drizzle a little honey over the final thing (which you could absolutely do), but a sturdy panini roll can handle a bit of dousing, and this honey and garlic butter is so good. Brush the sandwich with the melted butter while it's still piping hot. It might seem like overkill but honestly, more things should be brushed in honey and garlic butter. It's absurdly good.

Serves 2

2 panini rolls, sliced in
    half lengthways
4 slices of mortadella
6 slices of dry mozzarella
    (wet mozzarella is
    fine too, I just find
    the dry version melts
    particularly well)
olive oil
1 tablespoon butter
1 small garlic clove,
    finely sliced
1 teaspoon runny honey
flaky salt

First, toast your bread, either in a toaster or in a griddle pan if you want more of a char.

Lay 2 slices of the mortadella on the bottom half of each roll, folding it in, so it doesn't spill out of the bread too much. Arrange equal amounts of the mozzarella on top, then top with the other half of each roll. Squeeze the sandwiches down.

Set a large frying pan over a medium heat. When the pan is hot, drizzle a little olive oil over each sandwich and sit them – oiled side down – in the pan. Pop a piece of baking paper on top, then sit a heavy pan on top of the sandwiches to flatten them. Fry for 3 minutes, until the cheese is beginning to melt, then remove the pan and paper, drizzle the top sides with a little oil and flip the sandwiches. Cook for another 2 minutes or so, using the paper and pan again.

Meanwhile, melt the butter in a small saucepan over a medium heat. Add the garlic and cook for 1 minute, then add the honey and swirl the pan so that the honey and butter mix. Take the pan off the heat.

When the sandwiches are ready, use a pastry brush (or a teaspoon will do) to spread a little hot butter on the bread. Finish with a sprinkle of flaky salt. Cut the sandwiches in half and eat messily.

Grilled three cheese with jalapeños and lime-pickled onions

Sue Perkins was asked on her *Desert Island Discs* what she thought made a really great joke: 'Sometimes a really nuanced, really finessed type of sentence can make me guffaw, but equally, just a really well-timed burp.' Food is a bit like that, I think. A really intricate, beautifully prepared meal can be one of the best things, but so can a well-timed cheese sarnie. I don't want to speak too soon, but this might be the apex of cheese sarnies. Grated cheddar, crumbled up sheets of American plastic nonsense, full-fat cream cheese and finely chopped jalapeños. It's an ungodly mixture that would probably be terrible uncooked, but when hot and bubbling it becomes the most delicious sort of spicy cheese lava. The quick pickled onions cut through it. You could go for another kind of pickle – I find the hum of onion works particularly well.

This makes for the perfect late-night dinner, but it's also a great one to whip up for a crowd after a big weekend walk. Make the pickles and the cheese mixture in advance so all you have to do is assemble and fry rounds of fried-cheese sandwiches for the hungry hordes when you get home.

Serves 1

½ recipe quantity of Very Quick Pickled Onions (see page 23)
35g mature cheddar, grated
1 sheet of American cheese, crumbled
45g full-fat cream cheese
about 3 slices of brined jalapeño peppers (depending on how much chilli you like), finely chopped
a few coriander sprigs, roughly chopped
2 slices of bread, thinly sliced (something with rye would be particularly good)
a little soft butter, for spreading
flaky salt

Make the pickled onions according to the recipe on page 23 and leave them to sit for 20 minutes.

Mix the cheddar, American cheese and cream cheese together with a fork. Add the jalapeños and the coriander. Mix well.

Spread a little butter on one piece of bread and top the unbuttered side with the cheese mixture. Put another slice of bread on top and squeeze it down.

Set a frying pan over a medium heat. Get it nice and hot but not smoking. Use a fish slice to transfer the sandwich to the pan, buttered side down. Lay a piece of baking paper on it, then place a heavy pan on top. Make sure it's weighing everything down evenly. Cook for roughly 3 minutes, or until the bottom slice of bread is golden and the filling beginning to bubble.

Take the pan and baking paper off, spread a little butter on the top slice, then use the fish slice to flip the sandwich. Put the baking paper back on, followed by the pan, again making sure it's evenly weighted. Leave for 2 minutes. It's ready when the cheese is melted, bubbling and trying to escape the sandwich.

Serve sliced in half, sprinkled with salt and with a pile of lime-pickled onions on the side.

Silky scrambled eggs with tomato and coriander

Like shades of tea or the best David Bowie songs, everyone has an opinion when it comes to the firmness of scrambled egg. Some like the kind of consistency you could use to insulate a roof; others err on the side of a barely cooked scramble. Some use a wide frying pan and don't over stir, preferring elegant ribbons of egg, others like a closer texture. They all have their place, but when I want a more luxurious scramble, I'll use this technique.

With an extra yolk and flakes of cold butter beaten through the egg, plus a low heat and a continuous stir, you'll end up with super-silky, orange-yellow, quite creamy scrambled eggs. They're pretty rich, so often I'll just have them as they are with toast, but a nice way to freshen them up is to stir through some sautéed finely diced tomato and chilli and a little coriander just before serving.

Serves 1

1 tomato, finely diced
45g cold butter, plus extra
  for the eggs
½ small red chilli, finely
  diced
2 eggs, plus an extra
  yolk
a small handful of
  coriander, leaves and
  stems finely chopped
salt

To serve
slices of buttered toast
a lime wedge
hot sauce, for shaking
  over

Using a sieve, drain the diced tomato of excess liquid.

Melt half the butter in a small non-stick saucepan over a medium heat. Once melted, add the tomato and a little salt and cook for 3 minutes, or until well softened. Add the chilli and cook for another 1 minute. Remove the tomato and chilli from the pan and set aside.

Beat the eggs with a little salt. Add a knob of cold butter to the egg mixture in small chunks.

Put a separate small saucepan over a very low heat and add the rest of the butter. Once melted, pour in the eggs. Stir the eggs continuously as they cook. You want to get them to a point where they are still fairly uncooked and liquid, then take the pan off the heat and keep stirring until they firm up a little and come together. They should be super-silky.

Stir in the warm tomato mixture. Then quickly stir in the coriander and serve it all piled on to toast with lime for squeezing over and a sprinkling of hot sauce.

Sausage hash

The day after a big night is always better than the night before. Sure, parties are nice, but really I'm in it for the excuse to lie around drinking tea the next day. It's in the bleary-eyed sausage sandwiches the morning after a wedding; the coffee brewed amid the remnants of last night's party that the magic happens, I think. It's in the kitchen frying eggs and under a blanket watching *Titanic*, while you unpick every element of the night before.

I think strictly hash should be plainer than this. A traditional New England-style hash would use cooked meat (like corned beef), diced potatoes, onion and very little seasoning other than salt and pepper. I like the sauciness you get from cherry toms and lemon, but really it's all about the browned onion and nuggets of sausage. If I'm cooking for a crowd, I'll often make it in a paella pan, but you could make it in a roasting tin (as below), or a big frying pan or shallow casserole pan. It makes just as satisfying a dinner as it does a great morning-after brunch.

Serves 4

1.5kg potatoes (red-skinned, or a Maris Piper), cut into small chunks
olive oil
1 teaspoon sweet smoked paprika
4 garlic cloves, skin on
8 sausages
1 large onion, finely sliced
1 teaspoon fennel seeds
½ teaspoon dried oregano
1 tablespoon tomato purée
450g cherry tomatoes
1 large lemon, juiced
4–8 eggs
a handful of flat-leaf parsley or coriander, leaves and stems roughly chopped
salt

Preheat the oven to 220°C/200°C fan/Gas 7.

Put the potatoes in a roasting tin and toss them with a good glug of olive oil, the paprika and a good pinch of salt. Add the garlic cloves. Roast for 35 minutes, or until the potatoes are golden and crispy.

Meanwhile, strip the skins off the sausages and pinch them into chunks roughly the size of Maltesers. Set a large frying pan over a medium heat with a splash of oil. Cook the sausages until they're well browned and gnarly. Use a slotted spoon to transfer them from the pan to a plate – don't pile them on top of each other too much or they'll go soggy. Add another splash of oil to the pan and turn the heat down. Add the onion and a pinch of salt. Put a lid on the pan and cook for 12 minutes, or until the onion has softened and browned a little. Turn the heat up and add the fennel seeds. Cook for 1 minute. Then, add the oregano and tomato purée and a splash of water. Stir and cook for another 1 minute. Add the cherry tomatoes and cook for 10 minutes, or until the tomatoes pop. Squeeze a couple with the back of a spoon while they're cooking. Add the lemon, stir and cook for 1 minute.

Now get your grill on the highest heat it'll go.

Add the onion and tomato mixture to the roasting tin with the potatoes. Scatter over the sausage nuggets. Make 4–8 (one per egg) wells that you can nestle the eggs in. Crack an egg into each well, then pop the tin under the grill. Cook for about 2 minutes, or until the whites have firmed up but the yolks are still runny.

If you prefer (and your frying pan is big enough) you could add the sausages, potatoes and garlic cloves to the pan, stir everything, crack the eggs on top, pop a lid on and cook the eggs through on the hob.

Scatter herbs over the top and let everyone dive in.

Puddings to eat in the bath

We must risk delight. We can do without pleasure, but not delight. Not enjoyment. We must have the stubbornness to accept our gladness in the ruthless furnace of this world.

Extract from 'A Brief for the Defense'
by Jack Gilbert

Sundaes, Friday night cookies and frozen After Eights

I am not an especially glamorous person. I've never smoked, I don't really know how to do the back of my hair, and I don't know how to flirt enchantingly. Perhaps the closest that I have ever come to a moment of true, honest-to-goodness old-school glamour was the time I ate a perfect coffee éclair in a gold bath in Paris.

I went to do a week's work for the company I'd interned at on my year abroad and, as I had nowhere to stay, my old boss let me spend the week in one of his empty apartments in the Marais. It was unbelievably beautiful, and the bathroom was a kind of gilded affair. I think possibly it was only the taps that were actually gold, but in my memory the whole room, with its sunken bath tucked under the eaves, seemed to glow. On the first night I went out and bought a couple of cheeses and a bottle of wine, and then stopped at the boulangerie. Unable to walk away just with the crusty baguette I needed for my dinner, I left with a little box tied with a pink ribbon, containing a perfect coffee éclair. That night, I ate it in the bath, watching episodes of *30 Rock* until the water went cold around me, feeling like just about the most glamorous woman that ever lived.

You are not necessarily required to eat these desserts in the bath. Please feel free to enjoy them wherever you'd like; share them with a crowd or keep them to yourself. Make a tray of madeleines for one because you have a craving. See out the week in a blaze of trifle. Bake a batch of cookies to satisfy that need for something sweet with your movie night. Or spend a couple of hours making ice cream. Whether or not you end up eating any of these in the bath is up to you. The point is that puddings, in my mind, are to be savoured exactly as you want to. I tend to think if you're going to have one at all, you may as well really, really enjoy it.

I like a pud that is over the top, messy and piled high, with as much cream, custard and ice cream as I can legitimately fit in the bowl or on the plate. My friend Lara and I were once listing our top ten puddings (what d'you mean you've never done this?) and high on both our lists were tiramisù, ice cream, and chocolate mousse. Essentially, puddings for people with no teeth. Bring me clotted, Jersey, Chantilly, crème anglaise or a jug of Birds, and don't be shy; I like a heavy pour and a generous dollop. I don't actually understand the question: 'Would you like cream, ice cream or custard with that?' Obviously the answer is all three, and leave the jug. And while we're on the subject, whoever invented the coffee crème pâtissière you find in those perfect Parisian éclairs deserves a sainthood. That is some God-tier crème pat.

I don't think you need to serve dessert at a dinner party – a cracking cheeseboard wins any day. And if you want to offer something sweet, who is going to turn their nose up at some good chocolate (or, for that matter, not especially good chocolate ... I don't think I've ever knowingly turned down a Terry's Chocolate Orange)? But if you are going to do a dessert, you may as well really do dessert. I firmly believe that when it comes to sweet things, we are all essentially seven-year-olds pretending to be grown-ups anyway. Let everyone make their own knickerbocker glory, and they will be beside themselves with joy.

If you're on your own when a sugar craving strikes, it can be tempting not to bother making yourself a proper pudding – it could seem like all too much effort to bake an entire cake or a batch of cookies for one. Why would you go to the trouble of making a single individual tiramisù? To this I would merely venture two things. 1) You are absolutely worth making a personal pudding for. 2) Who says you can't make enough for eight and let the fruits of your efforts continue to bring you moments of joy over the days to come in the form of really excellent leftovers?

Nora Ephron once wrote in a *New Yorker* essay that in her twenties, when she was living in the Village and working as a reporter for the *New York Post*, she would cook herself 'an entire meal' from one of her cookbooks whenever she had a night at home alone. 'Then I sat down in front of the television set and ate it. I felt very brave and plucky as I ate my perfect dinner. O.K., I didn't have a date, but at least I wasn't one of those lonely women who sat home with a pathetic container of yogurt. Eating a meal for four that I had cooked for myself was probably equally pathetic, but it never crossed my mind.'

It doesn't sound pathetic at all. Quite the opposite. It's indulgent in the best possible way. It's generous and happy-making – the perfect use of an evening in.

Want not need

We rarely actually need pudding.

That's not why we have it. It's filed under 'want' not 'need'.
It brings out our childish side, tapping into that part of us
that secretly still prefers milk chocolate to dark and is always
hoping someone else at the table will order a dessert. I will
always choose an extra starter over a pudding if given the
choice. But when I really fancy dessert, nothing else will do.

I find it's the puds you loved as a child that you simply can't not
order if you're out and spot them on a menu. You weren't going
to have dessert but then you see they've got mint choc chip ice
cream. Sure, it's had an update with fresh mint steeped in raw
cream and shards of dark chocolate (and bears little resemblance
to the lurid scoops that peppered your childhood summer
holidays), but it's still mint choc chip, so you have to have it.
Maybe it's some sort of steamed number that does it for you,
bringing back hazy recollections of Sunday lunches that were
always signed, sealed and delivered with a jug of hot, skin-on
custard. Whatever it is, there is something about sweet things
that gets right to some indelible part of ourselves, which, once
triggered, cannot be ignored.

All of which is to say that I've never knowingly been able
to turn down an ice-cream sundae. It's right at the top of the
list of puddings that I can't not order. If you were to roll back
the years through my family photos, there are probably more
pictures of me looking exceptionally pleased with myself
sticking a long spoon into a tall sundae glass than there are
pictures of me with either of my siblings. I was genuinely a
bit devastated when our mum took our old electric blue sundae
glasses to the charity shop. They had matching spoons with blue
plastic fish and shells on the ends, for crying out loud.

I still love the whole ridiculous ceremony of a sundae – how
in a French bistro a coupe glacée is likely to come adorned
with some sort of flamboyant decoration no matter the age
of the diner, how you have to get through that first cloud of
whipped cream before you can start to dig down through the
layers. I loved them as a child. I love them still. I hope to still
be ordering an ice-cream sundae gleefully when I'm 90.

A case for the café liégeois

I know we've all gone potty for affogato in recent years (and rightly so, it's one of the greatest puds out there), but can I just put in a word for its extravagant cousin, the liégeois? It has to be the undisputed queen of the ice-cream sundaes. A chilled glass, a shot of espresso, scoops of coffee ice cream and a crown of Chantilly. I mean what's not to like? It's affogato plus. There is a time and a place for one perfect scoop of vanilla with a shot of hot coffee. But sometimes more is more. Sometimes you need to go full liégeois.

Whether you buy your coffee ice cream or make it, whip your Chantilly from scratch or reach for a can, this is pretty much guaranteed to be a good pud. If you are going to make your own ice cream, you'll need to either use an ice-cream churner (the easiest option if you have one) or commit to beating the mixture every couple of hours as it freezes. Diana Henry has lots of wonderful ice-cream recipes, including a fantastic one for a no-churn Turkish coffee number that involves whipping cream with condensed milk, thus getting round the need to churn. That method might be something to think about too. This recipe is custard-based and takes a little time but is very much worth the bother.

Serves 4

For the ice cream
300ml double cream
270ml whole milk
150g caster sugar
1 vanilla pod, split in
   half, seeds removed
   with a small knife
   (keep the pod)
2 teaspoons instant
   espresso powder
3 large egg yolks
180ml chilled strong
   coffee

For everything else
350ml double cream
1 teaspoon icing sugar
2 teaspoons vanilla
   extract
275ml chilled espresso
   or strong coffee
a few chocolate-covered
   coffee beans, roughly
   chopped (optional)

Heat the cream and milk in a wide saucepan over a low–medium heat with half the sugar, the vanilla seeds, the vanilla pod and the instant espresso powder. Stir occasionally to help the sugar dissolve. Bring the cream mixture almost to the boil, then turn the heat off and leave it to steep for 30 minutes. Then, remove the pod from the milk mixture.

Meanwhile, use an electric whisk to beat the egg yolks with the remaining sugar until they turn pale and frothy and they thicken a little.

Take a ladleful of the milk mixture and add it to the egg to loosen it. Then, put a low heat back on under the milk pan and add the egg, stirring all the time with a wooden spoon or spatula. Keep cooking and stirring until the custard thickens enough to coat the back of a spoon without entirely running off. Then take the pan straight off the heat.

Fill an empty sink with about 5cm of cold water and ice and carefully lower the pan into it, taking care the water doesn't come up over the sides. Let the custard cool down entirely, then add the cold coffee, beating it in to combine.

Chill the mixture for 30 minutes in the fridge, then churn it in your ice-cream machine, scrape it into a plastic container, pop on the lid and freeze until you're ready to serve. Or, if you're doing it with elbow grease, pop it straight into the container and into the freezer and take it out every couple of hours to whip it with electric beaters until it's set enough so that ice crystals don't form.

Put sundae glasses into the fridge to chill them. When it comes to assembling your sundae, whip the cream with the icing sugar and vanilla until soft peaks form to create the Chantilly. Take care not to overwhip it. Remove the sundae glasses from the fridge, then pour in the coffee, top with scoops of the ice cream and a dollop of Chantilly, and sprinkle with the chopped chocolate-coated coffee beans, if using.

Hot tahini fudge sundae
with sesame pine nut brittle

Frankly, more things should come with hunks of sesame pine nut brittle on top. This was a discovery I made when I was trying to caramelise pine nuts and ended up making a kind of messy but delicious shard of buttery toffeed nuts. I added sesame seeds and ended up creating something that tastes a bit how Butterkist toffee popcorn were to taste if it mated with a sesame snap. Safe to say, I've made it again and again since. Make a double batch, break it into shards and keep the shards in a biscuit tin for a little sweet something to reach for after dinner, or break them over a nutty, chocolatey sundae like this one.

I like tahini in the sauce, but you could use peanut butter or another nut butter. If you have leftover sauce, pour it into ramekins and pop it in the fridge – instant chocolate pots for the following day, perfect topped with a dollop of crème fraîche.

Serves 6

For the brittle
1 tablespoon salted
   butter
125g pine nuts
1½ tablespoons
   caster sugar
¼ tablespoon
   sesame seeds

For the sauce
160g 70% dark chocolate,
   broken into pieces
500ml double cream
2 tablespoons dark
   muscovado sugar
100g golden syrup
75g salted butter
100g tahini

For the sundae
2 scoops per person
   of vanilla ice cream
a little finely chopped
   70% dark chocolate
flaky salt

First, make your brittle. Set a small frying pan over a low–medium heat. Melt the butter. Add the pine nuts and toss them for a few seconds, then sprinkle over the caster sugar. Cook for about 1 minute, tossing occasionally, until the nuts are beginning to brown but aren't catching. Pour the caramel out on to a piece of baking paper, sprinkle over the sesame seeds and leave to cool and firm up. Break into pieces.

To make the sauce, put the chocolate in a large heatproof bowl and set aside. Put the cream, sugar and syrup in a small saucepan over a low heat. Stir until the sugar has dissolved, little bubbles are forming on the surface and the liquid is starting to tremble. Immediately remove the pan from the heat and pour the cream mixture over the chocolate. Leave to stand for a couple of minutes, then stir until the chocolate has melted. Add the butter and beat it all together with a wooden spoon until the mixture becomes nice and glossy. Using a balloon whisk, slowly add the tahini, beating until combined.

At this point, you could either serve the warm sauce immediately over your sundae or pop it back in the pan over a low heat and stir it for a minute if you want it properly hot. Next, crack on with assembling.

To construct the sundae, spoon a puddle of sauce into the bottom of each glass, then add 1 scoop of ice cream, a little more sauce, chopped chocolate, then a second scoop of ice cream. Top with more sauce, a shard of sesame pine nut brittle and a little flaky salt.

Bury me with this tiramisù

When a Friday night dinner party comes with a bit of warning (it's amazing how often I find I've accidentally invited five people over for dinner at 4pm on a Friday afternoon), you have the luxury of actually being able to get ahead with at least some of the meal. I am not an especially organised person, but if I know I'm having friends round and I have time, I'll try to make dessert the day before. There is just something very reassuring about knowing you've got your pud locked down before you've even bought the crisps. Tiramisù is perfect when you have time to make it ahead because it'll only improve with a day in the fridge – the cream firms up just as you want it to, the coffee and liqueur mellow a little, the vanilla becomes more pronounced. All you need to do is shake a little cocoa powder over the finished dish when you're about to serve.

I'm usually all for fripperies and extras when it comes to dessert, but I must admit with tiramisù I'm a bit of a purist. I'm just not sure you can beat that combination of boozy, coffee-sodden biscuits and almost mousse-like eggy mascarpone. You can make it as elegant or as functional as you like. There's an argument to be made for making individual tiramisù in glasses, layering it beautifully in a trifle bowl or cutting perfect squares to plate up and dust with cocoa. But there's nothing to stop you from fashioning the thing directly in your favourite pudding bowl.

Tiramisù tends to be something you'd make for lots of people, but I don't see anything wrong with making it for two (or, you know, for one, with a helping leftover… if you haven't eaten leftover tiramisù out of the fridge for breakfast then I'm not sure we can be friends). If I'm making a small one for two or three people as below, I often make it in a small rectangular enamel pie dish. There is usually only space for one layer of biscuits underneath the mascarpone, otherwise it all gets a bit fiddly. But it's just as delicious, and proof you don't need to have tonnes of people round to justify making a tiramisù.

This recipe serves two greedy people or three to four more abstemious eaters, but feel free to double, triple or quadruple it if you're feeding a crowd.

Serves 2–4 people,
  depending on greed

75ml cold strong coffee
2 tablespoons marsala
  wine
6 savoiardi biscuits
2 eggs, separated
40g golden caster sugar
185g mascarpone
1 teaspoon vanilla
  extract
1 tablespoon cocoa
  powder

Combine the coffee and marsala in a shallow bowl. One by one, dunk the biscuits in the mixture, really making sure they're soaking up the liquid, then lay them in the bottom of whatever receptacle you're using.

Use electric beaters, or a balloon whisk and a bit of elbow grease, to beat together the egg yolks and sugar in a bowl until they turn very pale, thick and glossy. A tablespoonful at a time, beat in the mascarpone to combine so you have a very smooth, thick cream. Add the vanilla extract and beat that in too.

In a separate bowl (or a stand mixer), use clean electric beaters to whisk the egg whites until stiff peaks form – just as if you were making a meringue.

Carefully but firmly, use a large metal spoon to fold half the egg whites into the mascarpone mixture. You want all the egg to be mixed through but for there to still be plenty of volume so that the mixture is beautifully light. Fold the second half of egg white into the mascarpone mixture. Keep folding until it's completely combined.

Sift half the cocoa powder over the savoiardi biscuits. Spoon the mascarpone over them. Even out the top, cover and refrigerate for at least 5 hours.

When you come to serve, sift the remaining cocoa powder over the top of the tiramisù.

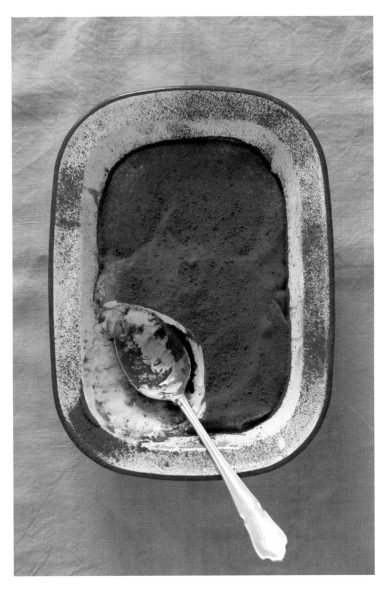

Salted brown butter honey madeleines

When I lived in Paris, I didn't have an oven. I did have something purporting to be an oven – it was smaller than a microwave and seemed to have two settings: cremate or warm through. A jacket potato took hours. You could just about use it to bake cookies if it was a very forgiving recipe, you watched them like a hawk, and you didn't mind slightly burnt edges. Cakes were an absolute no. For some reason I persevered, often attempting to bake an elaborate sponge when I should have been sitting outside a café smoking, reading Proust and looking extremely louche. I seem to remember a particularly bad coconut and rose water cake. You could have used it to spackle holes in your wall it was so sticky and stodgy.

That same year, Rachel Khoo's *A Little Paris Kitchen* came out. I cooked from it avidly, becoming obsessed with her recipes for boeuf bourguignon with baguette dumplings and salted caramel moelleux (executed with mixed levels of success in the dodgy non-oven …). There was a lemon raspberry madeleine recipe in the book which couldn't quite withstand my limited kit, but once I was back in England, I made them again and again. It was from Khoo's beautiful book that I learned to rest the batter properly, and to use honey for sweetness as well as sugar.

There is a fantastic, golden hued honey cake that you often find in French bakeries, where a simple sponge can be hard to come by in among the beautiful patisseries. I liked the idea of combining the light, butteriness of a really good madeleine with that rather sturdy honey cake. By using salted butter and browning it rather than just melting it, the madeleines take on a lovely butterscotchy flavour, which is going to make you want to dunk them, still warm, in an espresso.

These are great to satisfy a hankering for a late-night bake as they're pretty easy to whip up. They also make a lovely dinner-party pud. Make the batter the day before, leaving it in the fridge overnight. When people look as if they could be persuaded to have something sweet, put the oven on and whack in a tray of madeleines. Serve them warm, just as they are, or with a dollop of crème fraîche or whipped cream. You could bake them in a mini madeleine tray (you may need to reduce the cook time) and scatter a few over bowls of vanilla ice cream.

Makes 12

110g salted butter
2 tablespoons runny
   honey
2 eggs
85g golden caster sugar
100g plain flour, sifted
a pinch of grated nutmeg
1 teaspoon baking
   powder
salt

Preheat the oven to 200°C/180°C fan/Gas 6.

Melt the butter in a small saucepan over a low–medium heat. Keep going until the liquid is golden, the solids pale brown, and everything smells toffeeish and incredible. Take the pan off the heat. Reserve a dessert spoonful of melted butter in a little bowl – you'll use it to grease the madeleine tray. Stir the honey into the remaining butter. Pour the mixture into a heatproof bowl, making sure to get all the milk solids out. Leave it to cool.

Whisk the eggs with the caster sugar until they turn pale and foamy. Pour in the butter and whisk it in to combine. Then add the flour, nutmeg and baking powder along with a good pinch of salt and whisk on a low speed to combine again. Leave the mixture to stand in the bowl for at least 30 minutes (longer if you can – you can even leave it in the fridge overnight).

Use a bit of kitchen paper to grease the tray with the melted butter you reserved. Use 2 teaspoons to spoon the mixture into the tray. Don't overfill them – about two thirds full should do it. Bake the madeleines for 9–11 minutes, or until they are cooked through, a little risen and golden on top.

Leave them to cool on a cooling rack in the tin for 10 minutes. Then turn them out of the tin and leave them on the rack to cool entirely (or eat them warm ...).

Pyjama cannoli

It's 10.30pm on a Friday night in Boston's North End and there is a line at least 20 metres deep of people queuing for cannoli. It's the start of a weekend of festivities in this corner of the city as Boston's Italian community celebrates the Feast of St Anthony, which they have done every year since 1919. All the restaurants are crammed with people eating great bowls of spaghetti alla vongole and every side street is filled with food carts selling giant arancini, great pans of sausage and peppers, and all manner of pizza and gelato.

In the line for Mike's Pastry are sleepy, sweet-toothed children, a couple on a date, and a girl in her pyjamas, flicking through her phone. We have never heard of Mike's (though we'll later learn it has been renowned for its cannoli since 1946) but figure that when you're in a strange city and see a line of locals queueing for pastry in the middle of the night, you've got to join them. We have just eaten huge plates of seafood pappardelle and each had a gelato while strolling around the neighbourhood in search of a bar with a free table, but we do the sensible thing and follow the crowd. While the line edges forward, I watch the girl in the pink pyjamas and Ugg boots, wondering what sort of day she has had, and what series of events have led to this urge for a late-night cannoli run.

Inside, we have choices to make, and fast – there are scores of people behind us to serve. Do we want chocolate chip or pistachio, amaretto, chocolate ricotta, limoncello, hazelnut, Oreo or one of the million other options? How many? And do we want powdered sugar on top or not?

We opt for two choc chip and two plain ricotta, all with a liberal dusting, because why not? We leave with a little white box with a cobalt blue crown on it and eat the cannoli on the street, getting powdered sugar all over our faces and fingers. They are sweet and chubby and perfectly crisp, and filled with a velvety ricotta that I don't want to end. They are, quite simply, four of the best little things we've ever eaten.

If Mike's was at the end of my road, if I could walk there in my pyjamas at 10.30pm on a Friday night, buy a box of choc chip cannoli and take it home, I would. As I don't, I'll have to make them myself.

This is a recipe for one of those nights when you have a hankering for a baking project. Raid the contents of your store cupboard, make a dash to the nearest shop for ricotta, stick something good on Netflix (maybe Stanley Tucci doing his thing in *Big Night*, if you want to get meta about it) and start baking. About an hour and a half later, you'll have a plate of chubby, crisp cannoli filled with sweet, orange-flecked ricotta.

Makes roughly 15

For the shells
215g plain flour, plus
  extra for dusting
1½ tablespoons caster
  sugar
⅓ teaspoon bicarbonate
  of soda
45g unsalted butter
2 large eggs, separated
75ml marsala
plenty of neutral cooking
  oil, for deep-frying

For the filling
250g ricotta, drained
  of excess water
100g mascarpone
3 tablespoons icing sugar,
  sifted, plus extra for
  dusting
1 teaspoon vanilla paste
1 orange, zested

*Optional extras (for
  the cannoli ends)*
50g dark chocolate,
  melted
1 tablespoon nibbed
  pistachios to sprinkle
  on the chocolate

First, make the dough. Put the flour, sugar and bicarbonate of soda in a large bowl and mix well.

Add the butter in small chunks and rub it into the flour with your fingers until you have a fine sandy crumb.

Make a well in the middle of the flour and add the egg yolks and marsala. Using one hand, bring the dough together, then knead it until you have a smooth dough. Form the dough into a disc, wrap it in cling film and put it in the fridge to rest for 30 minutes.

Meanwhile, line a large baking tray with baking paper.

Take the dough out of the fridge, and dust your work surface and rolling pin with flour. Roll out the dough as thin as humanly possible – I'm talking wafer thin. To cut out the cannoli, either use a large biscuit cutter (about 12cm in diameter) to cut out rounds of dough, or use a sharp knife to cut round the rim of a mug. Lay the rounds on the baking tray and put them back in the fridge for another 30 minutes.

Meanwhile, make the filling. Put the ricotta and mascarpone in a large bowl and beat them together with a balloon whisk, then beat in the icing sugar. Finally, add the vanilla and the orange zest. Put the filling in the fridge until you need it.

When it comes to frying the cannoli, you can either wrap them around cannoli moulds, using a little egg

white to stick the edges of the cannoli together, or make your own makeshift ones like I do with silver foil. There are a couple of good YouTube videos on how to do this, but essentially you're just making a stiff tube about the width of your finger, rolled smaller at one end than the other, with a piece of folded silver foil. Make two or four of these so you can fry more than one cannolo at a time, reusing the foil tubes as you make your way through all your pastry discs, and you always have a cool pair handy.

Before you start frying, you should also get a cooling rack ready. You might want to stand it over a baking tray or some kitchen paper to catch any drips of oil.

Pour your frying oil into a deep pan over a medium heat, or into a deep-fat fryer. Don't fill the pan more than half the way up. Take a small piece of dough and add it to the pan. Once the dough has risen to the surface and is bubbling and turning golden brown, the oil is hot enough.

Fry the cannoli one or two at a time, using a slotted spoon to turn them as you see the dough turning brown underneath. When the cannoli are golden and slightly puffy, remove them from the pan and carefully transfer them to the cooling rack. At this point, you can use the tongs to carefully pull the foil or cannoli tubes out (be careful – the tubes will be superhot). Let the tubes cool before using them again. Keep going until you've finished frying all the cannoli shells.

When the cannoli are cold, you can fill them. If you don't mind a bit of a messy finish, you can just do this with a teaspoon. For a smoother look, use a piping bag. I sometimes spoon the mixture into a sandwich bag and snip the end off one of the corners, then squeeze the filling through the snipped hole into the tubes.

If you like, dip the cannoli ends (one or both ends, up to you) in melted chocolate and then sprinkle over the nibbed pistachios, before the chocolate sets and hardens.

Dust each cannoli with icing sugar and arrange them on a plate.

Friday night cookies

Sometimes, often far too late at night, I get a craving for cookies. Chewy ones, with chocolate and a little salt, but with a hum of cinnamon and vanilla too. I'm craving the scent as much as anything, I think – the way the kitchen fills up with warm, toasty sweetness. Sylvia Plath wrote in her diaries (from which a daily pearl of a quote can be found on the brilliant Twitter account @whatsylviaate) about eating cookies before bed: 'Toll house cookies will be most welcome,' wrote Plath, who is known to have considered baking a form of therapy. 'I'm too hungry to share many, so will eat them with my before-bed glass of milk.'

Occasionally, I give into this craving too. Though more often than not, I'll remember that late-night baking sessions also mean late-night washing up, which is far less appealing. When I do embark on a night-time bake, I need it to be a particular type of recipe.

The writer Matt Haig says you should get a routine 'baggy enough to live in'. I'd agree (possibly because I've never been able to keep anything resembling a routine) and would just add that the same should go for a late-night cookie recipe. It needs to do exactly what you want it to, but it also needs to have a certain amount of flexibility. Am I going to be bothered waiting for dough to firm up at 11pm? No. Am I going to dash to the corner shop when I realise I've run out of something? Also no. Am I going to measure out equal-sized portions? Probably not. Do I really want to have to wash up more than two bowls? Definitely not. Late-night cookie recipes need to be firmly on your team. They need to be baggy and satisfying, guaranteed to hit the spot.

I need chocolate, always. But I also want that intoxicating scent of cardamom and cinnamon baking, like when you walk into a café in Stockholm and the cosy thwack of spice and marzipan hits you full in the face. I love those ridiculously named snickerdoodle cookies, where the balls of dough are rolled in cinnamon sugar so that when they flatten out they retain this perfect coating that sparkles slightly once the cookies are baked. This cookie is like if a classic chocolate chip and a snickerdoodle eloped. Nutmeg and vanilla bring a custardy element that might make you want to have the cookies warm with vanilla ice cream. There's some essential salt, making everything make sense. And there's the nutty chew from a few oats. They've become a late-night staple, often keeping me company in the wee hours. See if they can do the same for you.

Makes 14 cookies

120g salted butter, room
    temperature
100g granulated sugar
85g light brown soft
    sugar
¼ teaspoon salt

Continued overleaf

Preheat the oven to 180°C/160°C fan/Gas 4. Put two large baking sheets in the oven.

Using either a stand mixer or electric hand mixer, cream together the butter, granulated sugar, brown sugar and salt. Beat them until pale and creamy, scraping down the bowl as necessary.

Add the egg and vanilla and beat on a low speed until the mixture comes together.

1 large egg, beaten
1 teaspoon vanilla paste
185g plain flour
½ teaspoon bicarbonate
  of soda
½ teaspoon ground
  nutmeg
100g 70% dark chocolate,
  roughly chopped
35g caster sugar
1 teaspoon ground
  cinnamon
¼ teaspoon ground
  cardamom
35g rolled oats
a little flaky salt

In a bowl, combine the flour, bicarbonate of soda and nutmeg. Add the dry mixture to the wet mixture and stir until everything just comes together. Then, add the chocolate and stir it through.

On a small plate, mix the caster sugar, cinnamon, cardamom and oats.

Take dessertspoonfuls of dough and roll each one into a golf-ball-sized ball. Roll each ball in the oaty sugar, lightly pressing the oats into the dough.

Take the baking sheets out of the oven, line them with baking paper and arrange the balls of dough over the sheets, leaving at least 6cm between each ball (bake in batches if you need to, depending on the size of your sheets). Bake each batch for 10 minutes, or until the cookies are a light golden brown. Remove them from the oven and drop the baking sheets on to your work surface from about 5cm above the worktop. This will help any puffiness in the centre of the cookies sink a little. Leave the cookies to cool on their sheets for 10 minutes.

Carefully move the cookies to a cooling rack and sprinkle them with flaky salt to finish.

Brown sugar pavlova with miso caramel peaches and bourbon cream

There is very little not to love about a pavlova, in my view. At its most simple, it's like a meringue love seat topped with a blanket of velvety whipped cream. I know it's a bit retro and can seem like a faff, but can I just make a case for it? For a start, you can make the actual pav at least a day in advance. Second, contrary to the meringue lore that would have you believe it will work in only a very specific set of conditions (there is a lot of chat out there about the temperature of the eggs, the tyranny of the accidental streak of yolk, and the cleanliness of the bowl), I don't think you can go too far wrong with fresh eggs and a bit of elbow grease. Make your meringue in advance and then all you really need to do is whip your cream and tumble over a few raspbs or cooked stone fruit. Or if you want to push the boat out, pre-cook something like these miso caramel peaches.

I have become slightly obsessed with adding miso to sweet things. The salty, funky tang works so well in this dark caramel sauce, which gets bailed over halved peaches. You can make them in advance too, perhaps just warming them through slightly when it comes to serving. This pav might even convert any naysayers who claim meringue is too sweet, as the peaches and miso cut through all the sugar.

Use caster sugar if you prefer rather than a mixture of caster and brown as below – I just like the slight toffeeness you get with the added brown sugar in this recipe, partly because it works so well with the bourbon and peaches. You can use vanilla extract for the meringue, but a nice trick is to pop a used vanilla pod in a jar of caster sugar. Next time you come to use it, you'll have homemade vanilla sugar.

Serves 6–8

For the meringue
4 egg whites, room
  temperature
185g golden caster sugar
50g dark muscovado
  sugar
1 teaspoon white wine
  vinegar
1 teaspoon vanilla
  extract

Continued on page 243

Preheat the oven to 150°C/130°C fan/Gas 2. Line a baking tray with baking paper.

First, make the meringue. Whisk the egg whites in a large, clean, dry bowl with an electric whisk until they turn into stiff peaks. Add the caster sugar one dessertspoonful at a time, whisking continuously. Keep going, whisking on high speed, until the mixture has turned super-glossy.

Break up any big lumps in the brown sugar, then whisk that through too. Keep whisking until you can no longer see any flecks of sugar in the mixture.

Add the vinegar and vanilla extract and fold it through with a large metal spoon.

Spoon the mixture on to the baking paper. You can be as neat or as rustic as you like. I like a rough

For the peaches
100g golden caster sugar
90g cold salted butter
not quite 1 teaspoon white
   miso paste
a pinch of salt
4 peaches, halved and
   destoned

For the cream
450ml double cream
1 tablespoon icing sugar,
   sifted
1 tablespoon Bourbon or
   rum

circle, about 6cm high. Make sure there's a good 1cm of baking paper left clear around the edge of the meringue.

Put the meringue base in the oven and bake it for 1 hour 10 minutes. Then turn the oven off, leaving the meringue inside to cool completely.

While the pavlova is baking, make the peaches. Set a large, heavy-based saucepan over a low heat. Sprinkle the sugar in the pan in a roughly even layer. Cook, watching the sugar until it first turns to liquid, then goes a pale amber, and finally turns a darker caramel. This could take a while (anything up to about 10 minutes). Don't be tempted to turn the heat up or stir the sugar. If the sugar is caramelising at vastly different rates, just gently swirl the pan a little. When it's a nice dark amber and smells caramelly, not burned, take the pan off the heat.

Add the butter to the pan and swirl it or stir with a spatula so it comes together as a thick caramel sauce. Now add the miso and salt and beat them into the caramel.

Put the caramel back over a low–medium heat and add the peaches, cut side down. Cook them for 6 minutes, then flip them and cook them for another 4 minutes, baling hot caramel over the fruit with a tablespoon. Then, take the peaches off the heat and allow them to cool to room temperature before using. You don't want to put them on top of the pavlova piping hot, but you don't want them cold either.

Whip the cream when you're almost ready to serve. Pour it into a large bowl and add the icing sugar and bourbon or rum. Use an electric whisk (or a balloon whisk if you prefer to do it by hand) and whip until you get soft peaks.

Spoon the cream on top of the cooled meringue and spread it around roughly with the back of a spoon. It can be helpful to create a bit of a lip if you can around the edge, so the peaches are less likely to slide off.

Place the peaches on top, spooning over the extra miso caramel. Serve straight away.

Sherry roasted plums
with clotted cream and crumbs

This pudding is like autumn in a bowl: a slump of hot, sherried, orange and cinnamon-spiked plums, cold clotted cream just beginning to melt at the edges, and dark caramelised crumbs. It's a handy one for dinner parties as you can make it in advance and then warm the fruit through. When making it for lots of people, I quite like serving the plums in the roasting tin, spooning cream and crumbs over the tin in a glorious mess and having everyone dive in quickly.

It's a lovely thing to cook just for yourself too. Make a batch of the plums and finish them for breakfast at the weekend with porridge or Greek yoghurt. I'd also make enough crumbs for six for one; trust me... having a supply of sweet, salty toffee-crunch crumbs to steal whenever you please is only going to be a good idea.

Serves 6

For the crumbs
155g bread (a dark rye, brown or granary would work well)
75g dark muscovado sugar
40g demerara sugar
95g salted butter
1 tablespoon olive oil
1 teaspoon caraway seeds (optional; if you like aniseed flavour, these work nicely)

For the plums
1 vanilla pod, split in half, seeds removed with a small knife (keep the pod)
3 tablespoons sweet sherry
1 orange
12–18 plums, halved and destoned
4 tablespoons light brown soft sugar
1 cinnamon stick
6 tablespoons clotted cream

Preheat the oven to 200°C/180°C fan/Gas 6.

First, make the crumbs. Pulse the bread in a food processor – you want a mixture of crumb sizes, some chunky, some fine. Put the crumbs in a bowl and add both kinds of sugar. Stir everything together.

Put a small saucepan over a medium heat with the butter. Once the butter has melted, pour it over the crumbs. Add the olive oil too and stir it all together.

Line a baking tray with baking paper. Scatter the crumbs on the tray, sprinkle over the caraway seeds if you're using them, and bake it all in the oven. (You can cook the plums at the same time, if you like – though the crumbs need to cool completely, whereas you might like to serve the plums warm.) Bake the crumbs for 10 minutes. Then, take the tray out and stir. Return the tray to the oven and bake for another 5 minutes, then take it out and stir again. Put the tray back for a final 5 minutes. You want the crumbs to be well-caramelised but not burned. Remove them from the oven and leave them to cool entirely on the sheet.

Make the plums. Put the vanilla seeds in a jug. Add the sherry and beat with a fork so the seeds disperse.

Slice each end off the orange and use a small knife to slice off three strips of peel. Juice the orange and add the juice to the jug with the sherry and vanilla.

Lay the plum halves in a large roasting tray in a single layer. They should fit fairly snugly without being piled on top of each other. Pour the sherry, orange and vanilla mixture over the plums.

Put a good pinch of the brown sugar in the divot in the middle of each plum. Lay the halved vanilla pod on top of the fruit, the strips of orange and the cinnamon stick. Bake the plum halves in the oven for about 40 minutes, or until the fruit has slumped a little but is still retaining its shape.

To serve, add spoonfuls of clotted cream to the tray, then spoon 4 or 5 plum halves, with the cream and a little cooking liquor, into a bowl. Top with crumbs.

Still-hot flapjack and very cold cream

Listen, all I can say is that when I first made this, I realised I'd been eating flapjacks wrong all my life. I'd thrown together a tin of flapjacks in a fit of 'Why is there nothing sweet in this house?!' hanger, and rather than wait for them to cool down and be sliced, I shovelled a still gloopy and hot heap of sticky oats into a bowl and covered it with fridge-cold cream. It isn't elegant, it isn't a great feat of culinary genius, it just hits the spot in the way that only an emergency pudding could.

Add extras to the mixture if you like – dried fruits or some chopped-up stem ginger. I'm a bit of a purist when it comes to flapjack and just like it to taste of toasty oats and golden syrup.

Serves 8

180g unsalted butter
220g golden syrup
140g dark brown soft
  sugar
½ teaspoon ground
  cinnamon
½ teaspoon flaky salt
255g oats
plenty of cold pouring
  cream, to serve

Preheat the oven to 180°C/160°C fan/Gas 4.

Put the butter, golden syrup, brown sugar, cinnamon and salt in a saucepan over a low–medium heat. Stir occasionally as the butter melts. It'll start to foam up – let it simmer for 2 minutes, watching the pan and occasionally stirring so it doesn't bubble over.

Put the oats in a big bowl and pour over the butter mixture. Stir so everything is well combined.

Line a 20cm square tin with baking paper. Scrape the oat mixture into the tin, put in the oven and bake the flapjack for 15 minutes.

By then, the flapjack will have firmed up at the edges and still have some wobble in the centre. Remove it from the oven and leave it to cool for 10 minutes, then scoop it – still hot – straight from the tin into bowls and pour over cold cream. Leave any leftovers to cool completely in the tin, cut into chunks and put them in a biscuit tin or plastic container for tomorrow.

Ginger, prune and PX cake with cardamom custard

The cake that I have made the most in my life is Nigel Slater's double ginger. It is unequivocally the king of ginger cakes. It's moist, sweet, perfectly spiced and never fails. For an impatient baker like me, it's the best kind of recipe – I can follow it to the letter or with only one eye on the book, make substitutions according to whatever I have in stock, and even forget to take it out of the oven for a few minutes. Somehow, whatever I do to it, it always comes out perfectly.

Coming in as a very close runner up for my go-to bakes is Nigella's Guinness cake. I make it again and again for the simple reason that a) it's delicious, not too sweet, gloriously moist and muddy, and b) it's just about the easiest batter in the world, as it all comes together in one pan.

This recipe is a paean to the Niges, pulling from both that perfect double ginger and failsafe Guinness cake but with added boozy, tea-soaked prunes for good measure. You could reserve the liquid from the prunes if you wanted to make a bit of icing, beating it with icing sugar and a little orange zest and juice and pouring it over the cake once it's cooled. You could have it just as it is. Or you could go the whole hog and serve it with a great puddle of warm cardamom custard.

Serves 8

For the cake
75ml PX or other sweet wine, such as marsala
50ml strong Earl Grey tea
175g pitted prunes
125g unsalted butter
125g dark muscovado sugar
150ml golden syrup
2 lumps of stem ginger, finely chopped
1 teaspoon ground cinnamon
2 teaspoons ground ginger
1 teaspoon bicarbonate of soda
250g self-raising flour
a pinch of salt
2 large eggs
150ml whole milk

Continued overleaf

Preheat the oven to 180°C/160°C fan/Gas 4 and grease and line the base and sides of a 20cm square baking tin with baking paper.

In a small saucepan, bring the PX, tea and prunes to a simmer over a low heat. Remove the pan from the heat and pour the hot liquid and prunes into a bowl. Set aside to cool, leaving the prunes to steep in the liquid while you do everything else.

In a large pan (much bigger than you think you'll need for the amount of butter and sugar), put the butter, sugar, golden syrup and stem ginger over a low–medium heat. Let it bubble up and cook for a couple of minutes, stirring so the sugar dissolves.

Sift the spices, bicarbonate of soda and flour into a large bowl along with the salt. Use a balloon whisk to beat all but a teaspoon of the dry mixture slowly into the liquid.

When it's well mixed, beat in the eggs. Then slowly pour in the milk, beating as you go.

Lift the prunes out of their liquid (reserve the liquid if you want to make a quick icing) and pop them in

For the custard
300ml double cream
300ml whole milk
150g caster sugar
1 vanilla pod, split in
  half, seeds removed
  with a small knife
  (keep the pod)
12 cardamom pods, bashed
  in a pestle and mortar
3 large egg yolks

the bowl with the remaining teaspoon of flour. Toss the bowl so the prunes get a light coating of flour. Then add them to the cake batter.

Pour everything into the cake tin, pop it in the oven and bake the cake for about 30 minutes, or until the centre springs back when you give it a light prod, or a skewer inserted into the middle comes out clean. You can either leave it to cool in the tin for 10 minutes and then turn it out and serve it hot, or if you're not going to eat it immediately, leave it to cool completely in the tin and then wrap it in baking paper or cling film. It'll be even better on day two.

If you're serving the cake with custard, it might be worth making the custard in advance and keeping it in the fridge, then reheating it gently if you want to serve it warm.

To make the custard, heat the cream and milk in a wide saucepan with half the sugar, the vanilla seeds and the pod and the cardamom (pods and any seeds that escaped during bashing). Bring the cream mixture almost to the boil over a low heat, then turn the heat off and leave it to steep for 45 minutes.

Strain the infused cream mixture through a sieve into a bowl. Discard the pods and seeds in the sieve and pour the mixture in the bowl back into the pan.

Use an electric whisk to beat the egg yolks with the remaining sugar in a large mixing bowl, until they turn pale and glossy.

Take a ladleful of the milk mixture and add it to the egg to loosen it. Then put a low heat back on under the milk pan and add the egg mixture, stirring continuously with a wooden spoon or spatula. Keep cooking and stirring until the custard thickens to the consistency you like it. Then, you can either remove the custard from the heat, pour it into a jug and serve it straight away or cool it and reheat it gently later. If you want to stop it cooking quickly, fill an empty sink with a few centimetres of cold water and ice and carefully lower the pan into it, taking care the water doesn't come up over the sides.

To serve, cut a generous cube of cake for each person and pour over a puddle of custard.

Proper chocolate mousse

As a general rule, I like any pudding that you might find on a trolley. I'm talking profiteroles, crème caramel, lemon meringue pie, chocolate mousse. I think maybe I was born in the wrong era. I'd have been happiest in a time when caramel oranges and cream horns were the height of sophistication.

A big bowl of chocolate mousse is still one of the best desserts you can serve a crowd. It's tempting to make individual mousses, but I love putting a great dish with a serving spoon on the table alongside a bowl of crème fraîche, and letting everyone serve themselves.

Serves 6

235g 70% dark chocolate,
  chopped
60g salted butter
6 eggs, separated
60g caster sugar

To serve
4 tablespoons full-fat
  crème fraîche or
  extra-thick cream
1 teaspoon icing sugar,
  sifted
1 small orange, zested
flaky salt

Put the chocolate in a heatproof bowl over a small saucepan of barely simmering water. Leave the chocolate to melt, stirring occasionally, then remove the bowl from the heat and add the butter. Stir as it melts, then set the chocolate mixture aside while you deal with the eggs.

Whisk the egg yolks with the caster sugar for a few minutes until they turn pale and thick. Keep the beaters going on a low speed and slowly pour in the chocolate mixture. Keep whisking until it's just combined.

Clean the beaters and whisk the egg whites until stiff.

Use a big metal spoon to fold half the egg whites into the chocolate mixture. Do it firmly but carefully. Keep going until the egg white is fully combined. Then, fold in the rest. Again, keep going until all the egg white is mixed into the chocolate. This could take a while – keep at it; you don't want to be left with any lumps of egg white.

Spoon the mousse into the bowl you're serving it in, cover it and put in the fridge for at least 4 hours, or overnight.

To serve, mix the crème fraîche or cream in a serving bowl with the icing sugar and orange zest. Sprinkle a little flaky salt over the bowl of mousse. Then, put both bowls on the table with a big spoon for scooping out mousse and another spoon for the orange-y cream.

Puddings to eat in the bath

Very thick hot chocolate

Sometimes I think I like the idea of hot chocolate, with all its cosy 90s American Christmas movie connotations, more than I like the real thing. I think it's because so often when you order one in a coffee shop it isn't actually chocolatey enough. If I'm going to have a hot chocolate, I really want to know about it. It needs to be thick and not too sweet or milky and preferably a little bit salty – somewhere between the kind of sauce you might have with churros and the velvety *chocolats chauds* you get in France that come with 'add-your-own' bowls of whipped cream. I probably have it only about once a year, but find it's one of those things that once the craving is there, nothing else will do.

Serves 2

35g light brown soft
    sugar
120ml double cream
1 tablespoon cocoa
    powder
a pinch of fine salt
a pinch of ground
    cinnamon
230ml whole oat milk
    or cow's milk
75g 70% dark chocolate,
    roughly chopped
2 shots of dark rum,
    brandy or Grand
    Marnier (optional)
flaky salt
2 dessertspoonfuls
    extra-thick cream (or
    use clotted or whipped
    single cream)

Put the sugar, cream, cocoa powder, salt and cinnamon in a small saucepan over a low heat. Whisk, and top up with half of the milk. Bring the mixture to a simmer, whisking occasionally to help the sugar dissolve and get rid of any cocoa lumps. When the mixture is simmering, add the chocolate and keep whisking until the chocolate melts and the mixture has turned very thick.

Meanwhile, put the rest of the milk in another small saucepan or a little milk pan if you have one. Place it over a low heat and bring it almost to the boil. Watch it – I always find milk suddenly comes to the boil and overflows if you don't.

Divide the thick chocolate cream between two large mugs. Use a teaspoon to stir a little hot milk into each to loosen it, then stir in a shot of booze if you're using it. Top up each mug with a bit more milk. Finish with a little flaky salt and a dollop of very thick cream.

Trifle (with poached raspberries and orange custard)

My parents' kitchen is filled to the rafters with stuff. Every shelf is stacked precariously, the mug collection features far too many early examples of homemade birthday presents (what guest wouldn't want their tea served in a highlighter-green mug with 'MUM' emblazoned across it and 'Luv Flora Age 6' on the bottom?) and most of the drawers require a knack to open them – pull too far to the left and you'll end up with 27 years' worth of utensils on your feet. It's full of bits of kit someone got for Christmas in 1992 and used once, treasured cookbooks, and serving platters handed down from grandparents. It's haphazard but it's home. Growing up, ours wasn't a house where children were scared to break something or spill Ribena all over the floor. If you broke a glass, you might receive an exasperated eye roll, but it was no big deal. The one exception, however, was when it came to Great Nanna Eleanor's trifle bowl.

It's funny how attached we become to objects when they hold the memory of someone we once loved. My mum's grandmother, whom I never met but am named for, had a famously sweet tooth. I am told, she kept a box of sweets by her armchair (Quality Street, liquorice and toffees that played havoc with her dentures) and always used to ask for 'just a sliver' of cake and then chastise you for giving her too small a portion. Her trifle, I'm told, was legendary. It was essentially trifle sponges soaked in a heavy-handed dousing of sherry, then raspberry jam, tinned Ambrosia and whipped cream – topped, of course, with glacé cherries and silver balls. It's her cut-glass trifle bowl that we still use every Christmas and Easter, and absolutely no one is permitted to get it down from the cupboard other than Mum. She goes up the step ladder and gingerly takes it off the shelf like she's picking up a newborn baby. We mock her for it, but if that bowl is still knocking about by the time we're making trifle for the next generation, I suspect the three of us will guard it like the crown jewels too.

These days, a trifle can be pretty much anything you want it to be. We make one at Easter with rhubarb and stem ginger; at Christmas I quite like a layer of clementine curd and might swap the sherry for something darker like sloe gin or rum. You can make every single element yourself, or buy most of the ingredients and simply assemble. I'm a jelly naysayer when it comes to trifle, but other than that, I don't prescribe to any particular rules, and I tend to think a hodgepodge number is going to end up tasting just as fantastic as something more finessed. It's trifle, it's literally always going to be a good thing.

This recipe requires a bit of cooking – you'll poach the raspberries in a little sherry, sugar and vanilla, and make a custard with orange zest. But you have full permission to cut a few corners with bits and bobs that you should be able to find in your nearest corner shop or small supermarket. I very rarely bother to make trifle sponges, reasoning that a shop-bought madeira is as good as the rest once it's been doused in sherry. And if you'd rather buy a pot of custard than make it, go for it. Incidentally, if you find you have some leftover cake ends, blitz or crumble them and put them in a freezer bag. In a couple of weeks when you remember you have

cake crumbs in the freezer, you can turn them out on to a baking tray with melted butter and a sprinkle of sugar and crisp them up in the oven. They turn into little sweet croûtons that you can scatter over ice cream.

I've given two versions of the same recipe here – one for a crowd, and one for those nights when you're in on your own and nothing but a private, individual trifle (that no one needs to know about but you) will do.

Feeding-the-five-thousand trifle

Serves 8

1 orange
700ml double cream
300ml whole milk
85g caster sugar
3 egg yolks
1 lemon, juiced
450g raspberries, plus
    extra for decorating
4 tablespoons sherry
2 tablespoons granulated
    sugar
2 teaspoons vanilla paste
190g plain cake
    (something like a
    madeira loaf), cut into
    2cm-thick slices
2 tablespoons Cointreau
1 tablespoon icing sugar

Slice the ends off the orange and, using a small sharp knife, remove the peel in strips. Juice the flesh.

Pour half the cream, with all the milk and orange juice into in a wide saucepan. Add the orange peel and half the caster sugar. Place the pan over a low heat and stir occasionally to help the sugar dissolve. Bring the cream mixture almost to the boil, then turn the heat off and leave the cream mixture to steep for 30 minutes.

Meanwhile, use an electric whisk to beat the egg yolks with the remaining sugar until they turn pale, frothy and thicken a little.

Take a ladleful of the cream mixture and whisk it into the egg to loosen it. Then, put a low heat back on under the milk pan and add the egg mixture, stirring continuously with a wooden spoon or spatula. Keep cooking and stirring until the custard thickens enough to coat the back of a spoon without entirely running off. Then, straight away, take the pan off the heat.

Fill an empty sink with about 5cm of cold water and ice and carefully lower the pan into it, taking care the water doesn't come up over the sides. Let the custard cool down for 10 minutes, stirring occasionally to help it cool. Then, add the lemon juice, beating it into the cooling custard. The lemon juice will thicken the custard slightly. Chill the mixture for 30 minutes in the fridge.

Meanwhile, poach the raspberries. Put them in a small saucepan with 1 tablespoon of the sherry, and all the granulated sugar and vanilla. Bring the mixture to a simmer over a low heat and cook it for 3 minutes. Then, pour the poached raspberries into a bowl and leave them to cool entirely.

Lay the cake slices in the bottom of a deep trifle bowl. Scatter the rest of the sherry and the Cointreau over the sponge and leave the sponges to soak up the booze for a few minutes. Then, evenly spoon over the cooled poached raspberries. Top with the custard. If you're not serving the trifle for a while, cover it and put it in the fridge.

When you're ready to serve, use an electric hand whisk to whip the remaining cream with the icing sugar. Spoon this evenly on top of the custard. Top with fresh raspberries (glacé cherries and silver balls are optional but encouraged).

Trifle for one

Serves 1

95g raspberries, plus extra to decorate (or use a cherry or two)
2 tablespoons sherry
2 teaspoons vanilla paste
½ orange, zest and juice
2 teaspoons granulated sugar
2cm-thick slice of plain cake (something like a madeira loaf)
2 tablespoons thick, fresh, shop-bought custard
150ml double cream
1 teaspoon icing sugar

First, poach the raspberries. Put them in a small saucepan with half the sherry and half the vanilla, and all the orange juice and granulated sugar. Bring the mixture to a simmer and cook it for 3 minutes. Then pour the poached raspberries into a bowl and leave them to cool completely.

Put the cake in the base of a tumbler, smushing it in so that it roughly fits in the bottom of the glass. Scatter over the remaining sherry and leave the booze to soak into the sponge for a few minutes. Then, spoon over the cooled poached raspberries.

Mix the custard with the orange zest and spoon the mixture on top of the raspberries. If you're not eating it for a little while, cover it and put it in the fridge.

When you're ready to serve, use an electric whisk or a stand mixer to whip the cream with the icing sugar and remaining vanilla. Spoon the mixture on top of the custard. Decorate with a couple more raspberries (or a cherry or two).

Puddings to eat in the bath

Hand pies

Towards the top of the list of most useful things I keep in my freezer (underneath peas and ice but arguably above fish fingers) is a sheet of ready-to-cook, all-butter puff pastry. It's the answer to so many last-minute cooking conundrums because it defrosts quickly and, unlike most other kinds of pastry, is a perfectly good stand-in for the real deal. Cover it in grated parmesan and black pepper, roll it up, slice and bake it and I've got instant cheese puffs for a dinner party nibble, or I can use it to crack out a batch of cheese and onion pasties or sausage rolls with a slick of mustard and onion marmalade for a winter walk.

The moment when an emergency scroll of puffed pastry really comes in handy, though, is when I get a craving for a pie. Not a deep-dish pie (for which I tend to think you need a different kind of pastry – something altogether sturdier, and more crumbly than flaky, like a French pâte sucrée or an unsweetened American pie crust, perhaps), rather, one of those sweet little hand pies like the kind you get in McDonalds.

These are so simple it's almost too good to be true. You can fill them with all manner of things (though be mindful about anything which is going to release too much liquid). Raspberry jam and clotted cream is one of my personal favourites among fillings. It makes these glorious syrupy pockets that are a bit like a cream tea crossed with a jam roly poly. Crack open a piping hot apple and cinnamon pie – all crunchy on top with demerara sugar – and you'll think you've walked into some sort of New England pie shop. Serve either of them with a puddle of custard, or channel your inner Sally Albright and have it *à la mode* ... though I never understood why she had hers with strawberry and not vanilla. Unacceptable.

Spiced apple hand pies

Serves 4

2 Granny Smith apples, cored and finely chopped (skin on or peeled, as you prefer)
1½ teaspoons ground cinnamon
grated nutmeg, to taste, plus extra to sprinkle
1 tablespoon caster sugar
2 teaspoons cornflour
a pinch of salt
1 x 320g sheet of all-butter puff pastry
1 egg yolk, lightly beaten
2 tablespoons demerara sugar

Preheat the oven to 200°C/180°C fan/Gas 6. Line a baking tray with baking paper.

Put the apples, spices, sugar, cornflour and salt in a large bowl. Mix well so the apples are evenly coated. If the mixture looks very wet (this may depend slightly on the juiciness of your apples), add a little more cornflour.

Divide the pastry into quarters by slicing a cross (one cut vertically, one cut horizontally) into the sheet. You should now have 4 rectangular pieces of pastry. Spoon a mound of the apple mixture on to one half of each of the pieces, making sure you leave about a 1cm border around the apple mound. Fold the other half of the pastry over the apple to create 4 pockets. Use a fork to press and seal the edges of the pastry together on the three open sides of each pocket.

Transfer the unbaked pies to the lined baking tray. Brush the tops of the pies all over with egg and sprinkle them liberally with demerara sugar. Bake them in the oven for 20 minutes, or until the pastry is golden brown. Remove the pies from the oven and transfer them to a cooling rack. Grate a little more nutmeg over them and leave them to cool for a minute or two before serving, as they will be piping hot inside.

I love these with the custard on page 250, but they're great with vanilla ice cream too.

Raspberry jam and clotted cream hand pies

Serves 4

4 teaspoons clotted cream
4 tablespoons raspberry jam
½ lemon, juiced
a pinch of salt
12–16 frozen raspberries
1 x 320g sheet of all-butter puff pastry
1 egg yolk, lightly beaten
2 tablespoons demerara sugar

Put the 4 teaspoons of clotted cream in individual mounds on a small plate (keep the teaspoonfuls separated) and place the plate in the freezer for 20 minutes or longer.

Meanwhile, preheat the oven to 200°C/180°C fan/ Gas 6. Line a baking tray with baking paper.

Mix the raspberry jam with the lemon juice and a pinch of salt.

Divide the pastry into quarters by slicing a cross (one cut vertically, one cut horizontally) into the sheet. You should now have 4 rectangular pieces of pastry. Spoon the raspberry jam on to one half of each pastry slice, spreading it out almost to the corners but making sure you leave about a 1cm border around the edge of the jam. Top with frozen raspberries – 3 or 4 per pie ought to do it. Take the clotted cream out of the freezer and pop one spoonful on top of the raspberries on each of the pies. Fold the other half of the pastry over the filling to create 4 pockets. Use a fork to press and seal the edges of the pastry together on the three open sides of each pocket.

Transfer the unbaked pies to the lined baking tray. Brush the tops of the pies all over with egg and sprinkle them liberally with demerara sugar. Bake them in the oven for 20 minutes, or until the pastry is golden brown. Remove the pies from the oven and transfer them to a cooling rack. Leave them to cool for a minute or two before serving as they will be piping hot inside.

Lemon ice cream with good olive oil and salt

The first time I made ice cream as a teenager (using a straightforward vanilla recipe I found on BBC Good Food, on which I've based all the ice creams I've made since), I felt like I'd cracked a code. I couldn't believe how good I could get it. It was the first time I'd made something that tasted as good if not better than something you could get in a restaurant. I find making ice cream to be extremely meditative, I think perhaps because you have to stay with the pan of thickening custard. You can't leave it, can't quickly wash something up or check an email; you have to stand there, stirring rhythmically round and round and round, never letting the mixture simmer or settle, keeping it moving as it cooks, watching to see how it thickens and starts to coat the back of your spoon. Then when it's thick enough, you have to act quickly, plunging the pan into ice-cold water and continuing to stir so that the custard cools down.

As with so many things that could be considered meditative, I think also it has something to do with the fact that you don't strictly need to do it. You can buy wonderful ice cream; you don't need to make it. If you choose to do it, then, it's because you really want to; because you have a stretch of free time and the inclination to get a pan out and watch the barely prickling custard as it thickens.

I particularly love making fruit ice creams. Apricot in the summer, raspberry with a slosh of rose water, and infinite citrus iterations in the winter months. I love how citrus ice creams can hold their own. You wouldn't really want them alongside a tart or cake, you just want to fill your mouth with that addictive, sherbet flavour, like those cylindrical lemon and orange ice creams from childhood summer holidays that you had to push up with a stick.

You could go super-retro with this lemon ice cream and pack it into hollowed-out lemon skins. At the end of a big meal, I like serving one scoop in a little bowl or glass with a drizzle of good extra virgin olive oil and a sprinkle of flaky salt – about as elegant a pud as any I can think of.

Serves 4

2 lemons
300ml double cream
300ml whole milk
150g caster sugar
3 egg yolks
4 dessertspoonfuls extra
  virgin olive oil
flaky salt, to serve

Slice the ends off the lemons and using a small sharp knife, remove the peel in strips. Squeeze the juice and set it aside to add later.

Heat the cream and milk in a wide saucepan with the lemon peel and half the sugar. Stir occasionally to help the sugar dissolve. Bring the cream mixture almost to the boil, then turn the heat off and leave it to steep for 30 minutes.

Meanwhile, use an electric whisk to beat the egg yolks with the remaining sugar until they turn pale, frothy and thicken a little.

Take a ladleful of the cream mixture and whisk it into the egg to loosen it. Then, put a low heat back on under the cream pan and add the egg mixture, stirring all the time with a wooden spoon or spatula. Keep cooking and stirring until the custard thickens enough to coat the back of a spoon without entirely running off. Then, take it straight off the heat.

Fill an empty sink with a few centimetres of cold water and ice and carefully lower the pan into it, taking care the water doesn't come up over the sides. Let the custard cool down for 10 minutes, then remove the lemon peel and add the lemon juice, beating it into the cooling custard. The lemon juice will thicken it slightly.

Chill the mixture for 30 minutes in the fridge, then churn it in your ice-cream machine, scrape it into a plastic container, pop on the lid and freeze it. Or, if you're doing it with elbow grease, pop the filled container in the freezer and take it out every couple of hours to whip it with electric beaters until it is frozen enough that ice crystals don't form.

Take the ice cream out of the freezer to defrost for about 15 minutes before serving. Then spoon individual scoops of ice cream into small bowls, drizzle over a dessertspoonful of olive oil and serve topped with a little flaky salt.

It isn't a birthday without ice-cream cake

Somewhere along the line, I ended up being the person who makes the birthday cakes.

I'm not sure how it happened – there are definitely better bakers among my friends and family. My friend Nandini is a prison governor who moonlights as some sort of icing virtuoso. For her sister's wedding, she made a bouquet of cupcakes that looked like ceramic roses, and honestly they were so beautiful they could have gone in the V&A. My sister Flo believes firmly that you should have cake with ice cream on birthdays, however old you are. She also believes Ketchup is the devil's work, speaks almost entirely in *Gavin and Stacey* quotes, and used to think the 'Rock' in 'Crocodile Rock' was Elton and Susie's son. Arguably, then, she's a dubious role model. She is, however, the best birthday-hype woman I know. She bakes incredibly beautiful cakes (she made me an apricot and lavender cake for my 26th birthday that my friends are still talking about) and can diffuse any birthday tension with a well-timed gag. She is, quite simply, a birthday guru.

I don't have the patience for detail and precision that either of them do, but I do really like telling people I love them with cake.

I used to go completely overboard with birthday cakes and plan all sorts of elaborate decorations that would have me up at 1am the night before swearing at melted chocolate. It took me far too long to realise that no one wants a cake you've slaved over like some sort of birthday martyr. They'd rather have a Colin the Caterpillar. I think I've just about learned my lesson, and these days if I do make a birthday cake, I'll tend to opt for something simple like Nigella's devil's food cake, perhaps iced with a coffee, caramel or tahini buttercream.

But if I have time and the hankering for a project, I love making (and eating) ice-cream cakes. They are about the least practical thing to bring to a party (though I have been known to pack an entire boot with ice in order to ferry one to a birthday do …)

but I firmly believe they're the best kind of celebration cake, if only because they bring out everyone's inner gleeful child. I still request one every August on my birthday, and I remain unconvinced that there's anything that can beat the messy joy of a rapidly melting ice-cream cake on a hot summer's day.

Blackberry and caramelised cake crumb ice-cream cake

There are any number of ways to go about making ice-cream cakes. You could make your own ice cream or use shop bought; you could do as the French do with their *gateaux glacés* and make a thin base of stiff meringue and pipe cream all around the outside; you could go for more of an Italian *cassata* vibe or take your inspiration from American-style ice-cream sandwiches.

If you're going to make your own ice cream, you could use the same principles as the lemon ice cream on page 261 or the coffee on page 229, using whatever flavourings you prefer. Just make sure that you give it a spin in an ice-cream machine first, or let it semi-freeze in a plastic container and beat it with an electric whisk. It needs to be at soft-scoop stage before layering it in your tin.

Serves about 16

For the cake
200g softened unsalted
  butter
200g golden caster sugar
4 large eggs
1 orange, zest only
2 teaspoons vanilla
  extract
200g self-raising flour
1 teaspoon baking
  powder
2 tablespoons whole
  milk

*For the blackberry
  compôte*
380g blackberries, plus
  extra for decoration
90g granulated sugar
1 orange, zest and juice
2 teaspoons vanilla
  extract

For the crumbs
1 tablespoon unsalted
  butter
1 tablespoon light brown
  soft sugar

Preheat the oven to 180°C/160°C fan/Gas 4. Grease and line a 25cm springform cake tin.

Make the cake. Use electric beaters or a stand mixer to beat together the butter and sugar. Keep beating until the mixture is pale and fluffy. Add the eggs one at a time, beating well between each one. If the mixture splits a bit, add a spoonful of the self-raising flour. Whisk in the orange zest and vanilla. Fold in the flour and baking powder with a large metal spoon. Do it firmly until everything is well combined. Finally, stir in the milk.

Scrape the batter into the cake tin, smoothing the top with a large metal spoon. Bake for 20 minutes, or until the centre of the sponge springs if you press it. Cool in the tin for 10 minutes, then turn it out on to a cooling rack and leave it to cool completely.

Meanwhile, make the compôte. Put the blackberries and granulated sugar in a saucepan, saving a few blackberries for scattering in among the filling. Add the zest and juice of the orange, and the vanilla. Bring the mixture to a simmer, stirring, and cook it for about 20 minutes, or until the juices have reduced and started to turn a little syrupy. It's fine if it's still a bit loose. Pour the compôte into a bowl and leave it to cool, then chill it completely in the fridge before using it.

When the cake is completely cool, slice it horizontally into three equal layers.

To assemble
300ml double cream
1 teaspoon vanilla
    extract
1 tablespoon icing sugar
2 x 460ml tubs of
    good-quality, firm
    vanilla ice cream
some sort of ridiculous
    sprinkle (optional)

Wash the cake tin and put the top layer of the cake in the base of the tin, cut side up. Break the middle layer of the cake into small chunks and crumbs. Reserve the bottom layer for now.

Preheat the oven to 200°C/180°C fan/Gas 6. Line a baking tray with baking paper.

Melt the tablespoon of butter for the crumbs in a small saucepan over a low heat. Mix the cake chunks and crumbs with the brown sugar and melted butter. Spoon the crumb on to the lined baking tray and bake them in the oven for 8 minutes, then stir them and bake for another 2 minutes, or until the crumbs have turned golden brown. Remove them from the oven and transfer them to a plate to cool completely.

Meanwhile, whip the cream for the assembly with the vanilla and icing sugar until soft peaks form.

Take the ice cream out of the freezer and leave it to soften for about 15 minutes, or until soft enough to scoop easily. Spoon the softened ice cream into a big bowl and add the caramelised cake crumbs. Mix everything together so that the crumbs are evenly distributed, then spoon a third of the blackberry mixture over the cake base in the tin. Top with two thirds of the ice-cream mixture, then spoon over a little more blackberry compôte (hold about half of it back for serving), and scatter over the reserved whole blackberries. Spoon the rest of the ice cream on top of that. Use your spoon to marble the sauce through the ice cream by dragging it back and forth. Don't over mix it; you want a nice ripple effect.

Place the reserved bottom cake layer on top and press it down lightly. Spoon the whipped cream on top and use a metal spoon to swirl it around on the top as you might if you were icing a cake with cream-cheese frosting. (You can pipe it if you prefer.) Put the assembled cake in the freezer straight away and freeze for at least 4 hours, or overnight.

Take the cake out of the freezer 30 minutes before serving. Run a palette knife around the outside of the tin and release the springform. Slide the whole thing on to a cake stand or board or just a nice plate. Top the cake with fresh blackberries (and sprinkles if you're using them). Run a very sharp knife under water that's just boiled from the kettle and use it to slice the cake. Serve with extra spoonfuls of blackberry compôte.

Rum baba French toast with whipped cream

You don't see rum baba enough on menus. A bready sponge soaked in rum syrup, with a cloud of whipped cream – what's not to like? It just doesn't come better than that. It's both ridiculous and over the top and oddly simple, and if ever I see one on a menu, I have to order it. This recipe has all the main components of a baba (chief among them being the boozy syrup) but it gets you there faster by swapping out the baba dough for brioche French toast. There's rum, cream and vanilla beans in the egg mixture that you'll soak the hunks of brioche in. There is a crunchy sugar coating and a hot rum syrup to pour over everything. This recipe will yield a bit too much syrup (depending, of course, on how heavy handed you are with your pouring), but then you have some on hand for rum cocktails. Just pop any leftovers in a jar and keep it in the fridge.

I like arranging the slabs of buttery French toast on a plate and putting them in the middle of the table, with a great bowl of whipped cream and a jug of syrup, so that everyone can help themselves.

Serves 4

For the rum baba
300g granulated sugar
1 vanilla pod, split in half,
   seeds removed with a
   small knife (keep the
   pod)
100ml dark rum
3 large eggs, beaten
85ml whole milk
50ml double cream
a pinch of salt
4 brioche slices, cut 2cm
   thick
65g butter

For the cream
220ml double cream
2 teaspoons icing sugar,
   sifted
1 teaspoon vanilla extract
   or ⅔ teaspoon vanilla
   paste

First, make the rum syrup. Set a small saucepan over a low–medium heat with 185g of the granulated sugar, 300ml of water and the vanilla pod (but not the seeds). Cook, stirring occasionally to help the sugar dissolve, until the mixture comes to the boil. Then, simmer it for 18 minutes, or until it becomes syrupy. This could take a little while – cook it for longer if you think it isn't quite syrupy enough. A good way to test it is to spoon a little on to a plate, leave it to cool for a minute and when you return to it, test how syrupy it feels with your finger. When it's a nice consistency, take the pan off the heat.

Reserve 1 tablespoon of the rum and then pour the rest into the syrup pan. Put the syrup back over a low–medium heat and cook it for another 2½ minutes, watching the pan as the syrup will bubble up. Then take the pan off the heat and pour the syrup into a heatproof jug or bowl.

In a large bowl, beat the eggs with the milk, cream, vanilla seeds, salt and the reserved tablespoon of rum.

Plunge the slices of brioche into the egg mixture, turning them over in the bowl. Leave them to soak for 10 minutes so they absorb as much of the mixture as possible.

Set a large frying pan over a medium heat and add the butter. Once the butter is melted and foaming, add the brioche. Cook the brioche slices for 4 minutes, then once they've turned golden brown, flip them and cook them for another 3 minutes until they are golden all over.

Meanwhile, scatter the remaining granulated sugar over a large plate. Place the cooked brioche on the sugar and press down. Turn the brioche slices over in the sugar, press and turn them again.

To whip the cream, pour it into a large bowl and add the icing sugar and vanilla. Use an electric whisk (or a balloon whisk if you prefer to do it by hand) and whip until you get soft peaks. Spoon the cream into a big bowl.

To serve, put a slice of brioche on a plate, spoon over an ungodly amount of syrup, and finish with a dollop of cream.

Apricot upside-down cake with basil sugar

In the vision I had for my adult life, my kitchen was meant to look far more like the kind you'd find in a Nancy Meyers house. It was supposed to have copper pans hanging neatly above a large gleaming range, beech shelves stacked with artfully non-matching crockery, jars filled with grains and flours, great bunches of fresh herbs in vases, marble bowls overflowing with citrus, and a cake stand topped with a glass cloche, in which there would be a steady rotation of perfect cakes. Given I am not – and never will be – a Californian millionaire, it was, I'll admit, a somewhat lofty, unrealistic vision for my future. But a girl can dream. I might not have the marble island or the range cooker, but the cake stand I can certainly muster, and one of the cakes in highest rotation in my kitchen is this apricot upside-down number. It's super-versatile as it seems to work just as well at teatime as it does for dessert. It's a keeper too – it's lovely on day one, fresh out of the oven and still a little warm, but it's just as good a couple of days later when the apricot syrup has really leaked down into the sponge.

I make a version of this cake throughout the year, depending on what's in season: rhubarb in the spring (roasting the fruit first with sugar and a splash of orange blossom water) and plums in the autumn, adding a teaspoon of mixed spice to the cake batter and swapping the granulated sugar in the base of the tin for demerara.

The basil sugar isn't essential but it's fantastic if you're serving straight away. The colour makes the cake look so beautiful, like a scattering of emerald glitter on top. It's worth it just for the smell as the basil hits the warm sponge. I serve this with thick cream or a little yoghurt mixed with icing sugar and orange blossom water.

Serves 8–10

For the apricot cake
80g granulated sugar
8 apricots, halved
  and destoned
200g unsalted butter,
  softened, plus extra
  for greasing
200g golden caster sugar
3 large eggs
125g self-raising flour
1 teaspoon vanilla paste
a pinch of salt
75g quick-cook polenta

For the basil sugar
10g basil
100g granulated sugar

Preheat the oven to 180°C/160°C fan/Gas 4.

Grease a 23cm cake tin with butter and line the bottom with a disc of baking paper slightly larger in diameter than the tin, so the paper comes up the sides by about 2.5cm. Sprinkle the granulated sugar over the baking paper in the bottom of the tin and arrange the apricots cut side down to cover.

Beat the 200g of butter and the caster sugar together with an electric whisk or in a stand mixer until pale and fluffy. Add the eggs one at a time, beating well between each egg. If the mixture looks like it's starting to curdle, add a spoonful of the 125g of flour. Beat in the vanilla paste too. Then, add the (remaining) flour, and the salt and polenta and fold in the dry ingredients with a large metal spoon.

Spoon the batter over the apricots and smooth out the top. Put the cake in the middle of the oven and bake it for 35–40 minutes, or until a skewer inserted into the middle comes out clean.

While the cake is baking, make the basil sugar. Wash the basil and dry it completely on a tea towel before blitzing it (any excess moisture will make the sugar stick together too much). Put the basil and sugar in a food processor (if yours comes with a small bowl, use that; or use a hand blender). Blitz it so that you get a bright green sugar – it'll stick together a little but should be sprinklable. If it doesn't feel as loose as you'd like it, add more sugar and pulse again.

Leave the cake to cool completely in the tin before turning it out on to a plate and peeling off the baking paper. There should be a fair bit of caramel and juice in the tin so watch out for any liquid when you turn the cake out. Or if you want to serve it warm, leave it to cool for about 20 minutes in the tin, then turn it out. Sprinkle the basil sugar over the cake, slice it and serve it with thick cream.

Spiced clementine gin

I make this gin every Christmas and pour it into seemingly endless little bottles with cork stoppers, either to give away as presents or force on people after dinner. I can attest to its ability to really get rid of any pre-karaoke jitters – all those friends who supposedly 'never do karaoke' (such a pointless hill to die on) will be up doing 'Don't Go Breaking My Heart' before long.

Makes a 750ml bottle

650ml gin
4 clementines, halved
1 lemon, just the peel
3 tablespoons golden
  caster sugar
4 star anise
2 cinnamon sticks

To serve
ice
tonic water
strips of orange peel
star anise

Pour the gin into a large jar or plastic container with a good seal on the lid. Squeeze the clementines into the gin and add the squeezed peel shells. Add the lemon peel, sugar and whole spices. Stir everything well, then put the lid on and leave the gin for a week, giving the container a brief shake every day.

After a week, strain the liquid through a muslin or a clean tea towel. You can pour it back in the bottle the gin came in and keep it in the fridge or pour it into smaller bottles (they make lovely presents).

When you come to drink it, either serve very cold shots (a little pre-pudding or after-dinner drink) or pour 40ml into a glass filled with ice, top with tonic and serve with a twist of orange and a star anise.

Chocolate, cherry and pine nut fridge cake

File fridge cake under 'break open in case of emergency'. It's the thing I make on nights when beating butter and sugar or watching a rising sponge or tray of biscuits through the oven door feels a step further than I'm willing to go. I can arrive home with a craving for a proper hit of chocolate and within minutes have raided the store cupboard, melted a couple of bars of 70-per-cent, and have a mixture packed with all manner of good things poured into a baking tray ready to firm up in the fridge. A couple of hours later and by the time I've made some real food and had a bath, it's ready to slice and eat.

There are any number of ways to make a fridge cake. Italians have an altogether more sophisticated version that resembles a long salami, rolled into a tight sausage and dusted with icing sugar to be sliced as needed. It often features chopped almonds, hazelnuts or pistachios and some kind of liqueur, like amaretto. What you put in your fridge cake is your choice alone; I find it tends to depend entirely on what I already have in stock. There should be some kind of broken-up biscuit, another form of crunch, whether from nuts, seeds or just a few Maltesers. You can make something that more closely resembles a childhood rocky road by substituting some of the dark chocolate for milk and adding a few marshmallows. I quite like this grown-up, slightly salty version with tart cranberries and sour cherries.

Cut yourself a generous square and devour it on the sofa with a mug of tea the size of your head, or dust it with icing sugar and divide it into thin slices roughly the size of a biscotti and serve alongside strong coffees and some sort of sweet wine at a dinner party.

Makes 16 pieces

200g 70% dark
   chocolate
200g salted butter
140g golden syrup
1 teaspoon vanilla
   extract
120g pine nuts
180g dried cranberries
170g dried cherries
100g digestive biscuits,
   broken into bits
3 x 23g Crunchie bars,
   roughly chopped
a pinch of flaky salt

Line a 20cm shallow, square tin with cling film (leave some hanging over the edge).

Set a small saucepan of water over a low heat. Put a large heatproof bowl on top. Melt the chocolate, butter and golden syrup together, stirring occasionally, until smooth. Remove from the heat and add the vanilla extract.

Set a small frying pan over a medium heat and toast the pine nuts. Watch they don't catch. Remove them from the heat and add them to the chocolate. Add the cranberries, cherries and biscuits too. Finally, add the Crunchie (you're best off mixing this in once the chocolate has cooled a little so the chocolate coating on the Crunchie doesn't melt too much).

Pour the mixture into the tin and refrigerate it for 1½ hours, or until it's set. Sprinkle a little flaky salt on top before you slice it into pieces and serve.

Risking delight

The brilliant food writer Ruby Tandoh once compiled lists of 'Good Food Things' on Twitter.

They were moments of delight found in the everyday – not necessarily great culinary triumphs, but the little wins, the brief moments of bliss. Her followers soon weighed in, adding their own perfect food things – Wotsit dust, accidentally finding a waferless KitKat, the crispy edges of a lasagne, sandwiches cut into four by someone who cares too much. Those lists were so wonderfully revealing – a reminder that when we let it, eating has the power to be this great conduit for delight and memory making. You might feel it when you're cooking – one of your perfect food things might be the nostalgic scent of onion hitting hot oil, or the unrivalled satisfaction of making a bacon sandwich exactly when you want one and exactly how you like it. But it's also just there in the way you approach eating a Mr Kipling Bakewell tart, nibbling the edges first, then scraping off the thick layer of icing with your two front teeth before eating the weighty little cup of pastry, jam and sweet almond filling in two bites. It's in the unadulterated ecstasy of those first few McDonald's fries, still piping hot and perfectly salty. It's the toast buttered at exactly the right temperature, the correct ratio of roast potato to mint sauce, the sweet milk at the bottom of the cereal bowl, the feeling as you slowly rip a bag of salt-and-vinegar crisps down the middle to be shared at a pub table. It's all about pleasure. And pleasure is something I think we need to be reminded to prioritise sometimes. We need to stop overthinking whether we really need that packet of Hobnobs and 'risk delight'.

I'd probably be lost without cooking – it's how I enter the world. The pleasure I get from making a meal for myself or for the people I love is a kind of invaluable shelter belt that I'm so grateful I get to lean on again and again. But I also know that a lot of the time it's not really about the food, it's about the people. It's all those chaotic meals eaten on wobbly emergency chairs in a slightly too hot kitchen while you celebrate the big milestone moments in life; it's the long, meandering dinners that remind you how good it feels to sit around a table with people who mean something to you. I hope the stories and recipes in this

book give you some inspiration for your own gatherings. I hope you make some happy memories with them.

We can't always sit together, of course, and there isn't always something obvious to celebrate. It can be harder to find those moments of pleasure on an average day when you're mainly just moving through the world on your own or focusing on being responsible for others. It helps in the times in between to have people in your life who will remind you to put yourself in the way of joy, no matter what is happening. In the pandemic, my friend Christie and I would send each other mint-chocolate-flavoured things in the post every few weeks. A bar of Tony's studded with peppermint candy cane shards at Christmas, a box of mint chocolate Fingers, Bendicks or After Eights. If one of us seemed to be having a dicey moment, we'd send a gentle WhatsApp reminder to go to the shop and buy a Cornetto (it's amazing how you can turn an afternoon around with a mint Cornetto – their cheering powers know no bounds). It's just an ice cream, just a small thing, but isn't life made up of lots of small things? Isn't it measured in the endless cups of tea and chocolate biscuits? Sometimes, that's what love feels like. The well-timed glass of wine handed to you while you let your heart drop out on to the table, or the text from a friend giving you permission to cancel on them because they can sense you need a night on your own on the sofa. I hope you find recipes here to help with those sorts of nights too, when you need to find solace or bliss in a bowl of pasta, or want to show someone how much you care with a really good plate of chips.

Mostly, I hope you find within these pages some signposts to delight. I hope you lean into eating for the joy of it, whatever that means to you, wherever you find it, whether it's in a pot of tomato sauce blipping away on the hob, or in the rustle of an After Eight sachet as you take out the chocolate with your finger and thumb.

Frozen After Eights

Serves as many people as you like, but probably just you, on your own, on the sofa

1 box of After Eights

Put the After Eights in the freezer. Leave them for 45 minutes for a soft chew; longer for a tougher chew.

Index

Acknowledgements

This book started life as an iPhone note. It could very easily have stayed an iPhone note, buried among the ones that are part shopping list, part earnest plea to sort my life out ('lemons, eggs, pasta, a better bra, credit card bill, for the love of God go to the dentist, redownload Hinge??, milk, peas, really good jeans, loo roll ...). That it is actually a book you are is only because some very clever people made it happen. Thank you for taking my iPhone note and letting me turn it into a real, physical thing!

Thanks first to Rachel Mills, my brilliant agent, for inviting me for a coffee and gently asking why I wasn't pitching you a book about food but a different topic altogether. You believed I could write about cooking and feelings; I thought you were absurdly cool so I believed you might be right.

Thanks to Alice Vincent for being so encouraging through the proposal stage. Thank you to Kitty Stogdon, Rowan Yapp and everyone at Bloomsbury for saying yes!

Kitty, you have been such a reassuring voice at the end of a phone or email. Thank you for always responding to my panic with kindness and calm. Thanks for guiding me through this unfamiliar land. I'm so grateful for your belief in the book and in the power a Friday night can hold. Thank you to Jude Barratt for your forensic eye and your funny, warm emails. Knowing your brain is all over these words gives me so much confidence. Thank you to Sarah Epton for tying up every loose end.

Thank you to Mark Evans for your incredibly beautiful design. People used to ask what I would want a cookbook to look like if I ever wrote one; turns out it's this! Thank you to Wei Tang, Lesley Miller and Megan Thomson for sourcing such gorgeous props, often with little notice. Thank you for your hand modelling, Megan, and for the lols, Les. You were both so patient with me and made those days so fun.

Sophie Davidson – as if someone let me do a book and then suggested you should do the pics? After following you on Instagram, adoring your pictures and fan-girling from afar, I'm thrilled to discover you are a lovely, funny, silly human with a Diet Coke addiction and a penchant for Elton John. Thank you for giving your insane talent to this book and for those long days pottering about the kitchen, eating and talking nonsense. Also thanks for not hating my kitchen singing.

Thank you to Danny Boyle at the *Telegraph* for first suggesting I did a little recipe for his newsletter. Thank you to Vicki Harper for putting it in the paper and first bringing Friday Night Dinner to life. Thanks to Rob Mendick for letting me cook the best reporters on Fleet Street Christmas dinner every year. Thanks to my lovely features colleagues for listening to me talk about this book for months. I'm so lucky to have had all of your support.

Thank you to the friends who replied to my frantic WhatsApps ('Can you come for dinner on Friday and also by the way you might need to have your photo taken with some potatoes') with an enthusiastic 'Yes!'

To Mads, Dee and Paul, thank you for my lovely home. And to Granny Milly for all the treasures in this kitchen that we still use all the time.

To my Hood girls, Hannah and Amy, thank you for the best thing I did in my twenties – those nights cooking for 50-odd women in a shop are stitched through the book. To the Diss girls, my original loves, thank you for caring about this so much. To the Covs, thank you for teaching me what a proper, raucous, shouty dinner party is. Martha, thank you for coaching me through the writing as we swam through the seasons at the lido. Rach, thank you for sitting on the sofa with me when I was too scared to open the Word doc. Thank you to Kate, Will, the world's best godson, Alex, and Phoebe – knowing your love-filled home is just just around the corner is a constant source of comfort. To Christie, Reena, Mike and Marina, thank you for the laughs and bottles of wine that peppered this process. To Dini, thank you for your steady friendship, your funny, gorgeous brain and for caring about a good dinner as much as me.

To Rosie, thank you for your love. You have been my favourite person to mooch about a kitchen with for 14 years.

To Flo and Ols, thank you for being the biggest cheerleaders and the best people I know. Finally, to Mum and Dad, thank you for teaching me how to cook. Thank you for filling our home with infinite love, laughter, music and truly excellent food. I love you.

Cook's notes

Unless otherwise specified, use medium-sized vegetables, fruit and eggs, and fresh herbs.

Weights

Metric	Imperial
15g	½oz
20g	¾oz
30g	1oz
55g	2oz
85g	3oz
110g	4oz / ¼lb
140g	5oz
170g	6oz
200g	7oz
225g	8oz / ½lb
255g	9oz
285g	10oz
310g	11oz
340g	12oz / ¾lb
370g	13oz
400g	14oz
425g	15oz
450g	16oz / 1lb
1kg	2lb 3oz
1.5kg	3lb 5oz
2.5kg	4lb 8oz

Liquids

Metric	Imperial
5ml	1 teaspoon
15ml	1 tablespoon
30ml	2 tablespoons or ½fl oz
60ml	4 tablespoons or 2fl oz
90ml	6 tablespoons or 3fl oz
120ml	8 tablespoons or 4fl oz
150ml	¼ pint or 5fl oz
290ml	½ pint or 10fl oz
425ml	¾ pint or 16fl oz
570ml	1 pint or 20fl oz
1 litre	1¾ pints
1.2 litres	2 pints

Length

Metric	Imperial
5mm	¼in
1cm	½in
2cm	¾in
2.5cm	1in
5cm	2in
10cm	4in
15cm	6in
20cm	8in
30cm	12in

About the author

Eleanor Steafel is a features writer and columnist for the *Daily Telegraph*. Her popular column 'The Art of Friday Night Dinner', and her love of getting friends round for dinner to see in the weekend, is the inspiration behind this, her first cookbook.

BLOOMSBURY PUBLISHING
Bloomsbury Publishing Plc
50 Bedford Square, London, WC1B 3DP, UK
29 Earlsfort Terrace, Dublin 2, Ireland

BLOOMSBURY, BLOOMSBURY PUBLISHING
and the Diana logo are trademarks of Bloomsbury Publishing Plc

First published in Great Britain in 2023

10 9 8 7 6 5 4 3 2 1

Publisher and Editor: Kitty Stogdon
Project Editor: Judy Barratt
Designer: Mark Evans
Photographer: Sophie Davidson
Prop Stylist: Wei Tang
Indexer: Hilary Bird

Printed and bound in China by C&C Offset Printing Ltd.

To find out more about our authors and books visit www.bloomsbury.com and sign up for our newsletters